Connecting Windows™ for Workgroups 3.1

Doug Bierer
Steve Hansen

Connecting Windows for Workgroups 3.1.

Copyright© 1993 by Que® Corporation.

Library of Congress Catalog No.: 92-81757

ISBN: 1-56529-146-8

95 94 93   4 3 2 1

Interpretation of the printing code: the rightmost double-digit number is the year of the book's printing; the rightmost single-digit number, the number of the book's printing. For example, a printing code of 93-1 shows that the first printing of the book occurred in 1993.

This book is based on Microsoft Windows for Workgroups 3.1.

Publisher: Lloyd J. Short

Associate Publisher: Rick Ranucci

Operations Manager: Sheila Cunningham

Book Designer: Scott Cook

Production Team: Debra Adams, Jeff Baker, Julie Brown, Jodie Cantwell, Paula Carroll, Laurie Casey, Brad Chinn, Michelle Cleary, Lisa Daugherty, Brook Farling, Howard Jones, Heather Kaufman, Bob LaRoche, Jay Lesandrini, Caroline Roop, Linda Seifert, Sandra Shay, Johnna VanHoose, Phil Worthington

This book was the product of many a long sleepless night on behalf of myself and my coauthor, Steve Hansen.

I want to dedicate this book to my long-suffering wife, Eileen, who has stood by me through thick and thin. She was my first editor, has listened to my complaints and offered solutions, and has served as a sounding board for ideas.

I also want to dedicate this book to my mother, whose example served to spark my interest in writing. As a kid I remember her pounding away at the typewriter every Sunday, week after week, sending letters to friends and relatives. When I left home the tables turned and I am now the recipient of those highly treasured letters. Mom's gift for writing makes me feel as though I am just around the corner from her. She has sent me a letter every week for the past 10 years. Well Mom, here's to you!

Acquisitions Editor
Chris Katsaropoulos

Title Manager
Walter R. Bruce III

Product Director
Timothy S. Stanley

Production Editor
Susan M. Dunn

Editors
William A. Barton
Elsa Bell
Barb Colter
Jane Cramer
Donald R. Eamon
Lori A. Lyons
J. Christopher Nelson
Susan Pink

Technical Editor
Robert L. Eidson

Composed in *ITC Garamond* and *MCPdigital*
by Que Corporation.

About the Authors

Doug Bierer

Doug Bierer is a Certified NetWare Instructor who works for Vitek Systems Education, based in San Jose, California. By day he teaches working professionals how to set up and maintain local area networks. By night he does contract programming work involving a variety of languages, including C++, C, Pascal, dBASE IV, Clipper, BASIC, and FORTH. Doug has been a speaker for a number of NetuCon (NetWare Users International) conventions. His specialty is Windows in the Novell NetWare environment.

You can contact Doug through his voice mail at Vitek Systems at 800-366-6655, extension 1507. Alternatively, you can reach Doug through CompuServe Mail. His CompuServe ID is 72600,3110.

Steven Hansen

Steven Hansen contributed to this book. Steve started in the networking industry in 1981 using some of the first Novell networks and CP/M workstations. In 1987, he became a Certified NetWare Instructor (CNI), one of the first Certified NetWare Engineers (CNE), and recently completed the requirement for Enterprise Certified NetWare Engineer (ECNE). Steve now teaches for Vitek Systems Distribution, Systems Education division, at locations throughout the United States.

Acknowledgments

I want to acknowledge the following people:

Ron Person of Ron Person & Co., who helped me get a start in the writing business. I contributed a chapter to his fine work, *Using Windows 3.1*. Ron has helped me with comments and advice on my writing style. He was the one who encouraged me to produce this book.

Rick Hellewell, president of the Sacramento PC Users' Group. Rick got me into writing professionally in the first place.

I also want to thank the editors at Que for their patience and helpful advice:

Tim Stanley has been instrumental in guiding me in the direction of this book.

Walt Bruce helped me develop the original outline for the book.

Chris Katsaropoulos stayed with me through thick and thin in getting this book to print.

Susan Dunn has been very patient and helpful.

Contents at a Glance

Table of Contents

Introduction

Windows for Workgroups is an exciting new product that places you, the Windows user, in a network environment by adding local area networking features to Windows 3.1. This book will show you how to set up your network, install and use Windows for Workgroups, and manage your workgroup.

With networks, there is good news and bad news. The bad news is that when sharing resources, such as a printer, workgroup users may have to wait until the printer is ready before they can print.

NOTE Networks present challenges over and above those presented by Windows for Workgroups. These challenges include cabling issues, network traffic, and incompatibilities between networking hardware (such as network adapter cards) and application software.

The good news is that Windows for Workgroups users can share information between computers. The great news is that Windows for Workgroups adds *workgroup management* features to the basic Windows 3.1 platform. These features include the capabilities to share files and printers, send electronic mail, chat, and perform workgroup scheduling.

Windows for Workgroups enables you to share directories on the computers on the network. Network users can set the *access type* for those directories. The access type enables you to share directories on your hard disk on a read-only or full access basis. (*Read-only access* is where other users can read files but cannot erase or change those files.)

The capability to share files in shared directories can save you quite a bit of time. The days of the "sneaker network"—where users had to pass around floppy disks to copy files between computers—are over. A computer can read files from another computer on the network quickly and efficiently.

The capability to share printers can save your company money. You no longer have to kick users off their computers to use their printers. The Windows for Workgroups Print Manager enables you to send print jobs to shared printers effortlessly. After a printer has been set up for sharing, the workgroup members can connect to the printer as though it were connected to their own computers. If a shared printer isn't accessible, the job goes into a *print queue* and is printed when the shared printer becomes available.

Who Should Read This Book?

Because *Connecting Windows for Workgroups 3.1* refers extensively to Windows 3.1 features and concepts, readers already should be comfortable using Windows 3.1. The following types of readers should benefit the most from this book:

- Any Windows 3.1 user who is curious about Windows for Workgroups

- Any person who will administer the office network using Windows for Workgroups

- PC support personnel

- Technical support staff

- Network engineers

- First-time network users

This book doesn't assume that you have any knowledge of networking. Networking concepts are introduced gradually, and a glossary of some of the more technical terms is included at the end of the book. For a comprehensive reference on Windows 3.1, see *Using Windows 3.1*, Special Edition, published by Que Corporation.

Windows for Workgroups Features

Windows for Workgroups is loaded with features. Over and above the features provided by Window 3.1, Windows for Workgroups offers networking features such as directory and printer sharing. Many utilities found in Windows 3.1 have been enhanced. Most Windows for Workgroups utilities, for example, include a feature known as the toolbar, which enables you to perform operations quickly.

The Windows for Workgroups Chat utility enables users to converse electronically over the network. When one user calls another, an icon of a phone ringing off its hook appears at the bottom of the screen. Click this icon to link the two computers over the LAN. During the Chat session, the words you type appear in a window at the top of the screen; the other user's words appear in a window at the bottom.

Windows for Workgroups also includes a scheduling program, Schedule+, which enables you to set up your own personal schedule and to access other users' schedules. Schedule+ also enables you to schedule meetings and book resources such as conference rooms. The scheduling program also includes some project management features, such as the capability to create *projects*. Projects are ongoing activities you are engaged in. Schedule+ allows you to create projects and keep track of what you have going on. You can assign *tasks* to the projects by priority. Tasks can be scheduled automatically.

The Mail program enables you to send and receive electronic mail. You create *folders* to store the messages. You can forward and send messages to multiple users. You can attach files to messages or embed objects, such as graphics or sound images, in the messages themselves. When recipients read a message with an embedded object, they can *activate* the object by clicking it.

Other Windows for Workgroups utilities include the ClipBook Viewer, Net Watcher, and WinMeter. The ClipBook Viewer is an expanded version of the Windows 3.1 Clipboard. You can view screen prints and items pasted out of application program windows, and store them in folders. ClipBook Viewer enables you to move this stored information into a shared file that other network users can view. Net Watcher displays connection information on your computer system, enabling you to find out who is connected to your computer and who is using which files in your shared directories. WinMeter monitors how much applications and the server are using the computer. By using this utility, you can gauge how much effort your computer is using to manage the needs of the network compared to the needs of programs running locally.

How This Book Is Organized

This book is divided roughly into three sections:

- Windows for Workgroups and networking concepts
- Detailed instructions on specific utilities
- Appendixes on installing and troubleshooting

Chapter 1, "Understanding Local Area Networks," explains some of the basic concepts of a local area network and how Windows for Workgroups fits into the picture. The basic concepts of workgroup features such as file sharing, printer sharing, and electronic mail are explained. The last part of this chapter uncovers some of the basic features of a LAN. Network adapters and cabling are among the issues discussed.

Chapter 2, "An Overview of Windows for Workgroups," gives you an overview of the features of Windows for Workgroups. The last part discusses some of the differences between Windows 3.1 running on a computer outside a network and Windows for Workgroups. You also walk through a sample implementation of Windows for Workgroups involving a fictitious network using Word for Windows and Excel. You also learn how to start up Windows for Workgroups.

Chapter 3, "Using File Manager in a Workgroup," covers the basics of directory sharing. You learn how to share a directory, set access rights, look at files on other computers, copy files between computers, and see who is using which files on the network.

Chapter 4, "Printing with Windows for Workgroups," discusses shared printers and print queues. You see how to pause and resume printers and print jobs. You learn how to connect to network printers and see which printers are busy. The chapter also consists of tips on how to optimize printing on your network.

Chapter 5, "Using Mail," covers the fundamentals of electronic mail and the Microsoft Mail program. You see how to set up a mail server and a post office for your workgroup. This chapter shows you how to send, receive, reply to, delete, store, and forward mail messages. You also learn how to attach files and embed objects in messages.

Chapter 6, "Using Schedule+," shows you how to manage your appointment calendar and keep track of projects and tasks. You see how to set up recurring appointments and tasks. Printing features covered show you how to print a daily, weekly, or monthly calendar in a variety of paper sizes. You also learn about workgroup scheduling features such as viewing another user's schedule, setting up meetings, and booking resources such as conference rooms.

Chapter 7, "Exploring Advanced Features of Windows for Workgroups," covers various utilities including the ClipBook Viewer, the Chat utility, Net Watcher, and WinMeter. You learn how to share information in the ClipBook with other users, converse electronically with them in Chat, and how to watch the network performance with Net Watcher.

Chapter 8, "Configuring Windows for Workgroups," shows you how to configure a variety of parameters in Windows for Workgroups so that you can customize and optimize the application for best performance.

Appendix A, "Installing Windows for Workgroups," covers how to install Windows for Workgroups on your computers. You also learn about setting up and configuring the network adapter cards.

Appendix B, "Troubleshooting Windows for Workgroups," goes through basic network troubleshooting procedures and some specific areas to watch out for when using Windows for Workgroups.

Appendix C is a glossary of technical terms you will encounter when dealing with Windows for Workgroups and LANs.

How To Use This Book

If you are new to networks, you first should read Chapters 1 and 2 and Appendix A. These chapters should give you ideas on how to implement Windows for Workgroups in your office. Chapters 3 through 7 give you step-by-step procedures to help you work through the basic operations you need to perform to set up directory and printer sharing and how to use the utilities provided by Windows for Workgroups.

More experienced users may want to skip to Appendix A, "Installing Windows for Workgroups." The next most useful chapters are 3 through 7, which take you through the utilities available in Windows for Workgroups.

Conventions Used in This Book

The conventions used in this book have been established to help
you learn to use the program quickly and easily.

You can access most commands and options by using the mouse
or the keyboard. Keyboard users can press Alt plus the hot key,
which is indicated in this book in boldface type (for example, from
the **Edit** menu choose **Copy**).

Words that you type appear in **lowercase boldface** or are set off
on a separate line. For example, type **net logoff**, or type

NET VIEW *computer*

Italicized words can represent variables. In the preceding example,
computer represents the computer name that you actually type as
part of this command.

Prompts or messages that appear on-screen are in `digital type`,
as are program file listings.

File names and DOS commands are in uppercase letters—for example, the CHKDSK command and the NET.EXE file.

Understanding Local Area Networks

One of the most important ideas to master when working with Windows for Workgroups is that of a LAN, or *local area network*. As the name implies, a LAN is a group of computers that are connected together in a small geographic location, such as in an office or in a building. A network consists of the following elements:

Computers

Network adapter cards

Cables (or other media)

Network operating system software

Network designers, including Microsoft, must consider these factors when designing a networking product. They also must consider the following:

Using communications protocols

Keeping track of users who are logged on

Controlling user access to shared resources

Before installing the Windows for Workgroups software, you must install the LAN adapter cards in each computer and cable the computers together. This chapter covers the following:

- File and printer sharing on a Windows for Workgroups LAN

- Types of LAN hardware

■ The advantages and disadvantages of different network adapters

■ Cabling options

After the network is up and running, your main job begins: managing the network. Beginning with Chapter 2, this book shows you how to manage the network using Windows for Workgroups. For newcomers to networking, however, this chapter gives you the background needed to start networking.

Working with stand-alone computers is vastly different from working with computers networked through a LAN. Networking offers advantages and disadvantages over using stand-alone computers. When computers are networked, you can share resources, including hard drives and printers. Networking requires careful planning, however, to ensure that users have quick access to files and printers.

> **NOTE** You can obtain further information about networks from many different sources, including *Introduction to Networking*, published by Que Corporation.

Sharing Directories

Two major issues to consider when letting users share directories are *security rights* and *multiple access*. The section "Providing Security" later in this chapter discusses security rights in more detail.

You should divide your files into two categories: program files and data files. Then create special subdirectories for these categories and copy the appropriate files into each subdirectory. The next sections discuss file sharing as it is related to each type of file.

Sharing Program Files

One of the most useful features of networking is sharing a directory that contains program files, which are the files required for an application to run. When operating a group of stand-alone computers, you must install on each computer an application that you want available to every user. With Windows for Workgroups, you have other options.

You can install one copy of the program on one computer and share the program with others. With this approach, you must consider how many people will use the program and the type of access they should have. More than four to eight people shouldn't share the same program. If too many people are using the program, it slows the computer on which the program is installed, which in turn causes a slower response time for the user.

You can install one copy of the program and use the network to copy it to other computers. This defeats the idea of being capable of sharing programs but speeds up the installation process. The advantage of having each person run programs from his or her own computer is that the LAN isn't bogged down with traffic. You must address legal issues, however, when installing more than one copy of a program on a network.

Understanding Legal Issues

An important legal issue when using a network such as Windows for Workgroups is how many copies of a program you should have. The most recent legal interpretation of copyright law is that you must buy one copy of the program for each computer that will run the program at the same time.

Software publishers have accommodated networking by making copies of their programs available in different forms, as follows:

- With a *site license*, you buy one copy of the software and a license for a certain number of users. WordPerfect is an example of a software publisher that uses the site license approach.

- A *network version* is a master version of the software containing all the necessary program files to run the program on a network. You then buy user upgrade modules, which generally are sold in increments of five. Each module enables five more users to use the software. When the number of users allowed matches the number of user upgrade modules, no additional users can use the program until a current user exits the program. Borland International's dBASE IV is an example of a program that uses this approach. (dBASE IV refers to the user upgrade modules as LAN packs.)

- *Starter kits* are another popular approach. The starter kit typically consists of two or more copies of the software bundled with hardware. Windows for Workgroups is sold in this manner. Two copies of the software are bundled with two Intel Ether Express network adapters.

continues

Understanding Legal Issues *continued*

If your software doesn't fit any of these categories, according to the law you must buy a copy for as many computers as will run the software at the same time.

Sharing Data Files

A problem associated with file sharing is multiple access to data files. The problem occurs not when many users *read* a file, but when more than one user tries to *write* to the same file at the same time. When two or more users try to write to the same file at the same time, the application momentarily must stop all the users except one. After the first user finishes writing data, then the remaining users, in turn, can perform their data writing.

The network software (for example, Windows for Workgroups) and the application program (for example, Word for Windows) must know who can and cannot write to the file. Usually the first person to open the file is given permission to read from and write to the file. (Access rights, discussed in the next section, also play a part in this decision.) The system places a *file lock* on the file for that user. Other users can read the file but they cannot write to it. After the original user has saved changes to the file, another user can reopen the file, which places a file lock on the file.

You can place a *record lock* on a single record in a database file. A database file, maintained by a database management system such as dBASE IV, is used to store information. A name and address list of clients is an example of a database.

The application program maintains file locks and record locks. The network software provides information to the application, including who is using the file, the user's level of security access, and the user's actions (such as reading the file or writing to the file).

Providing Security

A main function of network software is to provide security for network resources. Following are some network security considerations:

■ Can you delete or make changes to files on other computers?

■ Which files should be made visible to network users?

■ Can you print on this printer?

Security in the Windows for Workgroups environment is provided by sharing directories, sharing printers, assigning passwords, and limiting access rights. Only those directories specifically designated as shared are visible to network users. No other local directories are seen by network users.

When enabling users to share directories, you must decide the level of security that each user or workgroup requires. Windows for Workgroups has three levels of access rights:

■ *No access* is the default. Each user must designate specifically which of their directories other network users can share. If a directory is not designated as shared, it is not visible to the other network users.

■ *Read access* enables users to open and view documents but prevents them from deleting or changing documents. Read access is all you need to run a program.

■ *Full access* enables users to have complete access to the files in the shared directory.

Suppose that you have set up two workgroups for your network: SALES and ACCOUNTING. Users in the SALES workgroup need access to the inventory data file, which the ACCOUNTING workgroup maintains. If you give the SALES workgroup the read-only security level for the directory containing the Inventory files, the sales people can read the inventory files but cannot make any changes. The ACCOUNTING workgroup should be given a full-access security level so that they have full access to these files.

Careful planning is critical to making file sharing work well. You must decide who belongs to which workgroup, and what level of access to which directories the users will need. You can use the worksheet provided in figure 1.1 when gathering the information you need to make the proper decisions.

NOTE	The letters N, R, F, and P in the Security Level column of the worksheet represent **N**o access, **R**ead-only access, **F**ull access, and Depends on **P**assword access.

File Sharing Worksheet

User Name	Workgroup	Host Computer	Drive/Directory	Security Level
				N R F P
				N R F P
				N R F P
				N R F P
				N R F P
				N R F P
				N R F P
				N R F P
				N R F P
				N R F P
				N R F P
				N R F P
				N R F P

FIG. 1.1 *A file-sharing worksheet.*

Sharing Printers

Properly managing your printers can make or break the network. When printer sharing works well, you are regarded as a hero. The company saves money by buying a few high-quality printers rather than a printer for every person with a computer. The network users benefit from the flexibility of having a list of printers available for use. When printer sharing doesn't work well, however, frustrated users who cannot print their documents regard you as a villain.

For a well-managed network, you must plan which printers will be available to which users. Training is critical to make sure that the network operates smoothly. Be sure to train users on the use of the Control Panel's Printers option and Print Manager.

The two considerations when sending a job to a shared printer are the LAN and the print queue. Hardware problems with the LAN may prevent a job from successfully arriving at the shared printer. Print queue problems involve scheduling the order jobs print and on which printer they are printed.

The most frequent problems for network users are caused by the following:

- Cabling
- The network adapter card
- Loose connectors
- Outside interference (such as a power problem or lightning storms)
- Too many users on the network making heavy use of shared files and printers

One printing problem stems from retraining users in what is involved in sharing their printers. This problem is especially true where users are accustomed to operating a stand-alone computer. Network users must learn that when they share a printer, their print jobs are placed into a queue along with the jobs of other users sharing the printer. They also need to learn where the shared printers are located. A common problem is when a user prints to the wrong printer.

Users need to be taught how print jobs flow when printing to a shared printer, as described in the following steps:

1. Jobs first must be queued locally in Print Manager.

2. The job is sent over the network to the computer with the shared printer. If the network is busy, the job takes longer to send.

3. The job is queued in a hidden file on the computer with the shared printer.

4. If the shared printer is in use, the print job must wait. Impatient users who are unaware of how the system works often will send the same job repeatedly.

You can use the form in figure 1.2 to plan your network printing needs. List the following information in the appropriate column:

■ The workgroup the printer belongs to

■ The name of the shared printer

■ The name of the computer the shared printer is attached to (the host computer)

■ How many pages per day you estimate users will print on this printer. This estimation can help you determine the number and type of printers needed.

Sending Messages

A main advantage of using a network is the capability to send messages to other users. Using a network speeds up the information flow within a company. This way, users can get the information they need in a shorter timeframe. By cutting down on the amount of time exchanging information takes through the network, the process of operating a company speeds up.

Windows for Workgroups offers a sophisticated program called Microsoft Mail, enabling you to send electronic mail easily. An electronic mail message consists of the following elements:

■ A title indicating the subject of the message

■ A list of users or groups of users to whom the message is sent

■ The text of the message

■ Enclosed or attached files (such as document files or spreadsheet files)

Shared Printer Worksheet			
Workgroup	Printer Name	Host Computer	Estimated pp./day

FIG. 1.2 *A worksheet for determining shared printers.*

Messages are sent to user mail boxes—electronic areas where mail is stored. Users are notified that they have mail waiting when they start Windows for Workgroups.

Windows for Workgroups also offers the Chat utility so that you can converse with other users in real time. With electronic mail, you pick up your mail once or twice a day and reply about as often. When chatting, you interact with another user directly.

When you want to chat with another user, Windows for Workgroups gives you a list of computers now on the network. You can choose a computer in your workgroup or computers in other workgroups. The computer receiving the call starts beeping until the user answers or hangs up. Users comment that chatting over the network reduces the fear and intimidation that a face-to-face meeting can present.

Scheduling

Workgroup scheduling is an important tool that has emerged over the past few years. On a network, you can access the schedules of several users to coordinate meetings and other events. Normally, all events are considered public and are visible to network users interested in scheduling events. Users, however, manage their own personal schedules and can mark events as private.

Scheduling can be used by workgroup members in the following ways:

- Users can see a message that another person is busy on a particular date and time, without seeing the event the person has scheduled

- Users can see what events the other person has scheduled

- Users can schedule another person for an appointment

Using Network Operating System Software

The network hardware consists of network adapters and cabling; the network operating system software drives the network applications, such as scheduling and electronic mail. The operating system is the "glue" between the applications and the network hardware.

1

Windows for Workgroups is a network operating system that uses DOS for certain basic operations, such as managing files. Windows for Workgroups provides workgroup members with an attractive graphical user interface (GUI).

Network operating systems most often are studied in terms of the seven-layer OSI (Open System Interconnection) model, but a study of this model is beyond the scope of this book. Think of the software that connects computers in a LAN as a series of memory-resident drivers. At the top of the stack is the main user interface—in this case, Windows for Workgroups. Data communication between computers on a network involve hardware actions and software actions. Data is thought of as being sent as one large file. For the network to process this file, however, it must be broken up into manageable pieces and individually sent.

Communications drivers in the sending computer break that computer's information into *packets*, which are small fragments of information transmitted over the network. The receiving computer reassembles the packets into meaningful information.

One analogy is that of the telegraph system, which was introduced in the mid 1800s. To send information through this system, you wrote a letter and took it to the telegraph office. The telegraph operator converted it into Morse code and sent dots and dashes over the wire. The receiving operator translated the dots and dashes into letters, words, and sentences. A delivery person delivered the telegram. Table 1.1 relates this analogy to a LAN.

Table 1.1 The Telegraph-LAN Analogy

Telegraph	LAN
You write a letter.	You create a document in Word for Windows.
You tell the telegraph operator where to send the letter.	You pick the computer, shared directory, and file name for the document.
The operator converts the letter to Morse Code before transmitting it over the wire.	Windows for Workgroups converts the document into packets ready for transmission over the LAN. The packets are placed into a data frame suitable for the type of network adapter you are using.

continues

Table 1.1 Continued

Telegram	LAN
The operator transmits the dots and dashes using the telegraph.	Your network adapter card transmits the data frames as a series of binary 1's and 0's over the network cable.
The receiving telegraph operator listens to the dots and dashes and writes them down.	The receiving network adapter receives the 1's and 0's and stores them in a buffer as data frames.
The receiving operator translates the dots and dashes into letters, words, and sentences.	Windows for Workgroups on receiving computer translates the data frames into packets. The packets are reassembled into a copy of the original document.
The telegram is delivered to the recipient of the letter.	The document is stored in the designated drive and directory on the receiving computer.

Table 1.1 illustrates how information is created, broken into small parts, transmitted, and reassembled for the recipient. Unlike the telegraph system, however, networks predictably have been much more challenging to install. After installing a network adapter on your computer, you should note certain changes made to your CONFIG.SYS file. The network installation software has added commands to run drivers that make LAN communications possible at different levels. The following is a CONFIG.SYS file for an ARCnet adapter:

```
DEVICE=C:\WFW\WORKGRP.SYS
DEVICE=C:\WFW\PROTMAN.DOS /I:C:\WFW
DEVICE=C:\WFW\MSARC.DOS
```

The following drivers have been added:

- *WORKGRP.SYS.* Tells the other computers that this computer is available as a Windows for Workgroups peer.

- *PROTMAN.DOS.* Implements the Windows for Workgroups packet level protocol NetBEUI.

- *MSARC.DOS.* Activates the network adapter card.

Understanding Peer-to-Peer and Client/Server Networks

Such products as Windows for Workgroups, NetWare Lite, and LANtastic are examples of operating systems for a type of networking technology known as *peer-to-peer networks*. In such an environment, users can elect to share their own files and printers with other users connected to the same network, or they can choose to use the accessible files and printers of other computers linked to the network.

Unlike NetWare Lite or LANtastic, however, Windows for Workgroups makes no distinction between which workstation in the network is a client and which is a server. In fact, a workstation simultaneously can be a server to one user and a client of another. A *server* is a computer that makes resources such as shared files or shared printers available to other computers on the network. A *client* is a computer that uses resources from another computer on the network. (The next section gives more information about clients.)

With NetWare Lite, for example, you must run a program called SERVER.EXE to designate a specific computer on the network as a server. To designate a computer as a client, you must run a program called CLIENT.EXE. If you want a computer to offer shared resources to other computers on the network and use shared resources, you must run both programs on that computer. No such additional programs are necessary with Windows for Workgroups.

Every computer running Windows for Workgroups on a LAN can be termed a *peer*. Each computer running Windows for Workgroups on the network has the same status as any other computer on that same network. Each peer is the equivalent of a client and a server on other peer-to-peer networks.

You don't need to run any software on your computer other than Windows for Workgroups to make your computer a peer. After you install Windows for Workgroups, your computer can share files with other computers on the network when you designate its directories as shared directories.

A *client* is a computer that receives shared resources from another network computer but doesn't offer any services of its own to its peers. A computer running Windows for Workgroups is considered only a client if that computer receives shared files from other network computers but doesn't share any files or printers of its own with the network.

For a server to provide effective services, it must have resources that are in demand. These resource need to be made available to the other network users.

Client/Server LANs

A *server* is a computer that makes its services available to other computers on the LAN. Services include file services, print services, or any special resources such as modems or fax boards. In a workgroup, a server may be a computer with files that should be shared with other members of the workgroup. Any computer with a printer that should be shared also takes on the role of a server.

A *client* is a computer that uses services offered by a server on the LAN. In a workgroup, a client is any computer that uses a shared file or shared printer. Note that a single computer in a workgroup can be a client, a server, or both. A computer running the Workgroup Connection software is a client.

> **NOTE** Workgroup Connection is a new product from Microsoft that enables computers that don't have Windows for Workgroups installed to be clients in a workgroup. Chapter 8, "Configuring Windows for Workgroups," discusses Workgroup Connection in more detail.

Novell NetWare Versions 2.2 and 3.11 are *dedicated server* networks. In NetWare, one computer on the network is installed as the server. Computers that use the services provided by the server are installed as clients.

Client/server networks have certain advantages and disadvantages over peer-to-peer networks such as Windows for Workgroups. Advantages of a client/server network include the following:

■ *Faster access.* Because one machine is dedicated as a server, it is optimized to handle the client computers without having to handle other tasks. In the peer-to-peer environment, the operating system on each computer must handle not only the transfer of files over the network, but also all other tasks such as running application programs, handling the monitor, handling the keyboard, and so on. Client/server networks, for example, allow for faster file transfers.

■ *Better printing service.* Because the server-based operating system is not taking care of routine chores such as handling the keyboard, it can provide better printing service than the peer-to-peer network. Printing occurs faster and does not slow down any application programs you are running.

■ *Greater flexibility.* In a client/server network, servers provide services and clients use services, which enables you to have many different types of servers available. In a Novell NetWare network, for example, you can have many different types of dedicated servers, including the following:

Type of Server	Services Provided
Print server	Access to network printers
Database server	Processing database queries and access to databases
Fax servers	Shared fax machines, which can be used by any clients on the LAN
Communications servers	Dial-in and dial-out capabilities to service users dialing into the LAN using modems, or for users dialing out to access bulletin boards such as CompuServe

■ *Internetworking capabilities.* Client/server networks offer better capabilities to connect many different LANs. Connecting often is done using devices known as *routers*, which enable many different LANs to be connected together directly or over a wide geographic area through phone lines. With this capability, you can connect more users on larger networks without affecting network performance.

■ *Multiple protocol support.* Client/server networks now support many different types of communications protocols. With their internetwork capabilities, client/server networks can connect many different types of networks. A network of PCs running DOS, for example, can connect to a network of computers running UNIX and TCP/IP and to a network of Macintosh computers using AppleShare.

■ *Better security.* A client/server network has a single user (or a few users) who is designated network administrator. This person maintains security for the entire network or for a single server. Most client/server networks allow an elaborate security system with passwords that can be rotated over a daily, weekly, or monthly schedule. The network administrator can limit or not allow the capability to change the security structure.

■ *Single point of backup.* Because most critical data is stored on the server, backing up the server will back up all your data. In the peer-to-peer network, data is scattered throughout the network. Each user has the job of maintaining his or her own backup. Most users cannot be relied on to do their own backups.

The disadvantages of client/server networks include the following:

■ *More expensive.* Most client/server networks—including Microsoft LAN Manager, Novell NetWare, and Banyan Vines— are significantly (10 to 100 times as much) more expensive than peer-to-peer networks.

■ *Dedicated hardware.* Client/server networks require you to dedicate a computer as the server. Often the server must have more RAM, a faster computer chip, and a larger hard disk than on a peer-to-peer network. In most cases, this computer cannot be used as a client. If the computer can be used as a client, significant restrictions exist.

Peer-to-Peer LANs

In a peer-to-peer LAN, no computer has a special status over another computer. You can consider any computer running Windows for Workgroups a peer because the computer can be a client, a server, or both.

The advantages of a peer-to-peer network include the following:

■ *Less expensive.* Peer-to-peer networks use the local operating system (DOS, for example) for most basic functions. These networks have additional drivers to handle communications between network adapters and between computers. Because these networks use existing software, they are less expensive.

■ *No dedicated hardware required.* You do not need a dedicated computer to set up a peer-to-peer network. Any computer can talk to any other computer. This way, you have greater flexibility and can cut down on costs.

- *No single point of failure.* Because any computer is the peer of any other computer, no great inconvenience occurs if a computer goes down. Windows for Workgroups will continue to operate if a computer with a shared resource goes down—in off-line mode, if necessary. In a client/server environment, all clients in the entire network are affected if the server they are logged onto goes down.

The disadvantages of a peer-to-peer network include the following:

- *More difficult to troubleshoot.* In a client/server network, all communications go from the client to the server and back. The server always is involved in network communications. In a peer-to-peer network, every computer can be involved in network communications. If you have a problem accessing a file or printing to a shared printer, you need to know what computer has the shared directory containing the file or shared printer.

- *More difficult to manage.* A peer-to-peer network is like a house of cards: each computer depends on other computers for basic functions such as electronic mail, shared directories, and printing. If any one computer is down, problems can result on many other computers depending on that one computer. Although one downed computer will not bring the network down, like one would if that computer is the server in a client/server network, it will cause inconveniences for your network users.

- *More difficult to control.* By its very nature, peer-to-peer networking leaves many functions in the hands of the users. If a user has a shared printer attached to her computer, she easily can disconnect the printer from the network, thus causing the print jobs of other users to stop. Batch files accidentally can be erased or altered, a situation that can cause shared resources to be unavailable to other users on the LAN. Network security is mainly in the hands of each user.

- *Careful documentation required.* The major disadvantage of peer-to-peer networking is that the networking software must run with DOS. In many ways, unfortunately, DOS isn't well suited for networking purposes. DOS isn't designed as a multiuser operating system (unlike such systems as UNIX, which is designed specifically to enable multiple users to access resources simultaneously on a computer). DOS provides only limited support for file sharing in its SHARE program (which also provides some file-locking support).

DOS also incorporates no built-in support for multitasking (running multiple programs at the same time). Unlike systems such as NetWare 3.11, DOS doesn't offer multiuser file-handling capabilities.

Peer-to-peer networks slow down the network user's computer when sharing files, because DOS must split its efforts between each user who is sharing the same file simultaneously. Each user enjoys only a fraction of his PC's normal response time. The more users who are sharing a file, the slower the response time is for each user. This situation is true even if only one user is changing the file and all the other users are reading the file.

Using a disk-caching program such as SMARTDRV.EXE speeds up the file reading and writing process. Disk-caching programs perform disk operations through a memory buffer rather than directly to and from the disk drive. This capability enables the system to perform less critical disk operations at a later time.

Understanding Network Adapters and Cabling

You learned about the network operating system software earlier in this chapter. The following sections focus on network adapters and cabling.

> **NOTE** A computer set up with a network adapter card cabled to other computers is known as a *node* or a *workstation*.

Network Adapters

Network adapter cards come in several bus types. The older (and often less expensive) cards are 8-bit cards designed for the older PC data buses. Because these cards process information 8 bits at a time, throughput isn't as good as with cards with a greater number of bits. A 16-bit network adapter card can process information 16 bits at a time. The 8- and 16-bit cards can be used on AT or ISA bus computers.

You can use microchannel (MCA) cards on IBM PS/2 or compatible computers. These cards generally process information 32 bits at a time. The contacts that interface with the computer's data bus are typically half the size of an ISA bus contact.

EISA bus adapter cards also can process information 32 bits at a time. These cards are distinctive in that they have a staggered set of electronic pin contacts. The EISA slot on the computer has parallel rows of contacts.

The five most popular types of network adapter cards are EtherNet, ARCnet, token ring, FDDI, and wireless. The following sections briefly discuss the advantages and disadvantages of each network adapter to help you make a better decision when it comes time to set up your workgroup.

EtherNet

EtherNet is one of the most popular types of network adapters used in LANs. The main advantages of EtherNet are as follows:

- Moderate cost, with prices from $100 to $400.

- Excellent raw transmission speed of 10 million bits per second.

- Versatility. It can be used with coaxial or twisted-pair cable.

The official specification that corresponds to EtherNet is the IEEE (Institute of Electrical and Electronics Engineers) 802.3. This standard was developed from the original EtherNet specification developed jointly by DEC (Digital Electronics Corporation), Intel, and Xerox in the 1970s. The IEEE uses a series of additional specifications to differentiate the types of cabling that you can use with an EtherNet adapter. The most popular of these specifications are IEEE 802.3 10Base2, 10Base5, and 10BaseT. The following table lists some characteristics of each standard:

	Segment Length	Type of Cabling	Number of Segments
10Base2 (thin EtherNet)	607 feet	RG-58	5
10Base5 (thick EtherNet)	1,640 feet	RG-8 or RG-11	5
10BaseT (twisted-pair EtherNet)	325 feet	Twisted pair	1,024

EtherNet adapters use a technique called CSMA/CD. The EtherNet adapter waits until the LAN cabling system, or *bus*, is clear so that it can begin transmitting data. When ready, the adapter transmits its information as a series of packets. The adapter waits between each packet to check whether the bus is clear. If two adapters transmit simultaneously, a collision occurs.

By using thin coaxial cable (RG-58), you can cable together EtherNet cards using T connectors in a daisy-chain fashion. Each cable segment must be terminated on both ends, and one end should be grounded. You can join thin and thick EtherNet cable segments with a *repeater*. A repeater is bidirectional, which means it takes a signal from one side and retransmits it on the other side. The signal is boosted by the repeater and "cleaned up" so that it is as near to the quality of the original signal as possible.

> **NOTE** You can ground a segment by using a grounding terminator, which has a long chain or wire attached to the tip. You attach the end of the chain or wire to the center screw of the nearest electrical socket.

When used with twisted-pair cable, EtherNet cards often are re-ferred to by their IEEE specification: 10BaseT (pronounced *ten base tee*). If you are cabling two computers together, you can plug one into the other. If you have more than two computers, you need to use a signal-splitting device called a *concentrator* (also known as a *hub* or a *wire center*).

ARCnet

Datapoint Corporation introduced ARCnet commercially before EtherNet, but EtherNet eclipsed it in popularity. ARCnet's strong points follow:

- *Low cost.* Cost ranges from $50 to $200.

- *Long distances.* By using RG-62 coaxial cabling, you can have up to 2,000 feet between nodes or between a node and an active hub, and 20,000 feet maximum cabling between all nodes and hubs.

- *Robust.* ARCnet networks successfully transmit information despite a relatively high degree of electromagnetic interfer-ence (EMI).

The major disadvantage of ARCnet is its slow speed. It transmits at a raw transmission speed of 2.5 million bits per second. ARCnet typically uses a small packet size, which improves the efficiency of the LAN but decreases throughput.

Token Ring

IBM originated token ring in the early 1980s. In a token-ring network, a data frame known as the *token* is passed around the LAN from node to node in a logical *ring*. The token regulates which network adapter can talk next. Simply put, if a node wants to transmit information, it seizes the token and transmits its information. After the data token has returned, the sending node releases the token, giving its neighbor the chance to talk.

Token-ring adapters traditionally are wired to a Multistation Access Unit (also called MAU or MSAU), which looks much like the hub or concentrator used in 10BaseT. You can use a cable with a large connector on one end and a 9-pin connector on the other end. Alternatively, you can use RJ-45 connectors, which look like oversized modular phone plugs.

The main advantages of a token-ring network are as follows:

- It has a high data transmission rate. 4, 10, and 16 million bits per second are available.

- It has high data integrity. The sending node receives its data back before releasing the token so that it can check whether the data was received and whether it was received correctly.

- It works well under a heavy load. When many users on the network are sharing files and printers, all users get an equal slice of time, even when files and printers are shared by many users. EtherNet, on the other hand, may bog down when many users are sharing many files.

The main disadvantages of token ring are its high cost and short wiring distances without additional hardware. A typical token-ring adapter costs from $300 to $800. You can use twisted-pair cabling with RJ-45 jacks to keep the cost down. The length of a single cable is relatively short (hundreds of feet compared to thousands of feet for ARCnet). You can use repeaters to increase the distance for a single ring and a bridge to link and create new rings.

> **TIP** IBM has introduced new technology that increases the size of token-ring networks. The new technology involves replacing MSAUs with control access units (CAUs) and lobe access modules (LAMs).

Fiber Distributed Digital Interface (FDDI)

Fiber distributed digital interface (FDDI) uses a token-passing scheme similar to token ring. The main differences between FDDI and token ring follow:

■ FDDI adapters release the token immediately after sending data, whereas the token-ring network retains control of the token until the transaction is complete.

■ FDDI adapters enable two nodes to carry on a conversation with each other without first seizing the token.

■ FDDI uses fiber-optic cable rather than twisted-pair cable.

The main advantages of FDDI are as follows:

■ It has a high raw transmission speed of 100 million bits per second.

■ It is immune to electromagnetic interference, because FDDI uses a fiber-optic cable.

■ It's versatile. You can wire the adapter with two inputs and two outputs. The adapter maintains two rings, with data traveling on both at the same time. If a break occurs in one ring, the second ring takes over immediately.

■ It can be used over the longest distance. Nodes can be as far apart as 2 kilometers without a repeater. The entire LAN can have up to 200 kilometers of cabling, depending on how it is configured.

The major disadvantage is high cost. FDDI adapters cost $2,000 or more.

> **TIP**   Some vendors offer network adapters that use fiber-optic cabling but aren't FDDI cards. (An FDDI card is an adapter card that adheres to the ANSI specification.) Thomas Conrad offers the TCNS card, for example, which uses an ARCnet scheme over a fiber-optic line. The transmission speed is 100 mbps. The cost of a TCNS card is around $600.

Wireless

Wireless adapters give you the advantage of not having to deal with cabling. You can place computers anywhere in the office and move them freely. Manufacturers advertise distances of up to 3 to 5 miles. The disadvantage of wireless network adapters is their extreme sensitivity to electromagnetic interference.

Network Cabling

You can choose from various network cabling schemes, partly depending on the type of network adapter you choose (see the following table). If network cabling already is installed in your office, be sure that you choose a network adapter that works with the cabling.

Cable type	EtherNet	ARCnet	Token Ring	FDDI	Wireless
Twisted pair	X	X	X		
Coaxial	X	X			
Fiber optic		X		X	
No cables					X

The three main types of cabling are twisted pair, coaxial, and fiber optic. An alternative is to use wireless network adapters, which use radio transmission techniques to transmit information. This section describes the advantages and disadvantages of each type.

Coaxial

Hundreds of types of coaxial cable exist, rated according to their resistance (measured in ohms), conductivity, safety, and immunity to interference. The cost varies widely, from 10 cents per foot to $10 per foot (and up).

The typical end used on a network cable is the BNC connector, which resembles a cable TV connector without a threaded fitting. Standard types of coaxial cables often are associated with certain network adapters, as shown in the following table:

Network Adapter	Cable Type	Resistance Rating
Thin EtherNet	RG-58	50 ohms
Thick EtherNet	RG-8 or RG-11	50 ohms
ARCnet	RG-62	93 ohms

NOTE Cable TV uses RG-59 type cable rated at 75 ohms. Network adapters known as broadband adapters and a broadband EtherNet adapter (10Broad36) also use RG-59 cable.

Twisted Pair

Twisted-pair cable has the advantage of being very inexpensive. This well understood technology often is installed as a matter of course in new buildings.

The cable typically consists of two pairs of wires twisted around each other. An RJ-45 jack—similar to but larger than a standard modular phone jack—is crimped on each end of the cable. Most network adapters can be ordered to support twisted-pair wiring.

Twisted-Pair Wire's Twisted Appearance

Why is twisted-pair wire twisted? When electrical signals are sent over a copper wire, a magnetic field known as a standing wave form builds up. If left unchecked, the field would interfere with the data signals the network adapter cards are trying to transmit. Twisting the wire a certain number of times per foot breaks up the standing wave.

Fiber Optic

Fiber-optic cabling contains glass fiber strands. The fiber cable most often installed is called *plenum cable* and has 6 strands.

The main difference when using fiber-optic cabling compared to twisted-pair or coaxial cabling is that the transmitted signals are optical, not electrical. Now, few network adapters support fiber-optic cable. Because the information is transmitted in an optical form rather than electrical, most fiber-optic LANs have a higher transmission speed than the other types of networks. Fiber-optic cabling is also among the most secure because electronic bugging devices cannot tap a fiber-optic line.

A disadvantage is that the fiber-optic cable requires greater precision to install and is more expensive. Fiber-optic cable also is weaker physically than twisted pair or coaxial. The cable can break easily and cannot be bent at a right angle or beyond.

Wireless

Recent technological advances have brought the possibilities of wireless transmission techniques to the LAN world. The most popular technique uses radio waves on a special frequency band. Other techniques include infrared (the same technology used in remote controls for VCRs and televisions), laser, and microwave.

Several companies have marketed wireless network adapters. Windows for Workgroups soon will offer support for wireless adapters, such as the NCR WaveLan adapter and the Pure Data PDx90211 series adapters.

Wireless LANs follow the same rules for networking as other types of LANs, except that you have no wires to contend with. The current level of wireless LAN technology has several disadvantages: low EMI tolerance, slower raw speed of communications, and low security (network signals can be tapped from a distance).

Summary

In this chapter, you learned about LANs and how Windows for Workgroups fits into the network picture. An important part of using a network is sharing resources, such as printers or directories on other computers. This chapter also looked at network adapters and cabling.

Chapter 2, "An Overview of Windows for Workgroups," gives a general discussion on the features offered in Windows for Workgroups. You also learn about how to set up a workgroup in relation to the Windows for Workgroups.

An Overview of Windows for Workgroups

This chapter provides an overview of Windows for Workgroups. Topics include defining workgroups, the features of Windows for Workgroups, and the differences between Windows for Workgroups and Windows 3.1 running as a stand-alone program. Instructions for starting Windows for Workgroups complete the chapter.

Before you set up your Windows for Workgroups network, you need to give some thought to how you want to define a workgroup in your office. Some issues you read about in this chapter include defining a workgroup, cabling, and placing users on the network. Some initial start-up issues also are discussed at the end of this chapter, including specifying workgroup, computer, and logon names.

You also need to gain an understanding of exactly what Windows for Workgroups has to offer for you and your office. This chapter addresses, on a conceptual level, the key features of Windows for Workgroups. (The chapters that follow give you step-by-step instructions to perform specific actions.) You also learn about sharing directories and printers, electronic mail, and various aspects of scheduling, including individual scheduling and workgroup scheduling.

Readers who are used to using Windows 3.1 in a network environment, such as Novell NetWare or Microsoft LAN Manager, will see Windows for Workgroups as Windows with its own networking features. For those readers used to using Windows on their computers outside a networking environment, you learn some of the differences between Windows on the stand-alone computer environment and Windows for Workgroups.

Defining a Workgroup

The concept of the *workgroup* lies at the very heart of Windows for Workgroups. A workgroup can consist of a group of users, a unit of organization in your office, or even the computers used by the workgroup members. Working with Windows for Workgroups is much easier if you focus first on setting up your own workgroup instead of trying to deal with users and computers individually.

One of the first things you need to decide is what workgroups you want to define for your network. This decision influences everything else you do from this point on when setting up your Windows for Workgroups network. (Appendix A shows you specific pointers on installing Windows for Workgroups.) Initially, you need to ask yourself the following questions:

- How can you break the work in your office into groups?

- Whose work is similar to others in the office?

- How many people do you want in each workgroup?

- Can the network's cable reach all computers on the LAN?

Recognizing that users in one workgroup don't require a separate cable system from users in another workgroup is an important first step in organizing your workgroups. A LAN usually is organized so that *all* computers in the office are cabled together. A computer can belong to only one workgroup at a time, although many workgroups can operate on a single LAN.

The workgroup name you assign any particular computer when first starting Windows for Workgroups determines the workgroup to which that computer belongs. You can change this name at any time through the Windows Control Panel. Changing the workgroup name for a single computer in the network puts that computer into a new workgroup. (See "Specifying a Workgroup Name" later in this chapter.)

Every computer running Windows for Workgroups maintains a network data base containing the following information:

- The name for every computer on the network

- The name of the workgroup each computer belongs to

- The logon names and passwords of users on the network
- The default workgroup, computer name, and logon name usually assigned to each computer

When you change the workgroup name usually assigned to a specific computer, the database is updated accordingly. If the workgroup name doesn't exist, a new entry for the new workgroup is created in the database. If you change the name of a computer, the database is updated. If you change the logon name to a name that doesn't exist, you must give the network a new password, and the database is updated

You can change the name of a computer at any time. When it starts running Windows for Workgroups, other computers on the network are notified of any changes.

The database is "distributed" to all computers on the network running Windows for Workgroups. Computers carry a complete copy of all database elements specific to their workgroup. Computers carry a partial copy of database elements for other workgroups. If a computer needs to know more information about another workgroup, for example, when connecting a drive to a computer in another workgroup, it queries that computer at that time for the needed information.

Organizing Your Office into Workgroups

A LAN can accommodate hundreds of computers connected together. Because Windows for Workgroups operates atop DOS rather than a full-fledged network-operating system such as UNIX or LAN Manager, however, you may need to limit the number of users in a workgroup to fewer than 20 for the best results. A reasonable number of people assigned to a single workgroup ranges from 8 to 16. In small offices or departments, assigning everyone to the same workgroup often is the easiest way to set up your LAN.

Workgroups are usually logical groupings of users. The decision to organize workers in your office into specific workgroups generally is based on several factors, such as the following:

- Who needs to share files with whom?
- Who needs to share printers with whom?
- Which users must interact with the work of other users?

Often the very nature of the work in your office suggests a logical organization for your workgroups. In the case of a law firm, for example, work may fall clearly into certain categories determined by job description: attorneys, secretaries, paralegals, and administrative staff. In such a case, you may create workgroups for each work category, or you may decide to divide the office into two overall workgroups: LAW and ADMIN. Attorneys, paralegals, and secretaries then may be assigned to the workgroup LAW, and administrative staffers may be assigned to the ADMIN workgroup.

In this example, the attorneys, paralegals, and secretaries need to share files because of the way their work interconnects. Paralegals present technical summaries of case law to the attorneys; attorneys develop the information and produce rough drafts, notes, and dictation; and the secretaries review these drafts and organize the work into final form. The attorneys and paralegals then can review these final documents and suggest changes. The administrative staff has little or no interaction with the work of these professionals. Members of the workgroup ADMIN are concerned solely with such duties as accounting, office management, network administration, and PC support.

Sharing resources within a workgroup is far easier than doing so outside a workgroup. For your network to operate as efficiently as possible, therefore, you must determine which users in the network need to share files and printers most, making them candidates for the same workgroup. After you determine these needs, you can decide best what workgroups to set up and which computers to assign to each workgroup.

You can assign all LAN users to a single, large workgroup, of course. Such an approach, however, has a distinct disadvantage: To maintain a secure system, you must assign a separate password to every user with access to the workgroup's shared directories. This process not only consumes time but increases the likelihood of passwords becoming lost. Maintaining the network thus becomes more work.

In Windows for Workgroups, rather than create one single workgroup with many users, you can create several different workgroups each with fewer users, to keep your network more manageable. The advantage of keeping workgroups small is similar to the advantage of using smaller directories and subdirectories on your hard drive. Although you can store several hundred files in a single directory, you may find keeping track of all those files difficult. By creating several topical subdirectories for each directory and organizing files into the appropriate subdirectories, you easily can find the similarly grouped files.

Cabling Workgroups and Networks

Ideally, all network users are connected to the same network cabling system. In practice, however, connecting all users to the same network cabling system isn't always possible. Users on an especially extensive network may be located in different buildings, across town, or even in a different city from one another. (In such cases, you may want a more powerful network operating system than Windows for Workgroups—LAN Manager, for example, or NetWare 2.2 or 3.11).

Even within the same office or the same building, network cabling limitations may prevent you from placing all your computers on the same cable system. Thin, coaxial EtherNet cable, for example, limits the network to a length of 3,035 feet of cable (including repeaters), which may not be enough to reach all the computers you want to connect. You also must consider such physical barriers as office partitions, walls, drop ceilings, and so on when calculating how far your network's cable must reach.

NOTE According to the Institute of Electrical and Electronic Engineers, or IEEE (specification 802.3—10Base2), thin EtherNet is cabled together as 5 segments connected by 4 repeaters. (A segment is a portion of the entire cabling system.) Of the 5 segments, no more than 3 can contain active computers. Each segment cannot be more than 607 feet long. The 5 segments combined equal the 3,035 feet possible with this type of cable.

When necessary, you can use a hardware device known as a *bridge* to extend your network beyond the physical limitations of the cable. A bridge joins two cable systems, enabling Windows for Workgroups to treat the two LANs as one. When using thin EtherNet cable, for example, a bridge can extend the maximum cable length of the network to 6,070 feet.

A bridge is sold in several different configurations, depending on the vendor. Some vendors sell a "plug and play" box. This bridge is about the size of a small computer with two built-in network adapters, or a network adapter and an adapter to be used with a remote phone connection. Phone connections can include a standard dial-up line, or a dedicated or leased line. With these types of bridges, all you need to do is plug them in.

Other vendors sell you the software and, sometimes, specialized hardware. This style of bridge must often be installed on a regular PC. Often you must supply your own network adapters. This type of bridge often costs less but has a more involved installation procedure.

You can use as many bridges as you want within the specifications of the type of network you are setting up. Thin EtherNet, for example, can have no more than 30 nodes on a single trunk segment, which means you can have up to 30 bridges on a single trunk segment. If you also have computers on the same segment, subtract the total number of computers from 30. The remainder is the number of bridges you can have on that trunk segment.

You also can extend a network's cabling limitations by using a device called a *concentrator*, available from such vendors as Synoptics. Synoptics has developed a concentrator that you can use to cable twisted-pair (10BaseT) EtherNet adapters together. You can connect each Synoptics concentrator to another concentrator separated by as much as 1.24 miles of fiber-optic cable.

Most concentrators have a BNC connector (or, in the case of Synoptics, a fiber-optic connector) that enables them to be cabled together in a bus fashion, one after another. You attach a T connector to the BNC connector on each concentrator and cable the concentrators together T to T. Like bridges, the limit to the number of concentrators on a single thin EtherNet trunk segment is 30 nodes. Because a concentrator counts as an active node, you can have a maximum of 86 concentrators cabled together using thin EtherNet cabling. You also can connect concentrators using twisted-pair cabling. Due to timing problems, however, any 2 workstations should have no more than 4 concentrators between them.

Placing Users on a LAN

Users are people in the workgroup who are logged onto the network. After users log on, Windows for Workgroups can track them. Windows for Workgroups uses the logon name mainly to set up users' schedules, send electronic mail, and allow access to shared resources. (You assign a logon name for a user during that user's first Windows for Workgroups session.)

The physical location of users on the LAN doesn't matter when you are using Windows for Workgroups in your network. Five users sitting in a row in the same room each can belong to a different workgroup, and two users in separate rooms across the building can belong to the same workgroup. A particular computer located anywhere on the LAN functions just as effectively as any other computer connected to the network.

All network adapters on the LAN listen to the transmissions from the other adapters. Each adapter is much like a miniature citizens band radio that broadcasts and receives information on one channel. When one computer sends out information, all computers get the information regardless of their locations on the network. If a message is addressed to a particular workstation, however, the network card in that workstation alone processes the message.

Understanding Network Messaging

Each computer running Windows for Workgroups is part of a community of computers that send out messages to verify that every computer on the network is still active. Each computer needs to know that the other computers—especially those that share resources—are still available for access. Computers sharing files and printers with other computers also need to transmit data over the LAN. *Network messaging* is the term used to describe such computer-to-computer communication.

All communication between networked computers takes place in short bursts of information known as *packets*. If you copy a shared file from one computer to another, for example, Windows for Workgroups breaks the overall file down into smaller pieces, or packets, of information. These packets are transmitted in sequence from the sending computer to the receiving computer. The receiving computer reassembles the individual packets back into the original file.

Networked computers use such packets to prevent one computer from tying up the entire LAN while transmitting a large file (a process known as "hogging the bus"). Using packets makes communications over the LAN smoother.

Limiting the Number of Users on the LAN

In theory, a LAN can accommodate hundreds of users. In practice, however, the network starts to slow down when many users are accessing the LAN heavily. The more users need to read or write shared files, the greater the usage of the LAN. Finally, the LAN reaches a saturation point, where too many users are sharing files at the same time and the LAN seems to slow down. In some cases, you may see error messages appearing in programs running on users' computers. These error messages can include `Network Drive No Longer Accessible` or `Network Printer Unavailable`.

The LAN doesn't have problems reading and writing to files on your own hard disk. The problem—and the subsequent slowness of the LAN—arises mainly when you share files with other computers on the network. A copy of the shared file has to travel over the LAN from the source computer into the memory of your computer. Data traveling on the LAN is referred to as *traffic*.

> **NOTE** In network terms, "slow" doesn't mean that the transmitting speed of the network adapters changes. The term actually refers to a slowdown of response time on the LAN—that is, each user on the network must wait a longer period of time while the LAN handles the needs of so many users.

To understand network traffic better, think of the LAN as a one-lane highway. Each computer on the network is like an exit that doubles as an entrance. Each packet of information is like a car trying to access or leave the highway. Your "car" cannot get onto the highway until the next car has gone by—especially if that other car is now entering or exiting the highway through your entrance. The more cars using the highway, the longer you must wait to get on, just as with a very congested highway. Conversely, the fewer cars passing your entrance, the faster you can get on. After you are on the highway, you must drive at a certain, set speed (the network's "speed limit"), because—unlike on real highways—everyone on the LAN highway travels at the same speed. (You cannot break the network's speed limit to reach your destination computer sooner.)

Certain types of programs cause greater network traffic congestion than do others. Database programs, for example, tend to place the heaviest amount of traffic on the LAN, because such programs make frequent reads and writes to files. (Database programs include dBASE IV, Paradox, FoxPro, and R:BASE.)

Windows for Workgroups puts no set limits on the number of users who can connect to a network. Certain warning signs do exist, however, that the network is becoming too congested. Watch for the following conditions:

■ More than 60 users are logged onto and using the same LAN.

■ More than 50 percent of the users sharing files on a LAN are using a database program.

■ Users are starting to complain that the system seems slow when they share files or printers.

To resolve the problem of congestion, try these solutions:

■ Split the network into smaller, separate networks. Doing so reduces traffic but doesn't enable *any* user on one LAN to exchange data with other users on another LAN. This option lightens network traffic, thus reducing congestion but also reducing flexibility.

■ Split the network into smaller networks connected through bridges. A bridge filters out traffic not meant to go onto another network. You can split up the network by workgroups, for example, and place a bridge between the networks. This option enables any user to exchange information with any other user. Bridges can cost anywhere from $1,500 to $10,000.

■ Migrate to a faster type of network adapter such as FDDI, which transmits at a speed of 100 million bits per second (mpbs), compared with 2.5 mbps for ARCnet and 10 mbps for EtherNet. This option is very expensive. FDDI cards and concentrators can cost up to 10 times that of EtherNet. Switching the cable to fiber is also expensive.

■ Redistribute the programs and data to the computers that use them the most. Although the least expensive of the available options, this option can be time-consuming and defeats the purpose of having a network in the first place.

■ Migrate to a higher-powered operating system such as NetWare 3.11 or 4.0, or LAN Manager. This option can be expensive, however.

Certain programs are available to monitor the use of a LAN. One such program, included with Windows for Workgroups, is called WinMeter. Chapter 7, "Exploring Advanced Features of Windows for Workgroups," describes this program in more detail.

Programs that monitor other network operating systems (such as NetWare or LAN Manager) also exist. You can use these programs also with Windows for Workgroups if the programs are DOS based and compatible with the packet structure used by Windows for Workgroups. Unfortunately, many network monitoring programs written for other operating systems (such as UNIX) enable you to monitor the health of the LAN but don't give you information about Windows for Workgroups packets. Be sure that you are aware of the extent of such programs' compatibility with your system before you buy any for your network.

> **NOTE**   The packet structure used by Windows for Workgroups is the same as that of LAN Manager. The name of the protocol driver file is PROTMAN.DOS. The drivers for the network adapter cards are NDIS drivers, which have been used by many computers systems in the past 10 years and are an industry standard. Some LANs—NetWare networks, for example—use another type of protocol known as IPX (Internetwork Packet eXchange). NetWare adapter card drivers follow Novell's ODI (Open Data-link Interface) specification, which is compliant with the Open System Interconnection (OSI) reference model.

Understanding the Features of Windows for Workgroups

Four features make Windows for Workgroups stand apart from other versions of Windows (3.0 and 3.1): file sharing, printer sharing, electronic mail, and workgroup scheduling. These features transform the Windows interface into a powerful tool to enhance the productivity of a workgroup. The following sections discuss these features.

Understanding Directory Sharing

One of the most important features of Windows for Workgroups is the program's capability to enable workgroup users to share directories and files. *Directory sharing*, as the term implies, enables workgroup members to access a single directory at the same time.

The primary reason behind sharing directories is to enable members of the workgroup to access the files stored in the shared directory. This capability is called *file sharing*. The several types of files that workgroup members may want to share include the following:

- Workgroup data files

- Common forms, such as masters or templates

- Documents, spreadsheets, or other working files that more than one user needs to review

When first setting up your workgroup for directory sharing, you should provide workgroup users access to selected directories (or all directories) on the hard drives of computers in the workgroup. After you provide this access, the files in every shared directory (as well as all files in the subdirectories of any shared directories) are available for sharing among the workgroup members.

Setting up your workgroup involves not only installing network adapters and cabling but moving logically related files into appropriate directories and assigning various access types to directories. These access types are *read-only*, *full*, and *Depends on Password* access. The following sections describe each access type; Chapter 3, "Using File Manager in a Workgroup," discusses how to assign each access type to a directory.

Read-Only Access

Read-only access is assigned to workgroup members who only need to view a file or to run a program in the shared directory. Read-only access gives you a degree of protection from unwanted changes or deletions being made to files in the shared directory on your computer.

Directories requiring this type of protection include those containing forms, templates, and program files. Read-only access enables other users in the workgroup to gain access to such files in the shared directory without you or the user having to fear that someone may erase or modify these vital files accidentally.

> **NOTE** Normally you can change a file's attributes through File
> Manager by selecting a file and then choosing
> Properties from the **F**ile menu. You then can designate
> a file as read-only from the Properties dialog box.
> Although this procedure protects you from overwriting
> a file on your computer, it isn't the same as placing a
> file in a shared directory that is designated as read-
> only. You can change file attributes only for files that
> are stored in read/write shared directories. You cannot
> change any part of a file in a read-only shared direc-
> tory, however, including the file's attributes.

Suppose that you have created a master form in Excel that enables
users to formulate price quotations for customers. If the file containing the master form doesn't reside in a read-only directory, a
careless user can read the form into Excel on his computer, fill in
the blanks on the form, and then accidentally save the file under
its original name. As a result, users who subsequently access the
form find it already filled in.

To prevent such a problem, you can change the access rights for
the directory containing the form to read-only. Then users cannot save the modified form under its original name. Windows for
Workgroups also prevents users from saving *any* file to a shared
directory to which the user has read-only access. Users can save
such files on their own computers, however. Users always have full
rights to any directory on their own computer.

Full Access

Full access enables workgroup users to access freely any files in a
directory so designated. Workgroup members can delete files, create new files, and modify existing files in that directory.

Files placed in a full-access directory usually are shared data files
or any other file that more than one person needs to modify, such
as a database. Normally, many users in a workgroup require access
to a database, perhaps to add or change information.

Problems can occur with full-access file sharing when more than
one person at a time needs to make changes to the same file. Suppose that one user spends hours working on a file. If another user
opens the same file and makes changes, the last user to save his
work will prevail. Windows for Workgroups acts as a platform for

sharing files but doesn't control who can make changes to the file. The application program is what actually controls the changes users can make to a file after the file is accessed.

Most database programs, for example, have file- and record-locking capabilities. Most Microsoft applications have at least a file-locking capability. The section "Shared Data Files" discusses file and record locking in more detail, as does Chapter 3, "Using File Manager in a Workgroup."

Depends on Password Access

Depends on Password access may enable users to obtain read-only or full access to shared directory files, depending on their passwords. When users try to access password-protected directory files, they are asked for their password. If the user types an invalid password, that user cannot access the files in that directory at all. If the user types a read-only password, the files can be shared only on a read-only basis. If the user has a full-access password, full access is granted to all the files in that directory.

For information on how to assign password access to a directory, refer to Chapter 3, "Using File Manager in a Workgroup."

Shared Data Files

Shared data files may include accounting files, mailing lists, inventory files, order/entry files, and so on. Such files contain information of importance to everyone in a company. Data files are created by using a database management system (DBMS) such as dBASE IV or Paradox. Programs of this type feature file- and record-locking capabilities.

A *file lock* is a feature by which the DBMS grants exclusive use of a file to one user. This user alone has the right to make changes to the file. All other users can read from the file but cannot write to the file. The integrity of the file's data is thus ensured.

A *record lock* is a feature by which the DBMS grants exclusive use of one record (one part of a file) to a user. In the case of a personnel file, for example, eight people may need to review the file at the same time. If the first person reviewing the file wants to change the record now under review, the DBMS grants that user a lock for that particular record. If any other users access the same record at the same time as the user with the lock, those users can only read the record; they cannot make changes of their own to the record until the DBMS releases the record lock.

> **NOTE**   How any one database program grants file and record locks isn't within the scope of this book. Recognize, however, that Windows for Workgroups enables more than one user to access a database file at the same time. Windows for Workgroups provides the platform on which a database program can operate but doesn't interfere with the operation of an application program. If you want to protect the integrity of your database, you must rely on the database program to provide that security.

Understanding Printer Sharing

Printer sharing is the term used when more than one user on a network shares a printer. Windows for Workgroups enables you to share any or all printers attached to computers on the network. If your workgroup engages in printer sharing, you usually send your print files to a network printer other than the one attached to your computer—unless, of course, your printer is the one being shared.

Using a shared printer in a workgroup generally follows this sequence:

1. You create a document in an application on your computer (Word for Windows, for example).

2. You print to the shared printer defined when you first installed Windows for Workgroups.

3. Print Manager queues the document up as a print job.

4. Windows for Workgroups sends the print job over the LAN to the computer connected to the workgroup's shared printer.

5. The document is printed on the shared printer.

How your current application is configured determines what printer you use as defined from the Windows Control Panel. After you define the printer the program uses, you *connect* the printer to a port on your computer. You can choose to connect the printer to any port that Windows for Workgroups recognizes.

Chapter 4, "Printing with Windows for Workgroups," provides more information about how to print and use Print Manager in

Windows for Workgroups. The following sections discuss print
sharing in more detail.

> **NOTE** When you "connect" to a printer, the printer doesn't
> have to be attached physically to your computer. This
> setup is the beauty of Windows for Workgroups. You
> actually are connecting to a printer in a logical sense.
> You can connect to, disconnect from, and reconnect
> to any shared printer on your network (depending on
> your access rights).

Sharing Printers through Print Manager

Windows for Workgroups enables you to connect to shared printers as easily as you connect to your own printer. Whenever you
connect to your own printer or a shared printer, you first must
choose a local printer *definition*. This definition consists of a
driver for the printer you intend to use and a port assignment for
that printer (LPT1 or COM2, for example). After you define for
your software all the shared printers on your network, you can
connect to any shared printer on the LAN.

Printers connected to computers on the LAN appear on the list of
available network printers in Print Manager. Shared printers that
aren't attached physically to your computer appear by shared
printer names. The printer names that first appear on-screen are
those of your own workgroup. You also can browse through the
other workgroups on your LAN to find a shared printer to use.

> **TIP** You can restrict access to any shared printer by
> assigning password protection to that printer. Only
> those on the network who know the password can use
> a password-protected shared printer.

Using Print Manager has several other advantages:

- You can view the status of a print job at any time.

- You are notified when the printer runs out of paper or experiences other interruptions.

■ You can view other network printer queues to determine whether the printer you want to use is now available.

Print Manager also enables you to choose whether to print *separator pages* with a print job. Separator pages appear at the beginning of each print job and help to identify the owner of a particular print job. Some users see the use of separator pages as a waste of paper. In some cases, however, you may find separator pages beneficial, especially when many users share one printer.

> **TIP**   Windows for Workgroups offers a new feature that enables you to print more quickly to shared printers— printing directly to the network. This way, you bypass the local print queue function of Print Manager but still can view and manage jobs in shared network print queues. See Chapter 4 for more details.

Choosing Network Printers

To decide how many printers you need and the best locations for the printers on the network, you first must determine who in a workgroup needs to use a particular printer and approximately how often each person can be expected to print. After examining your printing needs, you may decide that you need several different printers in your office.

Each different type of printer prints a certain type of document well. Laser printers are excellent for printing nice-looking documents, memos, charts, graphs, and so on. Dot-matrix printers are well suited for printing rough drafts, long reports that require a full box of paper, or multipart forms.

If you need to connect several shared printers to your workgroup, assign each printer a logical, descriptive name. Workgroup members should be able to figure out, from its name alone, which printer to use and, if possible, where the printer is located. Some network managers name their printers according to function— INVOICE PRINTER, for example.

Limit the number of users sharing a single printer to three or four wherever possible. The exact number of users assigned to each printer must depend on each user's printing needs.

In most offices, the printing needs of different people can vary widely. An accounting clerk, for example, may need to print a lengthy report once a month. The type of paper used by the clerk is most likely multiple-part forms, which require a dot-matrix printer. The best choice of printer for this clerk's use, therefore, is a dot-matrix printer, located in the Accounting department. As a result, all personnel in the Accounting department are assigned to their own workgroup and given access to this printer.

A secretary, on the other hand, may need to print a dozen two-page letters of a very high quality every day. The type of paper the secretary uses is single-sheet high-grade bond. The printer producing this output must be quiet. For this secretary, the best printer is a laser printer, located within convenient access of the entire secretarial staff. Three or four secretaries may be assigned this laser printer as a default, and all the secretaries in the office can be assigned to their own workgroup. If this particular laser printer is tied up printing a large document, the secretaries then can view the status of other printers on the network and pick a printer that isn't busy.

Understanding Electronic Mail

Electronic mail, or *E-mail*, has become an important tool to many companies, providing a quicker and easier method of distributing memos throughout the company. With the advent of LANs connected by phone lines over wide geographical areas (called *wide area networks*), E-mail can enable even companies with branch offices located around the world to communicate more effectively.

Windows for Workgroups includes an E-mail program called Microsoft Mail (see fig. 2.1). By using Mail, you can create and send messages from one network computer to another. You can scan a list of incoming messages to determine which messages you need (or want) to read immediately and which can be read later. After you read an incoming message, you can delete, print, forward, reply to, or move the message to a folder. (Chapter 5 provides detailed instructions on using Microsoft Mail.)

Microsoft Mail includes provisions for managing folders, address lists, and attachments. As the name implies, *folders* are designed to store important messages. You can create folders as needed and retrieve at any time messages stored in a folder.

Address lists consist of the E-mail users with whom you correspond regularly. You can send messages to several users at the same time by sending the message to all users on a designated address list. You can create new address lists, add new names to an existing list, and delete names whenever you want.

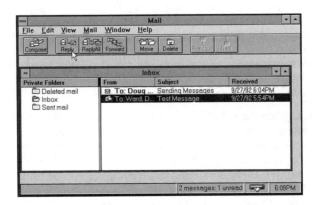

FIG. 2.1 *The main screen for Microsoft Mail.*

Attachments are copies of files. You can send a message to a supervisor, for example, and attach to the message a copy of a letter you propose to send to a client. The supervisor can read the message, save the attachment, and review the letter itself on a word processor.

One computer in each workgroup must manage all the E-mail on the network for the other computers in its workgroup. This computer is called the *mail server*. The mail server contains the *post office*, where all electronic messages for the workgroup are stored.

The primary job of the mail server is to broadcast periodic messages (computer messages, not E-mail messages) on the LAN informing other computers that this computer is the host to a post office. When users send E-mail along the network, their computers actually communicate directly with the mail server. The mail server then handles the messages for the post office, informing the other computers in the workgroup that the post office contains messages for their users.

Chatting with Other Users

The Chat utility of Windows for Workgroups enables you to carry on direct electronic conversations with other users on your network. *Chatting*, as such communication is called, is similar to, but different from, electronic mail communication. E-mail is static: After you deliver a message, no further action occurs until the receiver of the message reads it and sends a reply. Chatting, on the other hand, is an "on-line," or *interactive*, process. Chatting thus enables you to exchange ideas quickly, in writing, and get immediate feedback from other users in your office.

Many companies are discovering that such computerized "chatting" has an advantage over more direct forms of communication in that voice tones don't come so much into play. To a listener, direct vocal variations often may signify anger or displeasure on the part of the speaker, whether intended or not. The lack of such aural clues makes Chat conversations more neutral in tone, which, in turn, often encourages freer expression among users.

The button icons on Chat's toolbar (under the menu bar) resemble a phone (see fig. 2.2). Buttons are available for the following actions:

- Dialing
- Picking up the phone
- Hanging up

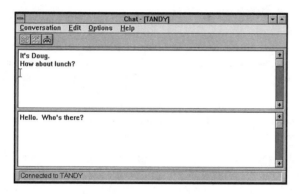

FIG. 2.2 *The Chat screen.*

You can initiate a Chat conversation by "dialing" another user now logged on the network. To do so, click the Dial toolbar button. The other user's computer beeps to signal your call, and an icon of a phone with the receiver ringing off the hook appears at the bottom of the other user's screen. The other user can click the phone icon to "pick up the phone" and start the conversation with you.

If the other user accepts your Chat call, the Chat utility splits the screens of both users horizontally into two windows, as shown in figure 2.2. Your words appear in the top window, and the other user's words appear in the bottom window. You both can type at the same time. After you finish chatting, you click the Hang Up icon to end the session.

> **NOTE** You may not always be answered when you use Chat. The user with whom you want to chat may be busy in a conversation with another user, for example, or may not want to talk right now. If the user is having another conversation, you are notified. If the other user chooses not to answer, much like a telephone, you can keep "ringing" that user as long as you want.

For more information on Chat, refer to Chapter 7, "Exploring Advanced Features of Windows for Workgroups."

Setting Up Individual Schedules with Schedule+

Schedule+, the Windows for Workgroups scheduling program, is an integrated time-planning tool. The Schedule+ Appointment Book enables you to work with your own private schedule and the schedules of any network user registered with your workgroup post office (depending on your access rights). You can display events in the Appointment Book by month, by week, and by day using the Schedule+ Planner. (For details on how to use Schedule+, refer to Chapter 6, "Using Schedule+.")

Schedule+ has what looks like divider tabs across the left side of the screen. The divider tabs replace the toolbar used in other applications. These tabs are organized, from top to bottom, as follows:

- Today
- Appts
- Planner
- Tasks

Figure 2.3 shows the Today window of the Schedule+ Appointment Book, which lists all the current day's appointments. The next few sections give you an overview of the various parts of Schedule+.

FIG. 2.3   *A Schedule+ window.*

The Today Tab

The Today window (part of the Schedule+ Appointment Book) shows you the current day at a glance. This daily planner lists appointments for the day. You can maximize the window to view up to 10 rows at one time. Each row represents a half hour of time. (Time settings other than the half-hour-per-row default are possible.)

You can enter appointments in your schedule by highlighting the desired time and typing in the name or description of the appointment. You can set an audible alarm for any appointment to remind you that the appointment is imminent. To the lower right of the window is a Notes text box in which you can type comments for the day.

The Appts Tab

The Appointments window is similar to the Today window, except that the schedule shown is for a day other than the current day. You can change this window from one day to another by changing the month, year, and date in the upper right section of the screen. Evening and weekend slots are indicated on all appointment days, including the current one, as shaded.

You can schedule appointments for one time only or for recurring times. You don't have to schedule recurring appointments individually. When you schedule them once, indicate the time frame (for example, the 15th of every month), and the recurring appointments appear on your schedule automatically.

The Planner Tab

The Planner, which you access by clicking the Planner tab, shows you another view of your schedule. Rather than view a single day, you can view from one to three weeks at a glance. The days of the month are listed across the top of the window. Down the left side are time slots in half-hour intervals.

The Planner window shows the appointments or events created in any of the other screens (Today, Appts, or Tasks), marked as black lines running down each day's column. An appointment can span days, weeks, or months. Gray areas represent off hours, such as evenings and weekends. (You can adjust through the Options menu the hours in a day or week that are considered off hours.)

The Tasks Tab

Tasks are similar to appointments, differing mainly in that tasks have a Due By date—that is, a date when the task must be completed. An appointment usually is set for a specific date and time. Tasks have no fixed starting date and time, although you can schedule a suggested starting date and time.

You can assign tasks a *priority* level, from 1 to 9 or A to Z. Tasks are displayed in the Task window in rows, listed by Priority, Due By date, and a *description* of the task. You can mark tasks in the Task list as completed after you finish each task. You can set any task with an alarm, like you can with appointments, to remind you when you are scheduled to begin work on the task.

You also can group tasks by *project*. A project is an overall heading that appears at the top of a group of associated tasks on the Task list. You can sort related tasks by priority, due date, or description within their projects.

You can add tasks to your schedule after you finish editing the details of a task. After you add a task to your schedule, the task appears in your Appointment Book and Planner. Schedule+ examines the due dates and the number of days before the due date you indicated you need to start the task, and assigns to each task the appropriate dates and times on your schedule.

You even can designate a task as *recurring*—that is, one that must be handled on a regular basis. Setting up a recurring task in your schedule can help remind you to pay that bill you always forget, for example. You can schedule recurring tasks as occurring daily, weekly, biweekly, monthly, or annually—for example, a meeting that occurs on the second Tuesday of each month. You can set the first occurrence and the last occurrence of this task, and Schedule+ fills in the occurrences between those dates. You can even leave the task open-ended so that the task has no last occurrence, and Schedule+ continues to list the task at the appropriate date and time on your schedule.

Understanding Workgroup Scheduling

One of the most powerful features of Schedule+ is its capability to coordinate scheduling for your workgroup, a feature that falls into the category of *groupware*. (Groupware is software that facilitates the coordination of efforts between members of a group.) Schedule+'s groupware features include the following capabilities:

- Scheduling meetings
- Scheduling resources
- Sharing individual schedules with the workgroup

Schedule+ works in conjunction with the electronic Mail program. Requests for meetings are sent out as E-mail messages, and replies are received the same way.

Scheduling Meetings

You can schedule meetings easily by clicking the Request Meeting button in the Planner. The request for a meeting goes by E-mail to those individuals in the workgroup you want to attend the meeting. Potential attendees may accept, decline, or tentatively accept the request. You also can cancel or reschedule meetings. Schedule+ even has a feature that enables you to set the program to pick the best date and time for the meeting for everyone who is to attend.

Scheduling Resources

Schedule+ can schedule the use of various resources, such as conference rooms and equipment, as well as meetings. You can schedule a meeting in a particular conference room by including the room name or number in the meeting attendee list along with the potential attendees. You also can schedule conference rooms through a member of the workgroup you have designated as your assistant. Users can book their conferences directly or go through a network user you have designated as an assistant.

In a law firm, for example, resources to be scheduled may include an overhead projector, a slide projector, two small conference rooms, and one large conference room. The scheduling assistant in the firm's workgroup takes requests from the attorneys to schedule conferences. The attorneys must indicate how many people are to attend, the preferred date and time, and acceptable alternative dates and times. The assistant determines whether a large-enough conference room is available by checking the schedule for each conference room on the target date and time. If the right room is available, the assistant schedules the room by sending a meeting request to the list of attendees, which includes all the attorneys, staff, and others who are to attend.

Sharing Individual Schedules with the Workgroup

Schedule+ enables you to make your own schedule available to the workgroup as a whole. Similarly, you can give only selected users in the workgroup access to your appointments. That way, for example, a single secretary can manage the schedules of several managers. The managers give the secretary access to their entire schedules. The secretary then serves as a focal point for setting up meetings and confirming appointments for the managers. You still can keep certain appointments private, however, by marking them as such.

Schedule+ also enables one user to act as the *assistant* to another user. The assistant can make, change, or cancel appointments for the other user. If you give other users access to your schedule without designating those users as assistants, those individuals can add or change only those appointments they create for you. Without your permission, they cannot change or cancel appointments they didn't make. Only your designated assistant can make these changes.

When making your appointments available to the workgroup, you set up defaults that apply to all members of the workgroup. You also can give a certain user or users additional access rights to work with your appointments. If an appointment is marked private, however, no one can access that appointment, not even an assistant.

Understanding Differences between Windows 3.1 and Windows for Workgroups

Understanding the differences between regular Windows 3.1 and Windows for Workgroups 3.1 is critical to understanding how to set up a workgroup environment using Windows for Workgroups. You can use Windows 3.1 in many different environments and even can install the program in computers without network adapters or any other means of communicating with other computers. This environment is called the stand-alone environment.

You can use Windows 3.1 in conjunction with a LAN and a network operating system, such as Novell NetWare 2.2 or 3.11, LAN Manager, or Banyan Vines. Windows 3.1 is considered *network aware*—that is, if installed on an active network, Windows 3.1 can detect the network's presence and load the necessary support drivers, if these drivers are available. (For information on installing and using basic Windows 3.1 on a Novell network, refer to *Networking Windows 3.1*, published by Que Corporation.)

In actuality, Windows for Workgroups 3.1 *is* Windows 3.1—but with enhancements. The two programs share the same graphical user interface (GUI). If you look at the screens of two computers side by side, one running Windows 3.1 and the other running Windows for Workgroups, you cannot tell the difference between the two versions. Visually, the sole differences between the two programs are in their initial sign-on screens (one reads "Windows 3.1" and the other "Windows for Workgroups") and the different icons present in Program Manager's Main and Accessories groups of Windows for Workgroups: the Mail, Schedule+, Net Watcher, and WinMeter icons.

Because Windows for Workgroups is designed as a network operating system in its own right, several conceptual differences are evident between the two programs. A computer running Windows 3.1 is set up to act as "an island unto itself." A computer running Windows for Workgroups, on the other hand, is by definition part of a "user community." Windows 3.1 is designed only for a computer acting as a client; Windows for Workgroups is designed for a computer acting as a peer (a client and a server). Windows 3.1 "takes" network resources; Windows for Workgroups "gives" and "takes" network resources.

One conceptual difference between Windows 3.1 and Windows for Workgroups is in how the two programs handle files. Windows 3.1

relies on outside utilities to regulate access to its files. Windows for Workgroups provides that capability through File Manager. Restricting another user's access rights to a file in Windows 3.1 requires an outside utility such as Novell's FILER, which you can use to alter the access rights of users to certain files or directories.

Windows for Workgroups operating in stand-alone mode acts exactly like Windows 3.1. When operating on a LAN, however, Windows for Workgroup utilities such as File Manager change to reflect the network environment. New toolbar icons appear in File Manager when the program is running on a computer connected to a LAN. In this environment, Windows for Workgroups provides its users the capabilities of sharing directories and regulating access to those directories.

When setting up an office to use Windows for Workgroups, however, many LAN managers decide to "consolidate" their printers so that everyone in the workgroup shares the various office printers. Those users whose duties require them to have private printers still can retain their own devices, even under a shared-printer system. Office workers who don't require separate printers, on the other hand, readily can access all the shared printers of the workgroup whenever necessary.

Windows 3.1 has its own scheduling accessory that performs some of the functions of Schedule+ in Windows for Workgroups: the Calendar. The Windows Calendar enables you to schedule appointments and to view your schedule by month or by day. Schedule+, however, is a much more comprehensive package and is project-management oriented.

Schedule+ enables you to create a "project." You can create "tasks" that can be assigned to projects and prioritized. You can have tasks scheduled automatically by following the instructions in Chapter 6, "Using Schedule+." You can view at any time the projects you have created and their tasks in various ways. You can view only tasks that you haven't yet marked completed, for example. You also can view tasks by priority.

Because Windows for Workgroups is on a LAN, Schedule+ enables one computer to share its schedule with other computers. This way, workgroup members can coordinate their schedules in a way that the Windows 3.1 Calendar cannot do.

Starting Windows for Workgroups

This section examines three critical means of identifying you, your computer, and your workgroup to Windows for Workgroups: the *workgroup name*, the *computer name*, and the *logon name*. More detail is provided in Appendix A, "Installing Windows for Workgroups."

You can start Windows for Workgroups from the DOS prompt by typing **WIN**. The first time you start Windows for Workgroups on your network, you are asked to supply a workgroup name and a logon name. Because the decisions you make regarding these names have a lasting effect on your network, carefully consider what names you want to assign before setting up your Windows for Workgroups network. The following sections discuss what is involved in specifying a workgroup name, computer name, and user logon name.

> **NOTE** You now also may want to designate a specific computer in the workgroup to act as the mail server. Designating a mail server is critical if you want to use the Mail program to send electronic mail to members of your workgroup or to schedule meetings among workgroup members. See Chapter 5, "Using Mail," for more information on designating a mail server.

Specifying a Workgroup Name

The *workgroup name* is used to identify a group of networked computers. You can name your workgroups any way you choose. You can name your workgroups after the departments to which the users belong—for example, SALES or EDUCATION—or you can name your workgroups by location, such as WEST or 3RD_FLOOR.

The workgroup name is at the top of the network hierarchy. Only the LAN itself is higher. Computer names and logon names fall within the domain of the workgroup.

The workgroup name is assigned when you first start Windows for Workgroups. You can change the workgroup to which your computer is assigned at any time by changing its workgroup name through the Windows Control Panel. If you change the workgroup name to a completely new name, you create a new workgroup.

Using the Computer Name

The *computer name* is first determined when you install Windows for Workgroups. The workgroup uses the computer name to identify on which computer a particular resource (a shared file or printer) is located. This computer name appears on the browse network list in File Manager or Print Manager when you go to share a file or printer. As your network starts to grow, the needs of the workgroup may change, or the location of your computers may change. You can change a computer name at any time through the Control Panel.

The ideal computer name is descriptive without being lengthy—names are limited to 15 characters and spaces. Avoid using users' names, if possible, because computer users often are promoted or transferred to another office, leaving their computers behind. You can use numbers as names, but users may have trouble recognizing number names. Naming computers by their location in the office often is a good choice—for example, RECEPTION, FILING ROOM, and so on. Another good source of names for computers is based on their (or their users') function—INVOICES or INSTRUCTOR 1, for example.

Specifying a Logon Name

When you first log onto the LAN, Windows for Workgroups asks for your *logon name* and password, as shown in figure 2.4. The logon name is a name that Windows for Workgroups uses to track access rights. The Windows for Workgroups network uses the logon name to represent a network user.

FIG. 2.4 *The initial prompt for a logon name.*

The logon name is limited to 20 characters and spaces. Most users choose their own names as their logon names. Because a person's full name may exceed 20 characters, however, many workgroup members use only their first name and last initial. DOUG BIERER, for example, may log on as **DOUG B**. If your office is small and informal, you even may consider using only first names. If you have a large, formal office, you may consider using the first initial and the last eight or so characters of the last name instead. STEVE HANSEN, for example, may log on as **S HANSEN**.

The *logon password* determines which resources a user can access. If you enter the wrong password when you log on, an error message appears. Windows for Workgroups doesn't load if you type the wrong password for a particular logon name.

Logging on serves three purposes:

- You are identified to other workgroup members, who may want to "chat" with you.
- You can share the resources of other computers on the LAN.
- You receive network connections that are permanent.

Network connections include any shared directories and printers on the network. These connections are assigned to you when you log on and are always available when you are working on the LAN. All network drives and shared printers specified Reconnect at Startup become available to you when you log on the LAN. Through File Manager or Print Manager, you can share a resource temporarily by not specifying the Reconnect at Startup option.

You can log on or off at any time when in Windows for Workgroups. You also can change whether you want the program to prompt you to log on when you first enter Windows for Workgroups. Network logon/logoff functions are available through the Control Panel. After you log off, you can continue to use Windows for Workgroups just as though it were stand-alone Windows; however, you are denied access to any network resources.

Setting Up Windows for Workgroups: A Scenario

Now that you have some idea of what Windows for Workgroups can do, you can put Windows for Workgroups to work. The following sections provide a case study to focus on using Windows for Workgroups with applications. The case study presents you with a scenario of setting up a Windows for Workgroups network.

Although detailed instructions aren't provided, you see how to set up a typical Windows for Workgroups network. Wherever practical, the discussion provides references to detailed instructions available in other chapters.

Determining the Example Firm's Needs

The case study focuses on Dewey, Cheatem and Howe, a small law firm that specializes in real estate law. The firm has three attorneys: Stan Dewey, Donna Cheatem, and Juan Howe. The firm also employs one secretary, Janet Dobson; one word processor, George Brush; and an office manager, Kathy Barnes. A part-time accountant, Jim Gonzalez, comes into the office twice a week to handle the company's accounts.

The firm has four IBM PC-compatible desktop computers on a LAN. Three computers are for the office staff: Janet, George, and Kathy. Each computer has a 10BaseT EtherNet network adapter card. The local phone company has wired the office with twisted-pair cable and installed two jacks in wall plates next to each desk. One jack is for the telephone; the other is for the LAN. In the telephone wiring closet, the phone company installed a 10BaseT concentrator with enough jacks to support as many as 16 computers, should the firm's network needs expand.

The fourth computer is used for two purposes: tape backup and accounting. Every night an automatic backup program copies shared data directories on all the computers to a tape backup unit. During the day, the computer runs the accounting program that records the finances of the firm. Jim uses this computer when he comes in twice a week.

Each attorney has a notebook computer that can be taken to depositions, client meetings, and court. When the attorneys are in the office, they connect their computers to the LAN, using portable network adapters that fit onto the parallel ports of the notebook computers. When the attorneys leave the office, they unplug the adapters and take the notebook computers with them.

The office has two printers: a Hewlett-Packard LaserJet IIId (HP) and a Star Micronix dot-matrix printer. Everyone in the office uses the HP. Because George uses the HP printer the most, it is attached to his computer. The dot-matrix printer is attached to Kathy's computer. Jim uses the dot-matrix printer to generate financial reports, print multiple-part forms, and so on. The other people in the office occasionally use the dot-matrix printer when they are printing rough drafts of documents or when others are using the HP.

The office has standardized on several application programs. Windows for Workgroups is used on all computers except Jim's. With this standardization, all network users can coordinate their schedules using Schedule+, exchange electronic mail using Microsoft Mail, and prepare legal documents using Word for Windows.

Jim has installed Workgroup Connection on his computer so that he can access network resources and Microsoft Mail. Kathy, the office manager, has programmed the automated tape backup program attached to Jim's computer to back up shared directories every night at midnight.

Kathy uses Excel to keep track of billable hours for the attorneys. Because she is the only person using Excel, however, the application isn't shared.

Planning and Setting Up the Workgroup

As the person responsible for maintaining the network, Kathy must set up Windows for Workgroups on each computer in her office. Kathy already had the phone company do the wiring for the telephones used by the firm and the LAN. She had a local computer reseller set up the computers in the office and install all the hardware, including network adapters. The reseller also tested the network connections, using network management software and other equipment.

Before Kathy can install Windows for Workgroups, she must develop a good design for her workgroup. She must decide what directories to create, which directories to share, what access rights to give to the users, and how to assign access to the printers. She must install Microsoft Mail and give each user an account with the post office. Kathy also must give some thought to workgroup scheduling. Finally, she must install Word for Windows and Excel.

Creating Names for the Workgroup

Kathy must establish several types of names. She begins by listing the types of names and then writing down the names she selects. She needs the following types of names:

- *Workgroup name.* Kathy decides to use DCH, the initials of the last names of the partners of the firm, as the workgroup name.

- *Computer names.* Kathy chooses to use the letters *PC* (for personal computer) and the last name of the person who would be using the computer—for example, PC DEWEY, PC BARNES, and PC GONZALEZ.

■ *Printer names.* Kathy chooses to use the brand names for the printers: HP IIID for the laser printer and STAR for the dot-matrix.

■ *User logon names.* User logon names are the person's first name. Kathy decides that if the firm hires someone with the same first name as a current user, the logon name of the new person will be the first name and first initial of the last name.

■ *Mailbox names.* The mailbox name for each person in the office is the same as the logon name. In the post office list, however, Kathy enters the person's full name.

Table 2.1 summarizes the names Kathy chooses for her office network.

Table 2.1 Workgroup Names

Item	Name Assigned
Workgroup name	DCH
Computer names	PC DEWEY
	PC CHEATEM
	PC HOWE
	PC DOBSON
	PC BRUSH
	PC BARNES
	PC GONZALEZ
Printer names	HP IIID
	STAR
User logon names	STAN
	DONNA
	JUAN
	JANET
	GEORGE
	KATHY
	JIM
Mailbox names	STAN
	DONNA
	JUAN
	JANET
	GEORGE
	KATHY
	JIM

To create the workgroup and logon names, Kathy must install and start Windows for Workgroups 3.1 on each computer. Windows for Workgroups first prompts Kathy for a workgroup name and then a logon name. She must enter the workgroup and logon names and a password for each user. Windows for Workgroups then creates a password file for each user "registered" on each computer. (The program consults this password file whenever someone uses Windows for Workgroups.)

Creating a Directory Structure for the Workgroup

The directories Kathy creates on the computers in her office depend on several factors:

- *Who will use this computer?* The person using the computer has a direct influence on the shape of the directory structure for that computer. Each person has different needs and a different function in the company.

- *What programs will this person use and how often?* The answer to this question determines whether Kathy installs the program on the computer or enables the person to share it from another computer. In the case of word processor George Brush, Kathy decides to install Word for Windows on his computer.

- *Will this computer share one or more directories with other computers?* Kathy must look over the needs of each person in the company and then decide where data will be stored. In some cases, data needs to be shared with others. Kathy creates, for example, an Excel spreadsheet with the billable hours for the firm. She saves this spreadsheet to a directory on her computer each day. Jim, the accountant, needs access to this data when he comes in to do the books.

Kathy must make some key decisions about how the computers in her firm are to be set up. She comes to the following conclusions:

- Each computer will have a directory called SHARED for *shared data.* This directory will be used for data that people need to exchange. If some of the data shouldn't be visible to everyone with access to SHARED, Kathy needs to create a separate subdirectory for the data that shouldn't be shared. The PC user providing the network access, of course, has access to all the data.

■ Each computer will have a directory for private data that is named the same as the user's name. Stan Dewey's computer, for example, will have a directory called STAN.

■ Each computer will have a directory for Windows for Workgroups (except for Jim's computer, which will not run Windows for Workgroups).

■ Kathy will install Word for Windows on George and Janet's PCs. George's PC will be shared as the main source of Word for Windows for the rest of the office. Janet's Word for Windows will be used as a backup in case George's computer crashes. Kathy bought four copies of Word for Windows for the office. Although seven people work in the office, no more than four people will be using the program at one time, and the firm is protected from copyright violation.

■ Kathy decides to keep all client files on one computer. Otherwise, everyone would have files for clients scattered all over the office, increasing the odds that one file could overwrite a more recent revision or that a file could get lost.

George's computer will have a directory called CLIENTS with a subdirectory for each client. These subdirectories will contain documents created for each client that everyone in the office will be able to share. Because George's computer is backed up every night by the automated tape backup system, the client files will be restored onto Janet's computer in case of disk failure.

■ Kathy has installed Excel for Windows on her computer. Because she is the only Excel user in the office, however, this directory isn't shared.

■ Kathy's computer will become the mail server (that is, her computer will contain the post office) when she sets up Mail for the office.

■ Jim's computer has the accounting program and the tape backup program for the firm.

Figure 2.5 shows the master directory structure Kathy chose. She designed her structure with the name of the workgroup at the left. The names of each computer come next, and then the subdirectories for each computer. Because George's computer has client data to be shared by the entire company, his computer has two disk drives.

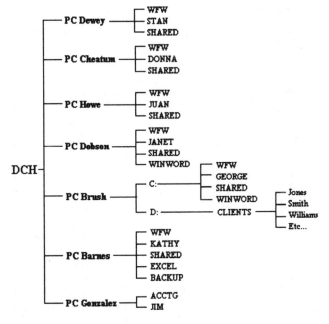

FIG. 2.5 *Dewey, Cheatem & Howe master directory structure.*

At this point, Kathy is ready to install Windows for Workgroups on each computer (except Jim's), using the names she selected.

Sharing Directories and Assigning Access Types

Now that Kathy has her directory structure planned for the company, she needs to share the appropriate directories and assign security rights. Because the copy of Word for Windows on Janet's computer exists only as a backup, Kathy will not mark this directory as a shared directory. To mark it as shared would only confuse the people at the company.

Before going into File Manager on each computer and making the directories shared, Kathy fills out the Directory Sharing worksheet introduced in Chapter 1. Figure 2.6 shows her version of the worksheet. In the left column are names of computers with shared directories. The second column lists drive letters and directories on each computer. The third column indicates which type of security access Kathy has decided to give the shared directory. These types include None (used for private directories that aren't shared), Read, Full, and D on P, an abbreviation for Depends on Password.

Workgroup Name	DCH		
Computer with Shared Dir.	**Directory**	**Security Level**	**Password**
PC Dewey	C:\SHARED	None ☐ Read ☐ Full ☒ D on P ☐	trout
PC Brush	C:\WINWORD	None ☐ Read ☒ Full ☐ D on P ☐	
	C:\CLIENTS	None ☐ Read ☐ Full ☒ D on P ☐	catfish
	C:\SHARED	None ☐ Read ☐ Full ☒ D on P ☐	snapper
PC Bames	C:\BILLHOUR	None ☐ Read ☐ Full ☐ D on P ☒	read=bass full=tuna

FIG. 2.6 *The Directory Sharing worksheet filled out for DC&H.*

The column on the right lists the passwords needed to access the shared directories. If the worksheet doesn't list a password, as in the Word for Windows directory in George Brush's computer (C:\WINWORD), the users don't need to enter a password to read files in the shared directory.

Kathy wants the attorneys to have access to the files in the C:\BILLHOUR directory on her computer but not the capability to alter them. Jim needs to look at the files, however, and may need to alter them. Kathy assigns the D on P access type to this directory. She then assigns BASS as the password for read-only access and TUNA as the password for full access. She gives the password BASS to the attorneys and the password TUNA to Jim.

To program each computer to share a directory and assign it access rights, Kathy must log onto each computer, one at a time. On each computer, she opens File Manager and selects the directory to share. From File Manager on George's computer, for example,

Kathy selects the C:\WINWORD directory and clicks the Share Directory toolbar icon, making the directory available to any network user. For access type, she selects read-only and doesn't assign a password.

To provide each user with the connections needed to do his or her daily work, Kathy connects a network drive for each user for each shared directory. From File Manager on Stan's computer, for example, Kathy chooses Connect Network Drive from the Disk menu. She then connects drive D to the \\PC_BRUSH\WINWORD directory. To make the connection permanent, she enables the Reconnect at Startup option. Kathy then places the icon for Word for Windows into the Applications group on Stan's Program Manager. From now on, when Stan is in the office he can use Word by sharing it from George's computer. When he is away from the office, Stan can use Windows Write to compose his notes. (For more information, see Chapter 3, "Using File Manager.")

Planning for Shared Printers

Kathy now must set up the shared printers. First, she needs to interview everyone in the office to get an idea of everyone's printing needs. As you may recall, the printers she has available in the office are an HP LaserJet IIId and a Star Micronix dot-matrix printer. After interviewing everyone in the office, Kathy determined the following printing needs:

Name	Items Printed	Pages Per Day	Print Quality
Stan Dewey	Personal schedule, outlines	2	Draft
Donna Cheatem	Personal schedule, outlines	2	Draft
Juan Howe	Personal schedule, outlines, memos	3	Draft
George Brush	Various legal documents	100	Letter
Janet Dobson	Formal correspondence, briefs	30	Letter or draft
Kathy Barnes	Billable hours spreadsheets, office schedule, memos	8	Draft
Jim Gonzalez	Financial reports	20	Draft

Kathy attaches the HP to George's computer because he uses the printer the most and needs letter-quality output. Because the HP is attached to George's computer, George is the manager of that printer; he is the local user of the HP.

Kathy decides to move the dot-matrix printer to Janet's computer because Janet is the second most frequent user of a printer. Janet can share the HP, but she also has the dot-matrix printer in case she needs to get a quick letter out when the HP is in use. Janet is now the local user of the Star printer. George and Janet have HP IIID as their default printer. The others in the office have STAR as their default printer.

During the initial installation, Kathy installed the printers for each person using Windows for Workgroups (everyone except Jim). She made the HP on George's computer a shared printer. She made the Star on Janet's computer a shared printer. On all other computers she must open Print Manager and connect over the network. To make these connections permanent, she enables the Reconnect at Startup option. (For more information, see Chapter 4, "Printing with Windows for Workgroups.")

Setting Up Mail

Kathy sets up the Mail system for the office in the two following stages:

- ■ Setting up the post office
- ■ Setting up the user accounts

Earlier Kathy decided to make her computer the Mail server, which contains the post office information. Because this computer should be running before any other users log on to the network for the day, she leaves instructions that the first person into the office on any day must turn on her computer. To set up the post office, Kathy first starts Mail on her computer. She then selects the option Create a New Post Office.

To set up the user accounts, Kathy installs Mail on each computer. She enters the user's logon name for the name of that user's mailbox. For each user she selects the option Connect to an Existing Post Office. She directs the users to the post office on her computer. She then fills in a data-entry screen with other information about that user.

Kathy also adds a new folder called COMPANY MAIL, a shared mail folder that anyone in the company can read from and write to. This folder provides company-wide mail access for common messages for everyone in the company. She also creates two shared subfolders under COMPANY MAIL called ATTORNEYS and STAFF. These folders are for any information pertinent to just the attorneys or just the staff, respectively. For more information, see Chapter 5, "Using Mail."

Planning for Workgroup Scheduling

One of Kathy's responsibilities includes scheduling for the office, a time-consuming task. She must coordinate the schedules of the attorneys, including their court dates. One missed date could cost the firm's clients thousands of dollars. She also schedules meetings with clients, general office meetings, holidays, and vacations.

Kathy decides to use Schedule+ to manage the scheduling needs of her firm. Each person in the office is responsible for entering his or her own appointments. Because the attorneys plug their notebook computers into the LAN when they come into the office, Kathy sets up the attorneys' computers to load Schedule+ when they first open Windows for Workgroups. She does so by moving the Schedule+ icon into Program Manager's Startup group, causing the master and individual calendars to be updated. The attorneys consult their calendars each morning to see what they are scheduled to do for the day. Their computers update the master calendar with any appointments they have entered. Meeting requests are circulated through the Mail system.

When Kathy installs Schedule+ on everyone's computer, she makes herself the assistant for everyone's schedule, giving her full access to everyone's schedule except for appointments that her coworkers have marked private. She can make, change, or remove appointments for anyone in the office. When someone makes changes on his own calendar, Kathy is notified. Everyone in the office can read each other's schedules. For more information, see Chapter 6, "Using Schedule+."

Summary

This chapter covered the basic features of Windows for Workgroups on a conceptual level. Network features of File Manager and Print Manager were covered. New applications provided with Windows for Workgroups were covered, including Mail and Schedule+. This chapter also discussed various concepts involved in organizing and managing a workgroup, covering such topics as directory and printer sharing, how to define a workgroup, and how workgroup names are selected.

The following chapters move from the conceptual arena into the practical realm of using Windows for Workgroups. Each main utility of the program is discussed in its own chapter. Chapter 3, "Using File Manager in a Workgroup," for example, discusses File Manager in relation to Windows for Workgroups.

Using File Manager in a Workgroup

As you saw in Chapter 2, one of the key strengths of Windows for Workgroups is its capability of sharing files. File Manager is the tool that accomplishes this task.

This chapter takes you through File Manager, emphasizing features that are unique to Windows for Workgroups. This chapter first covers some concepts that are critical to the development of a Windows for Workgroups network: network drives and directories. You learn how to work with network drives and shared directories, and how to view network users that are currently sharing your directories and files. Security access rights are discussed in detail. You also learn about the new File Manager tool bar.

Understanding Network Drives and Shared Directories

As you learned in Chapter 2, one use of File Manager is to share directories with other users. Just as you can share a directory on your hard disk, you also can use a shared directory. File Manager enables you to assign a drive letter to a shared directory from another computer.

As you know, DOS assigns drive letters to physical devices. Drive A, for example, is the first floppy drive, and drive C generally is your hard drive. A *network drive* letter, on the other hand, isn't the assignment of an actual drive. Using Windows for Workgroups, you assign a drive letter to a shared directory that you are connecting to.

Before you connect a network drive letter to a shared directory, Windows for Workgroups checks your security access type. If a password is assigned to the shared directory, you are prompted to enter it. After you connect to the shared directory, notice that you cannot see any directories above this directory. The network drive appears as though it is the root. You can see and change to subdirectories of the shared directory.

You can create network drives, remove them, and change them at any time. You also can make a network drive "permanent"—that is, you can choose to assign the same drive letter to the shared directory each time you start Windows for Workgroups.

The next sections focus on directory management issues, network drives, and shared directories. Network issues such as security and file sharing are discussed, as well as what happens when you connect or disconnect a network drive.

Understanding Directory Management

Setting up directories on networked computers is different than on stand-alone computers. You need to decide which computers offer shared directories. These computers must be running Windows for Workgroups and must be connected to the LAN. Security access types also must be assigned for the shared directories: will a directory be a read-only or a full-access directory, or will the access type depend on assigned passwords?

The shared directories should contain application program files or data files that other users need access to. Directories that remain private (not shared) can hold any kind of file that only one user needs access to. Files in shared directories are *public*. Files in directories that aren't shared are *private*.

Separating application files from data files is recommended. Assign read-only access to directories that contain application files, to prevent users from accidentally erasing those files. Most likely you would assign full access only to data files. If you must mix application and data files in a single directory, you can change the attributes of the individual application files to read-only through the Properties command on File Manager's File menu.

Understanding Network Drives and the DOS Last Drive

Windows for Workgroups enables you to assign as network drives only letters up to and including the last drive specified in DOS. The default DOS last drive is E. (DOS uses A through C for local drives.) You can gain additional drive letters by adding or changing the LASTDRIVE statement in your CONFIG.SYS file.

Windows for Workgroups doesn't change the LASTDRIVE statement during installation. If you don't have enough drive letters available for Windows for Workgroups, you see an error message when you first load Windows for Workgroups (see fig. 3.1).

FIG. 3.1 *Not enough DOS drive letters error message.*

> **NOTE** Every time you make a change to the CONFIG.SYS file, you must restart the computer before the change becomes effective.

In the following sample CONFIG.SYS file, LASTDRIVE is set to drive G. The user on this computer can assign drives D to G as network drives.

```
DEVICE=C:\WFW\HIMEM.SYS
DEVICE=C:\WFW\EMM386.EXE noems
DOS=HIGH,UMB
DEVICE=C:\DOS\SETVER.EXE
files = 99
buffers = 15
STACKS=9,256
device=C:\WFW\protman.dos /i:C:\WFW
device=C:\WFW\workgrp.sys
device=C:\WFW\PE2NDIS.EXE
LASTDRIVE=G:
```

> **TIP** If you plan to use Windows for Workgroups with other networks, you may have to put some thought into setting the LASTDRIVE parameter in the CONFIG.SYS file. Some networks, such as Novell's NetWare 3.11, assign drive letters *after* the LASTDRIVE. Other networks, such as Banyan Vines, assign drive letters *before* the LASTDRIVE. If you plan to use only Windows for Workgroups, set LASTDRIVE to Z. If you plan to use Windows for Workgroups and NetWare, set LASTDRIVE to G. (NetWare uses drives H through Z, and Windows for Workgroups can use drives D through G.)

Identifying Network Drives

Network drives appear in File Manager differently than local drives do. When looking at the File Manager window, you easily can identify network drives in the following ways:

- The drive icon you see in File Manager is different than the icon for a local drive.

- Two backslashes, the computer name, and the directory name appear in the title bar of the directory contents listing window for a network drive.

The drive list box in figure 3.2 shows that the computer TANDY and the subdirectory FARSIDE is assigned drive letter D. The computer TANDY and the subdirectory DOUG is assigned drive letter E.

Sharing Files

Be aware of the application that you use when sharing files. Some applications are *network aware*, which means that they sense the presence of a network and take steps to prevent users from overwriting the same file at the same time.

An application doesn't have to be network aware to run on a network. Notepad, an accessory that comes with Windows for Workgroups, for example, is not network aware. If two users have the same file open at the same time, one user can overwrite the other's work. The only safeguard you have in this situation is to

assign security access types carefully. Use read-only access whenever possible. Read-only access enables users to read the files in
the directory assigned but prevents them from saving changes to
files in the directory.

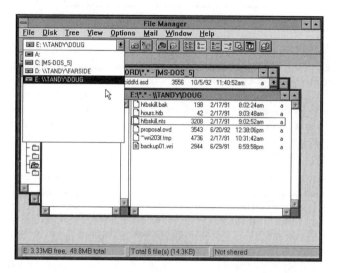

FIG. 3.2 *Identifying shared drives in Windows for Workgroups.*

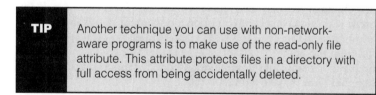

TIP Another technique you can use with non-network-
aware programs is to make use of the read-only file
attribute. This attribute protects files in a directory with
full access from being accidentally deleted.

Word for Windows is a network-aware application. When two users have the same file open at the same time, Word gives the first
user priority over all other users. This process is known as a *file
lock.*

If you open a Word for Windows file that another user has open,
you see a message box that enables you to open a *copy* of the file
or to wait (cancel the operation) until the file no longer is in use
(see fig. 3.3). You cannot make changes to the *same* Word file until the other user closes the file, and then you close and reopen
the file.

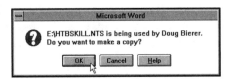

FIG. 3.3 *A message warning you that another user has the file open.*

When you load a document from a shared directory into Word, Windows for Workgroups transfers the document over the LAN into your computer's memory. When two users have the same document on-screen, three copies of the same file actually exist: the first copy is on your hard drive, the second is in the memory of your computer, and the third is in the memory of the other person's computer.

Network-aware programs such as Word keep track of who has "checked out" a copy of the file. When the first user closes and saves his copy of the document to his hard drive, Word updates its internal "checkout desk." As far as Word is concerned, you now have an outdated copy of the document in the memory of your computer. Word requires you to dump the outdated copy (by closing the document) and reopen it again to see the changes made by the other user. Now, as the exclusive user of the document, you are given priority over other users.

Any changes you may have made will be lost if you close the document without saving it. If you open a document that is in use by another user and want to save that document, you can specify a different file name. The danger here is that you could end up with multiple revisions of the same document. Trying to piece it back together later may be a difficult task.

When you try to overwrite a document in use by another user, you see a message like the one shown in figure 3.4.

Securing Your Directories

In Chapter 2, you learned that four kinds of security access exist: no access, read-only, full, and depends on password. The first access type, no access, is not assigned. If you do not share a directory, network users cannot access that directory. The only exception to this rule is that when you share one directory, network users can access its subdirectories. You can assign the other kinds of access through File Manager when you first prepare a directory for sharing. The person who is using the computer with the directories to be shared assigns access types.

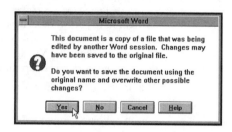

FIG. 3.4   *Preventing others from overwriting a shared file.*

> **TIP**   Don't share the root directory of a hard drive. Sharing the root directory of a computer's hard drive voids security on the drive. Workgroup members then can access *all* directories on the hard drive. Rather, share only subdirectories. You then can control the kind of access to individual directories—read-only access or full access.

The following sections explain how to assign the various access types to directories.

Assigning Read-Only or Full Access

To assign read-only or full access to a directory, follow these steps:

1. In File Manager, select the directory you want to share.

2. From the **Disk** menu choose Share **As**. The Share Directory dialog appears.

> **TIP**   To access the Share Directory dialog, you also can click the Share Directory icon on the toolbar. File Manager's toolbar buttons are described later in "Understanding the File Manager Window."

3. In the Share Directory dialog, enter the following information:

Dialog Item	Description
Share Name	A brief name you want to have appear across the LAN to other users when they connect through File Manager or through network-aware applications
Path	The drive\directory on your computer to be shared
Comment	A brief description that will appear next to the Share Name across the LAN to other users

4. In the Access Type section, choose **Read-Only** or **Full**.

5. Type a password in the **Read-Only** Password or **Full** Access Password text box.

> **NOTE** If you don't type a password, Windows for Workgroups assumes that you don't want to have a password for this directory.

6. Choose OK.

In figure 3.5, the directory CCMAIL is set up as a shared directory with read-only access. The password EMAIL is assigned to gain access to the directory.

Assigning Depends on Password Access

The Depends on Password access option in the Share Directory dialog enables you to assign read-only and full access to the same directory. You assign each access type through a separate password. If the user enters the password that specifies read-only, Windows for Workgroups enables access to the directory on a read-only basis. If the user knows the password for full access, full access to the directory is granted.

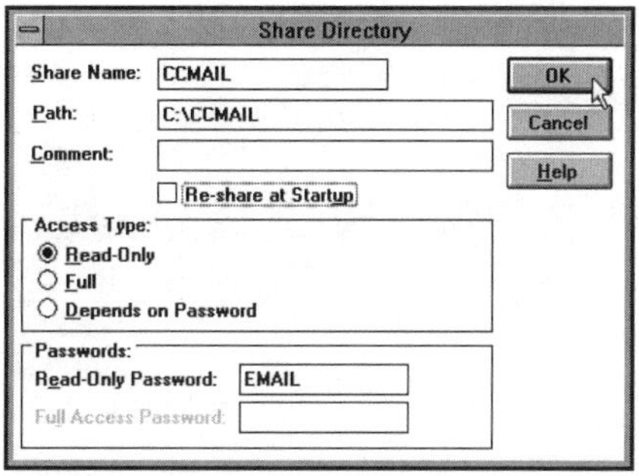

FIG. 3.5 *Assigning a shared directory with read-only access.*

> **NOTE** You don't have to choose **D**epends on Password to assign a password. You can choose read-only or full access and still specify a password. In that case, the user is prompted to enter a password but gets only read-only or only full access.

To assign depends on password access, follow these steps:

1. In File Manager, select the directory you want to share.

2. From the **D**isk menu choose Share **A**s.

3. In the Share Directory dialog, fill in the appropriate information in the **S**hare Name, **P**ath, and **C**omment text boxes, as explained in the preceding section.

4. Choose the **D**epends on Password radio button.

5. Type a password in the Read-Only Password text box.

6. Type a different password in the Full Access Password text box.

> **NOTE** Passwords can be up to eight characters long. Any character you can type is acceptable.

7. Choose OK.

Now to access this shared directory, users must enter a password at the prompt (see fig. 3.6). Without this password, unauthorized users cannot access information in the shared directory.

FIG. 3.6 *Accessing a directory that requires password access.*

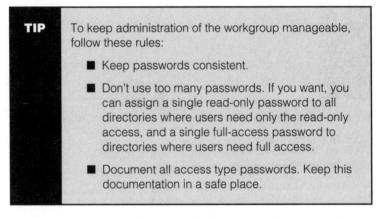

Your password is saved in a *password table* if you select the Save this Password in Your Password List check box in the Enter Network Password dialog. You never have to enter the password again when you reconnect, unless you change the password. This password applies only to read-only or full access types. If you assign depends on password access, users are prompted for a password every time they try to connect.

Each password you save with the Save this Password option is saved in the password file on your computer. The file is stored in the Windows for Workgroups program directory with a name consisting of your logon name and a PWL extension.

Changing a Directory's Access Type

Your needs may change as you continue to use your Windows for Workgroups network. Suppose that you install a program and assigned read-only access to its shared directory. When using the program, you discover that it writes temporary files to its directory. The local user can use the program because he has full access to any directories on his own computer, but other users cannot. To remedy the situation, you must change the access type to full.

To change a directory's access type, follow these steps:

1. In File Manager, select the shared directory to change.

2. From the **Disk** menu choose Share **As**.

3. In the Share Directory dialog, click the button next to the desired access type.

If you change a directory's password while users are using the directory, you will disconnect the users' network drives from the shared directory. The users still see the network drive listed, but no files are listed. Users who are disconnected because of a password change need to reconnect to their network drive and enter the correct password. If you don't change the password or have no password to begin with, users currently using this directory should have no problems.

If you have a document or spreadsheet open in a shared directory and are disconnected, the document or spreadsheet remains in the memory of your computer. You can save the document or spreadsheet to your local hard drive. If you have a large database file open, your changes may or may not be saved, and the database may become corrupted and unusable.

> **TIP**　When nobody is using the shared directory is the best time to make access-type changes. You can use File Manager to see who is using a shared directory (see "Displaying Users of a Shared Directory or File" later in the chapter). You also can use the Chat utility to warn users of impending changes. (Chapter 7, "Exploring Advanced Features of Windows for Workgroups," shows you how to use Chat.)

Using File Manager

File Manager, a utility installed in Program Manager's Main group, is a critical tool used for looking for files, creating directories, copying and moving files, and deleting files. In a workgroup environment, you also use File Manager to share directories, connect network drives, and assign security access.

The following sections introduce and explain how to use the File Manager features available in Windows for Workgroups. Specifically, you learn how to obtain directory information, connect network drives, make directories into shared directories, and display user information.

Understanding the File Manager Window

File Manager has a main window with menus and icons that enable you to perform actions without having to go through several menus. Through a series of directory windows, you also can view the directory trees of several drives at one time. The left window shows the directory tree, and the right window lists file names. Figure 3.7 shows File Manager's main window.

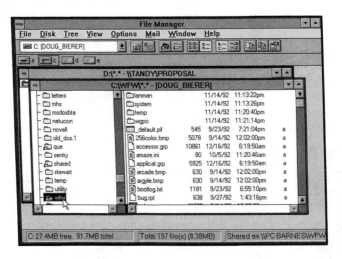

FIG. 3.7 *File Manager's main window.*

The File Manager window is divided into the following major parts:

- The menu bar
- The toolbar
- The drive bar
- The directory window(s)
- The status bar

The following sections explain the function and usage of each feature.

The Menu Bar

File Manager's menus consist of File, Disk, Tree, View, Options, Mail, Window, and Help. Table 3.1 describes each menu command. The Access Type column lists the access type you need to perform each File Manager function if you are accessing a shared directory on another computer. If you are working with directories on your own computer, the Access Type column is not relevant.

Table 3.1 File Manager Menu Commands

Command	Description	Access Type
File Open	Opens associated file under the associated application program	Read-only or Full
File Move	Moves a file from one drive\directory to another. If the drive is a network drive, moves the file over the LAN to the computer to which the network drive is assigned.	Full in source and destination directories
File Delete	Deletes selected file	Full
File Rename	Renames a file	Full

continues

Table 3.1 Continued

Command	Description	Access Type
File Properties	Shows information about the file, including date and time last changed, version, copyright (if available), and file attributes. The option Open By tells whether another workgroup user has the file open.	Read-only to see properties; full to change
File Run	Executes the selected application file	Read-only or Full
File Print	Prints the selected document file	Read-only or Full
File Associate	Creates an association for a file type (by extension)	Read-only or Full
File Create Directory	Creates a directory	Full
File Search	Searches for files in the currently selected directory or the entire disk drive	Read-only or Full
File Select Files	Enables you to select some or all files in the current directory	Read-only or Full
File Exit	Exits File Manager	Read-only or Full
Disk Copy Disk	Copies a floppy disk (doesn't work with network drives)	N/A
Disk Label Disk	Labels the local floppy or hard drive (doesn't work with network drives)	N/A
Disk Format Disk	Formats a floppy disk (doesn't work with network drives)	N/A

Command	*Description*	*Access Type*
Disk Make System Disk	Transfers system files to a floppy disk (doesn't work with network drives)	N/A
Disk Connect Network Drive	Assigns a drive letter to a shared directory on another computer	Read-only or Full
Disk Disconnect Network Drive	Disconnects a drive letter from a shared directory on another computer	Read-only or Full
Disk Share **As**	Turns a local directory into a shared directory	N/A
Disk Stop Sharing	Removes a local directory from the shared directory list on the LAN	Read-only or Full
Disk Select Drive	Changes viewed drive to another drive letter (also can click a drive icon)	Read-only or Full
Tree Expand One Level	Expands the directory structure one level deeper	Read-only or Full
Tree Expand **Branch**	Fully expands the selected branch	Read-only or Full
Tree Expand **All**	Fully expands all branches	Read-only or Full
Tree Collapse Branch	Reduces the branch so that you see only the main directory and no sub-directories of this branch	Read-only or Full
Tree Indicate Expandable Branches	When the branches aren't fully expanded, places a plus sign (+) inside the icon to indicate that this directory has more branches	Read-only or Full

3

continues

Table 3.1 Continued

Command	Description	Access Type
View Tree and Directory	Displays the directory tree and directory contents	Read-only or Full
View Tree Only	Shows only the directory tree	Read-only or Full
View Directory Only	Displays only the directory's contents	Read-only or Full
View Split	Redefines the split point between the directory tree and the directory contents listing	Read-only or Full
View Name	Lists only file names in the directory window	Read-only or Full
View All File Details	Shows all file details (name, size, date and time file was last modified, and attributes)	Read-only or Full
View Partial Details	Enables you to choose only the file details that you want to see	Read-only or Full
View Sort by Name	Lists files sorted alphabetically by file name	Read-only Full
View Sort by Type	Lists files by file type (by file extension)	Read-only or Full
View Sort by Size	Lists files by file size, largest to smallest	Read-only or Full
View Sort by Date	Lists files by the date last modified	Read-only or Full
View By File Type	Lists files by type, such as Pattern (*.ZIP), Directories, Programs, Documents, and Other Files. Also shows hidden and system files.	Read-only or Full

Command	Description	Access Type
Options Confirmation	Suppresses confirmation on File Delete, Directory Delete, File Replace, Mouse Action, and Disk Commands. Usually, File Manager asks you to confirm deletion of a file (to prevent accidental deletion). Often, this option is inconvenient. To delete 100 files at a time, for example, you must choose OK 100 times, thus consuming time.	Read-only or Full
Options Font	Enables you to change fonts used in File Manager	Read-only or Full
Options Customize Toolbar	Enables you to choose buttons that appear on the toolbar	N/A
Options Toolbar	Enables you to display or hide the toolbar	N/A
Options Drivebar	Enables you to display or hide the drive bar	N/A
Options Status Bar	Enables you to display or hide the status bar	N/A
Options Open New Window on Connect	Enables you to determine whether a directory window is created when you connect a network drive	N/A
Options Minimize on Use	Reduces memory and CPU use by turning File Manager into an icon when you run an application from within File Manager	N/A

continues

Table 3.1 Continued

Command	Description	Access Type
Options Save Settings on Exit	Enables you to save the last File Manager settings so that when you return to File Manager, you see the same settings	N/A
Mail Send Mail	Takes you to the Send Mail portion of the Mail program, where you can send the selected data file to the desired user as mail	N/A
Window New Window	Creates another directory window	N/A
Window Cascade	Cascades the directory windows	N/A
Window Tile Horizontally	Tiles the directory windows top to bottom	N/A
Window Tile Vertically	Tiles the directory windows left to right	N/A
Window Arrange Icons	Improves the appearance of the directory windows that were reduced to icons—no overlap	N/A
Window Refresh	Updates the directory window. Useful when many users are sharing the same directory and creating many new files. Usually, Windows for Workgroups automatically updates the directory windows.	N/A
Window 1	Assigns a number to each active directory window according to the order the window was created so that you can switch between directory windows	N/A

Command	Description	Access Type
	With a mouse, you can click any part of a directory window (or press Ctrl+Tab) to make the directory active.	
Help	Presents a help screen. Like all Windows applications, File Manager has extensive help available. You can get help on menu items by highlighting the menu item and pressing F1.	N/A

The Toolbar

The toolbar is a set of buttons below the menu bar that makes using File Manager easier. Each toolbar button is like a visual macro. (Unlike a macro, however, you cannot change the function of a toolbar button.) By clicking the button, you can access an option that otherwise may take you three or four menus or dialogs to access.

Table 3.2 lists all available toolbar buttons and their corresponding menu commands. Commands marked with an asterisk (*) appear by default in the File Manager toolbar.

Table 3.2 File Manager Toolbar Buttons

Toolbar Button	Equivalent Menu Command
[X]	File Delete
[a.b]	File Rename
[⊞]	File Copy

continues

Table 3.2 Continued

Toolbar Button	Equivalent Menu Command
	File Move
	File Print
	File Properties
	File Create Directory
	File Search
	File Select Files
	Disk Connect Network Drive*
	Disk Disconnect Network Drive*
	Disk Share As*
	Disk Stop Sharing*
	View Name
	View All File Details
	View Partial Details
	View Sort by Name

Toolbar Button	Equivalent Menu Command
	View Sort by Type
	View Sort by Size
	View Sort by Date
	View By File Type
	Options Font
	Window New Window
	Window Cascade
	Window Tile Horizontally
	Window Tile Vertically
	Help Contents
	Mail Send Mail

You can customize the display and order of toolbar buttons by selecting Customize Toolbar from the Options menu. In the Customize Toolbar dialog, you see a list of available buttons on the left
and buttons now in the toolbar on the right (see fig. 3.8). The Customize Toolbar dialog also enables you to add or remove buttons.
By using the Separator option, you also can insert space between
buttons.

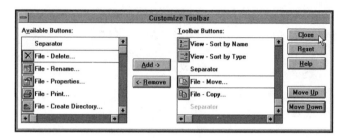

FIG. 3.8 *Customizing the toolbar.*

The following table describes the function of other options found in the Customize Toolbar dialog.

Button	Function
Add	Adds buttons from the Available Buttons list to the Toolbar Buttons list, thus adding buttons to the toolbar. The Toolbar Buttons list contains buttons already on the toolbar by default. (These buttons are marked in table 3.2 with an asterisk.)
Remove	Opposite of the Add button, moves buttons from the Toolbar Buttons list to the Available Buttons list, thus removing buttons from the toolbar
Move Up	Moves the selected toolbar button in the Toolbar Buttons list up one item on the list, thus changing its order of appearance on the toolbar
Move Down	Moves the selected toolbar button in the Toolbar Buttons list down one item on the list
Close	Saves changes and returns you to File Manager
Reset	Restores the default toolbar buttons
Help	Displays a help screen on customizing the toolbar

The Drive Bar

The drive bar displays icons of each drive now in use. Depending on the kind of drive available, three icons are available. The following table shows these icons:

Icon	Drive
▭ a	Local floppy drive
▭ c	Local hard drive
▭ d	Network drive

Clicking the desired drive icon produces a listing of the drive's directory contents in the active directory window. New icons appear as drives become available. If you connect to a shared directory over the LAN, for example, an icon appears for the new drive letter that is assigned to the shared directory.

The Directory Window

The directory windows show you information about the currently selected drive. The information and the order in which the information is displayed depends on the current View options. You can display, for example, the directory tree and the directory contents. You can sort files by name, type, size, and date. You can view as little file information as the file name, or as much information as the full file option presents.

You also can tile or cascade directory windows by choosing the appropriate Window menu option. You even can open two or more windows on the same hard drive by choosing New Window from the Window menu. The New Window option is especially useful if the drive has many files and/or subdirectories.

To change drives, click the desired drive icon or from the **Disk** menu choose **Select Drive**. In the directory tree, you also can click the desired directory or press the arrow keys to select the desired directory.

If the screen becomes too cluttered, you can minimize a directory window by clicking the Minimize button (the down triangle at the right end of the title bar) or by choosing Minimize from the window's Control menu.

The Status Bar

The status bar at the bottom of the File Manager screen is divided into three sections. The information that appears on the status bar depends on whether you have selected a directory or one or more files. The following table shows you what you should see on the status bar, depending on your selections.

Selection	Information in Left Section	Information in Middle Section	Message in Right Section
Directory	Drive, total megabytes free, total megabytes	Total number of files and how much available disk space is taken	`Not Shared` or `Shared as` `\\computer\-` `directory`
Single file	File size (in bytes), date and time of last change	Total number of files in directory and how much disk space is taken	`Not Shared`
Many files	Number of files selected and how much disk space the files take	Total number of files in directory and how much disk space is taken	`Not Shared`

TIP   Files display a **Not Shared** message, even when the files can be shared. You can determine whether a file is open and who has the file open by following these steps:

1. Select the file in question.

2. Choose Properties from the **F**ile menu.

3. In the Properties dialog, choose the **O**pen By button.

You see a list of all users—and each user's access rights—who now have the file open.

Viewing Information in a Directory Window

A major difference exists between viewing a local drive and viewing a network drive in File Manager. You have full access rights to your local drives and will not be prompted to enter a password to access a directory on your own computer. You can see all directories and can copy, delete, and move files at will. You also can create and remove directories. When working with a network drive, however, you are restricted to the access rights that have been assigned to the workgroup. If you have full-access rights, you can treat the network drive as a local drive. If you have read-only access rights, you can only view the files in the shared directory and run applications.

Information in a directory window consists of two sections: a directory tree and directory contents. Depending on the View menu setting you select, you can view as much or as little information as you want, as follows:

- The directory tree only, the directory contents only, or both

- Only file names, full file details, or partial file details

- Files sorted by file name, file type, size, or date

You can set these options by selecting the desired combination from the View menu. You also can adjust the placement of the dividing line between the directory tree and the directory contents by choosing Split from the View menu.

The View By File Type command enables you to change what defines a file type. The default file type is the file's extension.

Opening a New Directory Window

Often, you may want to open a new directory window while viewing another drive. You can do so in two ways: from the Window menu choose New Window, or from the Disk menu choose Connect a Network Drive. To view directory windows on more than one drive, switch to one window or the other and click a drive button.

> **NOTE** After you change a drive letter, you don't have to open a new window. Changing drives changes the display in the currently active directory window.

When you first open a window by using the New Window command, you see a display that duplicates the currently active window. This command is useful if you want to see more than one part of the directory structure for a single hard drive. Figure 3.9 shows a two directory windows displaying views of the same hard disk.

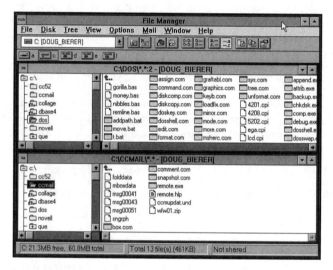

FIG. 3.9 *Two directory windows for the same hard drive.*

Updating a Directory Window

Windows for Workgroups updates information in a directory window every few seconds. If you have many application windows open, however, you may not see the most current information because refreshing the directory window is a low-priority task for Windows for Workgroups.

You can update the information in a directory window in the following ways:

- Press the F5 key, or from the Window menu choose Refresh.

- Change to another drive and then back again. To change drives, you can click another drive icon, or from the Disk menu choose Select Drive and then select another drive from the list.

■ For network drives, disconnect and reconnect the drive. (On a busy network, changing to another drive may not fully refresh the directory window.)

Remember that if you don't choose the Open New Window on Connect command from the Options menu, you don't get a new directory window for the shared directory. You will see information about the drive you just connected in the active directory window.

Sharing Directories

If you want to make directories available to users in the workgroup, learning the procedure for sharing directories is essential. You can share directories temporarily or permanently. Permanently shared directories are made available every time the user goes into Windows for Workgroups. The following sections discuss these two types of sharing.

Permanent Sharing

To share a directory permanently, follow these steps:

1. Select the directory on your hard drive.

2. Click the Share Directory toolbar button or choose Share As from the Disk menu. The Share Directory dialog appears.

3. In the Share Name text box, type the name under which you want this directory listed for the reference of workgroup users.

4. In the Path text box, type the local drive letter and directory to be shared.

5. In the Comment text box, type all comments you want to make. The text you type here is only for your reference.

6. Mark the Re-share at Startup check box.

7. In the Access Type section, choose one of the following options:

    Read-only

    Full

    Depends on Password

8. Enter a password or two, if desired. If you enter a password, the user must enter a password before he or she can connect a network drive to this directory.

9. Choose OK when done.

Figure 3.10 shows a completed Share Directory dialog.

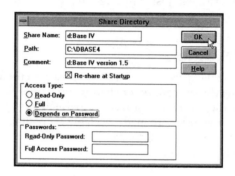

FIG. 3.10 *The Share Directory dialog.*

Temporary Sharing

To share a directory temporarily, follow the same steps as in the preceding section, but don't mark the Re-share at Startup check box (step 6). This procedure makes the directory temporarily available to workgroup members. After a user exits Windows for Workgroups, however, the directory again becomes unavailable.

Connecting to Directories

As a workgroup member, you can connect a network drive to any shared directories to which you have access. The minimum access required is read-only. If the access depends on a password, you are prompted to enter a password. The password you enter determines the access type, read-only or full. If you don't know the password or if you enter an invalid password, you cannot access the directory.

You can connect to as many shared directories as you have drive letters available. The drive letters you have available are controlled by the LASTDRIVE parameter (explained in more detail earlier in the section "Understanding Network Drives and the DOS Last Drive"). The network drives you connect can be on any computer you have on your Windows for Workgroup network.

The next sections give you detailed procedures on how to connect and disconnect network drives.

Connecting to a Shared Directory

To connect to a shared directory, follow these steps:

1. From the **Disk** menu choose Connect Network Drive, or click the Connect Network Drive toolbar button. The Connect Network Drive dialog appears (see fig. 3.11).

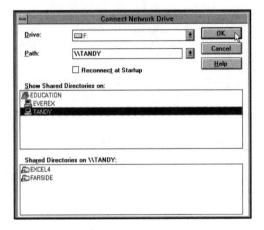

FIG. 3.11 *The Connect Network Drive dialog.*

2. Type the desired drive letter in the **Drive** text box or scroll through the **Drive** drop-down list to select the drive.

3. Type the path, if known, in the **Path** text box, using the syntax *computer\path*. If the computer to which you want to connect is named DOUGS_PC, for example, and the directory name is WINDOWS\TEMP, type the following:

   \\DOUGS_PC\WINDOWS\TEMP

   If you are unsure which computer and which directory to specify, use the Show Shared Directories On (computer) and Shared Directories On (selected computer) list boxes.

4. If you want to have this drive available every time you start Windows for Workgroups, mark the Reconnect at Startup check box.

5. Choose OK.

Disconnecting a Network Drive

You may want to disconnect a network drive after you are done using an application or file on another computer. Disconnecting is also a good practice if you know the user on the other computer plans to turn off the computer. If you leave the drive connected and the other user turns off his computer, you will notice only if you are running an application on the shared directory. In this case, an error message will appear, telling you to terminate the application.

To disconnect a network drive, follow these steps:

1. From the **Disk** menu, choose **Disconnect Network Drive.** You also can click the Disconnect Network Drive toolbar button. The Disconnect Network Drive dialog appears.

2. Select the drive to disconnect the network drive.

3. Press Enter or choose OK.

Selecting Files and Directories

Selecting items in Windows for Workgroups is no different than in Windows. Highlighted files and directories are considered to be "selected." This section describes several methods of selecting groups of files and directories at once.

To select a directory, you click the desired directory icon at the left side of the directory window. If you double-click a directory icon, subdirectories of the directory appear. Double-clicking expands the directory branch. If you also want to see the contents of the directory, from the View menu choose Tree and Directory.

You can select files using one of several methods, as described in the following sections.

Selecting Files with the Mouse

To select a single file, click the file name. To select multiple files with a mouse, however, you can use several different techniques. Follow these steps:

1. Click to select the first file.

2. Hold down the Shift key and click a second file to highlight all files between the first and second files. You also can hold down the Ctrl key and click to highlight additional individual files.

Selecting Files with the Keyboard

You also can use the keyboard to select files by following these steps:

1. Use the arrow keys to highlight the first file.

2. Press and hold the Shift key and press the arrow keys to highlight more consecutive files. Press and hold the Ctrl key to highlight a file that is not in consecutive order.

> **TIP** Use Tab and Shift+Tab to move between the tree and contents portions of the directory window.

Selecting Files with the Select File Command

The Select File command on the File menu enables you to select files by using DOS wild cards and file-name patterns. The selections you make affect only the active directory window. You can make as many selections in different directory windows as you want. Each selection is cumulative. You also can use this command to deselect files.

To select multiple files by using the Select File command, follow these steps:

1. From the File menu choose Select File. The Select Files dialog appears (see fig. 3.12).

FIG. 3.12 *The Select Files dialog.*

2. Type a file-name pattern in the File(s) text box. You can enter a pattern to narrow down the list of files you want to see. Patterns can include the following kinds of examples:

   ■ Complete file names with an extension, such as DOSKEY.COM

■ The beginning of a file name followed by asterisks, such as QB*.*

■ An asterisk and a file extension, such as *.CPI

■ All files, using *.*

■ A file name with question marks substituting for individual characters, such as MSG00??.DAT

3. Choose the Select button to select all files that match the Files(s) pattern.

4. Repeat steps 2 and 3 until you have selected all desired files.

Notice that, as you select files, the file names are underlined in the directory window. When you exit the Select Files dialog, the underlined files are highlighted.

Displaying Users of a Shared Directory or File

When workgroup users are using shared directories, Windows for Workgroups keeps track of who the users are and what files these users have open. You can obtain this information by using the Properties command on the File menu, as explained in the following sections.

Viewing Which Files are Open in a Shared Directory

The Network Properties dialog shows you network-related information about a file. This feature only works when you select a single file. If you select multiple files, this option isn't available.

You can find out which users are using a file in a selected directory, and network statistics on the file, by following these steps:

1. From the File menu, choose Properties (or press Alt+Enter). The Properties dialog appears.

2. Choose Open By. The Network Properties dialog appears.

The Network Properties dialog contains the following items:

■ The name of the shared directory (in the Share Name field)

■ The local drive letter and directory (in the Path field)

- The number of times this file has been opened since you started Windows for Workgroups (in the Open Count field)

The **Open By** scroll box in the Network Properties dialog includes the following information:

- The logon name of the user who has the file open

- The access type for the open file

- The name of the open file

Closing Files Opened by Workgroup Users

After you pull up a list of open files in a shared directory, you can select and close one or more files. You may need to close a file opened by a crashed application program, for example. In this situation, users may not be able to make changes to the file because Windows for Workgroups assumes the file is open and in use. Close the file by using the techniques described in the following steps. That way, other users can access and make changes to the file.

You also can use this technique to "yank" a file out of the grasp of a user you don't want to have access. Suppose that you go into File Manager and notice that a sensitive payroll file is open by the janitor.

You can close files opened by other users by following these steps:

CAUTION
If you close a file by using these steps, the user may lose data. You can warn users by using the Chat utility (described in Chapter 7). The users then can save changes before you close the file.

1. Get a list of open files by following the steps in "Viewing Open Files in a Shared Directory" earlier in this chapter.

2. From the directory window, select the file you want to close.

3. From the File menu choose Properties (or press Alt+Enter). The Properties dialog appears.

4. Choose the Open By button to open the Network Properties dialog.

5. Choose the Close Files button; then choose OK to return to the directory window.

The application program returns an Access Denied error message to users with an open file that has been closed.

Viewing Different Directory Levels

Directories can contain other directories called subdirectories. A directory and the subdirectories that it contains is a branch. Several techniques are available to view subdirectories. You can expand one or more branches, depending on how much you want to see. Figure 3.13 shows a directory with all branches expanded.

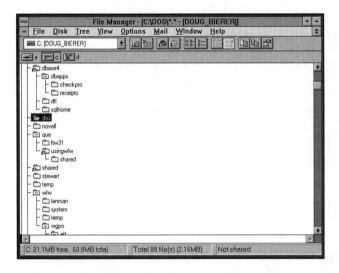

FIG. 3.13 *A directory tree with all branches expanded.*

The next sections describe how to expand and collapse your view of the directory tree.

Expanding One Level

Expanding a directory by one level reveals all the existing subdirectories one level down. Subdirectories in the same branch that exist two or more levels down don't appear when you use this option.

To expand a directory by one level, double-click the directory icon. Alternatively, select the branch to expand and then press the plus (+) key, or from the Tree menu choose Expand One Level.

Expanding One Branch

Expanding one branch displays all subdirectories in the selected branch. To expand one branch completely, follow these steps:

1. Select the directory that you want to expand in the directory tree.

2. Double-click the directory and all subdirectories one at a time until all are expanded.

   You also can press asterisk (*) or from the Tree menu choose Expand Branch.

> **TIP** If you want to view *all* directories and subdirectories on a drive, press Ctrl+* (asterisk), or from the Tree menu choose Expand All.

Collapsing a Branch

To keep a directory structure manageable, you may want to collapse a branch after you are done working with it. When you collapse a branch, the directories aren't deleted; their names just disappear from view. To collapse a branch, follow these steps:

1. Select the directory to collapse.

2. Double-click this directory and all subdirectories one at a time until all are collapsed.

You also can collapse a branch by pressing the minus key (–). Alternatively, from the Tree menu choose Collapse Branch.

Working with Files and Directories

This section discusses common actions that you can perform on files and directories, focusing specifically on what impact access types have on these actions. The following table lists the access types needed for directories when you copy or move a file. *N/A* indicates that access types aren't applicable.

Copy/Move From	Access Type	Copy/Move To	Access Type
Local drive	N/A	Local drive	N/A
Local drive	N/A	Network drive	Full
Network drive	Read-only or Full	Local drive	N/A
Network drive	Read-only or Full	Network drive	Full

The following table lists access types required for other various operations on network drives. Access types aren't an issue on local drives.

Action To Perform	Access Type Needed
Delete file	Full
Rename file	Full
Create new file	Full
Open file	Read-only or Full
Run application	Read-only or Full
Make changes to file	Full
Remove directory	Full
Rename directory	Full
Create new directory	Full
Move directory	Full

If you want to copy files or directories to other drives, the procedure is easier if you first make sure that a directory window is open for the destination drives. Be sure that you also have assigned the appropriate access types.

Printing Files

File Manager prints only files that are *associated* with applications (see the following section, "Associating a File"). You can tell that a file is associated when the document icon has lines inside the icon. When you print the file through File Manager, the application program first is loaded and the print option is activated.

Printing takes place through the default printer. To change the default printer, go to the Control Panel and choose the Printers option, or open Print Manager.

To print a file, first select the file or files to be printed. Then, from the File menu choose Print. The selected files print to your local Print Manager or to the network if printing to a shared printer. (Refer to Chapter 4, "Printing with Windows for Workgroups," for more information.)

Associating a File

Associating a file causes the associated application to load after you click the file. The file then loads into the application.

Association is by file extension, which means that if you associate one file with an application, all files with the same extension then become associated with this application. If you associate the file XYZ.DOC with Word for Windows, for example, all files that end with DOC become associated with Word for Windows, and selecting one of these files loads and runs Word for Windows.

To associate a file, follow these steps:

1. Select the file you want to associate.

2. From the File menu choose Associate. The Associate dialog appears.

3. In the Files With Extension field, verify that the file extension is the one you want to associate.

4. Choose the desired application from the list under the Associate With drop-down list box.

If you don't see the application with which you want to associate a file, choose the Browse button. The Browse dialog appears (see fig. 3.14).

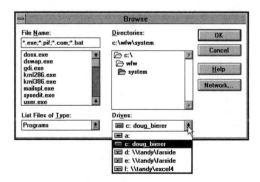

FIG. 3.14 *The Browse dialog.*

A list of all application files appears in the Windows for Workgroups SYSTEM directory. You can move up and down the directory structure for the currently selected drive by selecting the appropriate directory in the Directories box. You also can choose any currently connected drives, including network drives, by clicking the arrow next to the Drives box. You also can click the Network button, which enables you to access the appropriate network drive to browse for an application file on another computer in your workgroup.

Most application files have the extensions EXE, COM, PIF, or BAT. If the application you want to associate has a different extension than EXE, COM, PIF, or BAT, type the correct extension in the File Name text box.

Summary

This chapter took you step by step through File Manager's features in a Workgroup environment. You saw how to connect and disconnect a network drive, share directories, and secure directories. This chapter also showed you how to see the open files in a directory or to see who has a specific file open.

The next chapter continues the exploration of Windows for Workgroups. Chapter 4, "Printing with Windows for Workgroups," discusses printing in the workgroup environment.

Printing with Windows for Workgroups

As you know from your experience with networks or from Chapter 1, installing a LAN enables you to share printers. Rather than buy a printer for every person in the office, you can buy several good printers and have office workers share them.

One of the most important tasks for a LAN administrator is to set up the network's printers. This chapter explains how to set up shared printers in Windows for Workgroups and to enable users to access them. You also see how to manage the shared printers and print jobs by using Print Manager.

Understanding Shared Printers

Shared printers, also called *network printers*, are attached to one computer but used by more than one user. When sharing printers, a variety of issues become important. Consider the following questions:

- What is print queuing?

- Who should share printers?

- What printers should be shared?

- What kind of access to shared printers should you assign to users?

Printing from a network is different than printing from a stand-alone computer. If you are printing to a shared printer, your *print job*—the information that you send to the printer—must cross the LAN before it's printed. One analogy for stand-alone versus network printing is that of eating at home compared to going to a restaurant to eat. In both cases, you are eating food—perhaps even the same food. When you eat at home, you sit down at your table and eat. When eating out, you must

- Call the restaurant for reservations.

- Get into your car.

- Drive across town.

- Enter the restaurant.

- Wait for a table.

- Order your food.

- Eat your food.

When printing to a shared printer in a network environment, a print job must make a similar trek:

- The print job is queued locally by your Print Manager.

- Just like making a reservation in a restaurant, your computer must check with the computer attached to the shared printer (the host computer) and tell it that a print job is pending.

- In the restaurant analogy you get into your car, drive across town, and go into the restaurant. In the LAN environment, the print job must be packaged into smaller units known as *packets*. The packets are transmitted across the LAN. The host computer stores the packets and reassembles them back into the print job.

- After you arrive at the restaurant, you wait for a table to become free. In the network printing environment, your print job is queued by Print Manager at the host computer until the printer is ready.

- In the restaurant, you get a table and eat. On the computer side of this analogy, the job is printed.

Figure 4.1 shows the flow of printing across the LAN. In this diagram, the document is originated at your computer running Word for Windows. When you choose to print to a shared printer, the document first is queued by your local Print Manager. Print Manager checks with Print Manager on the host computer. When the network is clear and the host computer is ready, the print job is downloaded, through the LAN, to the host computer. (The LAN in the diagram is seen as a pipeline.) Print Manager on the host computer then queues the document. When the shared printer (the printer attached to the host computer) is ready to accept the job, the document prints.

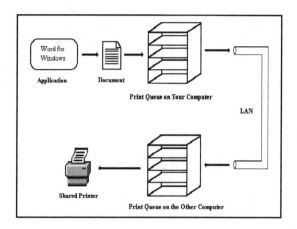

FIG. 4.1 *Network printing.*

Windows for Workgroups treats your print job differently, depending on whether you have a printer attached to your computer or are using a shared printer attached to someone else's computer. If you have a printer attached to your computer, Windows for Workgroups queues up the print job on your local computer. If you are connected to a shared printer, however, your document ends up queued on the computer with the shared printer.

Before you can use a shared printer, the printer must be set up correctly. Physically attach the printer to the computer, using the proper cable. Use the Control Panel's Printers option to install the printer driver. After the printer is set up locally, you then can share the printer using Print Manager. (Step-by-step instructions later in this chapter show you exactly how to accomplish the steps that involve Windows for Workgroups. You need to consult your printer manual for instructions on how to physically attach your printer to your computer.)

To print to a shared printer from an application program, you first must connect to the shared printer. After you connect your printers using the Control Panel, you can use the application's Printer

Setup option or the Control Panel to select the printer you want to print to. When you print, Windows for Workgroups redirects the printer output to the computer hosting the shared printer.

You can print to a shared printer even if you have no printer attached to your computer. This capability is one of the major advantages to networking. When you print to a shared printer, Windows for Workgroups intercepts the print job and then sends it across the LAN to the computer hosting the shared printer. After your print job arrives at this computer, one of two things happens. If your print job is the only one to print, it's sent immediately to the printer. If other print jobs exist, your job is placed in the print queue and must wait its turn.

The following sections discuss in greater detail print queues and sharing printers.

Understanding Print Queues

A *print queue* is a list of documents waiting to print. The print queue is created when you share the printer. Print Manager controls the print queue.

NOTE	The term *document* as used in this chapter can refer to any file that you print.

The computer that has the printer attached to it maintains the print queue. You have a certain amount of control over documents that are waiting to print. Actions you can perform on documents in the print queue include pausing a document, resuming a paused document, changing its print order, deleting a document from the queue, and using separator pages.

The following sections give you an overview of using the print queue. Later, the section "Using Print Manager" presents step-by-step instructions on the general issues introduced in these sections.

Managing Documents in the Queue

You can delete documents in the queue. Deleting a document from the queue stops the document from being printed but doesn't delete the document from disk. You may need to delete a document from the queue if, for example, you need to make changes to a document after sending it to print. Deleting the document from the queue saves time, paper, and ink.

You also can move documents up or down in the queue. Moving a document up in the queue causes it to print before other documents. Moving it down causes it to print after other documents.

You can add separator pages (also known as *banner pages*) in front of a document to be printed. By using separator pages, you quickly can identify jobs that are printed on shared printers. This feature is especially useful when you have many users sharing one printer. Separator pages can include the file name of the document, the logon name of the job owner, and the date and time the document was printed.

Not every user on the LAN, however, can perform or control all these actions on documents in the print queue. The following section explains who can delete and change the position of print jobs in the queue.

Determining Who Can Manage the Queue

From Print Manager's standpoint, three types of users exist: the remote user, the local user, and the job owner. The person who prints the job and the location from which he or she prints determine the type of user.

The remote user is a person on the LAN who prints a job using a shared printer that isn't attached to his computer. Remote users can control only print jobs that they originate.

The local user is the person who works at the computer to which the shared printer is attached. Local users always have priority when they print. If a remote user's job now is printing, however, that user's job can finish before the local user's job starts printing.

The job owner is the local or remote user who sent the job. The job owner has complete control over his own print jobs. If the job owner is a remote user, he has no control over jobs that aren't his own. If the job owner is the local user, however, he also can affect jobs printing on his computer that belong to others. Later, in the "Understanding Print Manager" section, table 4.1 explains actions that each type of user can perform.

> **TIP** One way to tell quickly whether you can perform an action is to look at the toolbar buttons. Buttons that appear to be dimmed indicate actions that you cannot perform. Likewise, dimmed menu options are actions that you cannot perform. Local users can perform all actions that pertain to their printer.

Sharing Printers

You must set up through Control Panel all printers used in your workgroup after they are installed. After all computers are set up, you need to decide which printers will be shared.

Windows for Workgroups is very flexible. Printing arrangements can range from having no to all printers shared. In many cases, you may have a mixture of shared and unshared printers. You can designate printers as shared or unshared at any time by using Print Manager.

You can decide which printers to share based on several factors:

- The type of printer
- The type of document
- How often users print (print volume)

The following sections describe each of the preceding points.

Printer Type

The most popular types of printers include dot-matrix, inkjet, and laser printers. Considerations for each type of printer include type of paper used, quality of print, and speed. The following table summarizes these considerations:

Printer Characteristic	Dot-Matrix	Inkjet	Laser
Speed (pages per minute)[1]	Low to moderate	Moderate	Moderate to high
Quality (dots per inch)[2]	Moderate	High	High
Use of continuous-form paper	Yes	No	No

Printer Characteristic	Dot-Matrix	Inkjet	Laser
Use of single-sheet paper	Yes[3]	Yes	Yes
Use of multiple-part forms	Yes	No	No
Type of ink used	Ink ribbon	Ink cartridge	Toner cartridge
Cost of operation[4]	Low	Moderate	High

[1]*Some dot-matrix printers approach the speed of the slower inkjet printers. A high speed is considered 15 to 20 pages per minute. An average laser printer can print close to 10 pages per minute. Expensive laser printers and high-speed printers found in mainframe installations can print close to 20 pages per minute.*

[2]*A typical laser printer has a 300 dpi resolution. A low-end dot-matrix may have less than 100 dpi. Some higher quality laser printers have 600 dpi resolution.*

[3]*For dot-matrix printers, you usually must hand feed single-sheet paper one sheet at a time.*

[4]*Cost of operation includes the cost of paper and the cost of replacing parts such as print heads or drums, ribbons, ink cartridges, and toner cartridges.*

4

Document Type

The type of documents you plan to print is a factor in printer sharing. An accounting workgroup, for example, needs to print specialized forms, such as checks and invoices. You may decide not to share a printer that prints checks.

Other considerations include quality of print and multiple-part forms. A sales workgroup, for example, needs high-quality printing for its promotional documents. A purchasing workgroup, on the other hand, may need a printer that can print multiple-page forms. In these cases, assign a laser printer for the sales workgroup and a dot-matrix printer for the purchasing workgroup.

Print Volume

The volume of printing also may be an issue. The more printing that takes place across the LAN, the slower the LAN becomes.

Think of the LAN as a pipe. You can send only one item through at a time. If many users need access to the pipe, they must wait until the pipe is free. The host computer is also slower when many users are using the shared printer. Users who print frequently should have their own printers. Users who print less frequently should be assigned to shared printers.

Figures 4.2 and 4.3 are worksheets that you can use for determining your printing needs.

Workgroup	Logon Name	Shared Printer(s)	Type of Printing	Amount of Printing (High, Medium, Low)		
				H	M	L
				H	M	L
				H	M	L
				H	M	L
				H	M	L
				H	M	L
				H	M	L
				H	M	L
				H	M	L
				H	M	L
				H	M	L
				H	M	L

Determining Printing Needs of Users

FIG. 4.2 *A worksheet for determining the printing needs of users.*

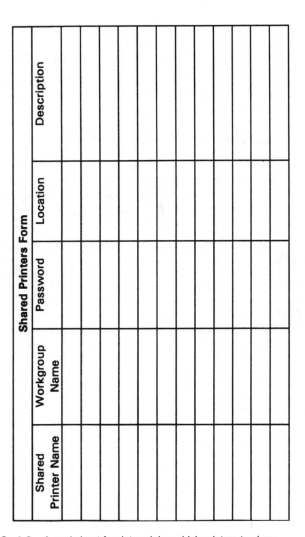

FIG. 4.3 *A worksheet for determining which printers to share.*

Securing Printers on Your System

You can assign individual passwords to shared printers. If a password isn't assigned, users can connect to the shared printer without being challenged. If a password is assigned, users are prompted for it when they try to connect to the printer.

In an example given earlier, if you are setting up a printer to print checks, assign a password to the printer. This password should be given to users in the accounting workgroup who have the authority to print checks. You can keep track of passwords using the Shared Printers Form in figure 4.3.

Introducing Print Manager

You use Print Manager to manage printers and documents queued to be printed. With Print Manager, you can monitor the status of documents queued to print on your printer or on shared printers. You can access Print Manager from Program Manager in the Main group.

> **NOTE** This section introduces you to the major features of the Windows for Workgroups Print Manager. Step-by-step instructions are presented in the section "Using Print Manager."

You can perform the following actions in Print Manager:

- Set up new printers
- Share printers
- Pause and resume printers
- Set a printer as the default printer

On a queued print job, you can use Print Manager to perform the following:

- Pause and resume printing of the document
- Delete the document from the queue
- Move the document up or down in the queue

Table 4.1 lists all actions you can perform using Print Manager. This table focuses on the menu commands and includes a column listing the type of user who can issue this command: a local user, a remote user, or a job owner. Some commands pertain to printers and others pertain to documents waiting to be printed.

Table 4.1 Print Manager Menu Commands

Menu	Option	User Type	Description
Printer	Pause Printer	Local	Stops the printer; similar to switching the printer manually to off-line. Print jobs stay in the queue until you delete them, exit Windows for Workgroups, or resume them.
	Resume Printer	Local	Enables the printer to resume printing
	Connect Network Printer	Local or remote	Enables you to connect to a network printer
	Disconnect Network Printer	Local or remote	Disconnects you from a network printer
	Share Printer As	Local	Turns a printer attached to your computer into a shared printer
	Stop Sharing Printer	Local	Stops sharing a printer; printer becomes a local printer only
	Set Default Printer	Local or remote	Enables you to set the default printer, which should be the printer you use most often. If you want to use another printer, use File Printer Setup from the application you are using.

continues

Table 4.1 Continued

Menu	Option	User Type	Description
Document	Pause Printing Document	Job owner	Causes the document to stop printing but continues with the next queued job
	Resume Printing Document	Job owner	Returns paused documents to active status in the queue
	Delete Document	Job owner or local user	Removes the document from the queue but doesn't delete it from disk. Local users can delete *any* print job; remote users can delete only their own print jobs.
	Move Document Up	Job owner or local user	Moves the document higher in the queue, giving the document priority over documents lower in the queue. Remote users can move documents only relative to their own documents. Local users' print jobs always get first priority.
	Move Document Down	Job owner or local user	Moves a document down in the print queue so that it prints after documents listed above it
View	Time/Date Sent	Job owner	If checked, displays the time and date the job is sent

Menu	Option	User Type	Description
View	Print File Size	Job owner	If checked, displays the file size of the print job
	Status Text	Job owner	Displays the job status. Status conditions include no status (queued), Printing, Paused, or Error.
	Refresh	Job owner	Refreshes the Print Manager screen with the status reported by the various network printers you are connected to
	Other Network Printer	Job owner	Enables you to view other shared printers available in your workgroup that your computer isn't connected to
Options	Toolbar	Job owner	If checked, displays the toolbar
	Status Bar	Job owner	If checked, displays the status bar
	Font	Job owner	Enables you to change the font displayed on the Print Manager screen
	Set Column Widths	Job owner	Enables you to adjust column widths on the Print Manager screen
	Background Printing	Job owner	Enables you to bypass the local print queue on your computer

continues

Table 4.1 Continued

Menu	Option	User Type	Description
Options	Separator Pages	Local	Inserts an extra page before each job, specifying the file name, the logon name of the job owner, and the date and time of the print job
	Printer Setup	Local or remote	Enables you to set a printer attached to your computer. If the driver files are not loaded already on your computer, you need to supply the appropriate Windows for Workgroups floppy disks when prompted.
Help		Any	Displays the Print Manager help screen

Enabling Print Manager

You don't have to use Print Manager for printing; you may find, however, that Print Manager is a very useful tool. Print Manager enables you to send more than one document at a time to a printer. You then can monitor the status of your print jobs queued up to print on a local or shared printer.

In some cases you may encounter a computer where a prior network administrator or user has disabled Print Manager. You easily can enable Print Manager using the Control Panel. Follow these steps:

1. Start Control Panel from the Main program group.

2. From the Control Panel window, click the Printers icon.

3. In the Printers dialog, select the Use Print Manager check box to enable Print Manager (see fig. 4.4).

4. Choose the Close button.

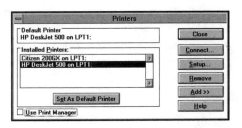

FIG. 4.4 *The Use Print Manager check box in the Printers dialog.*

Understanding Print Manager's Window

The Print Manager window consists of the standard Windows elements such as the title, menu, and status bars. The Print Manager window also has a toolbar, unique to Windows for Workgroups. The following sections give brief explanations of each part of the window.

The Title, Menu, and Status Bars

Like the Print Manager window in Windows 3.1, the Windows for Workgroups Print Manager has the standard title bar, complete with a Control Menu box, the title of the utility (Print Manager), and the Minimize and Maximize buttons.

The menu bar gives you access to the Print Manager menus: Printer, Document, View, Options, and Help. The Printer and Document menus are unique to Windows for Workgroups.

The status bar displays helpful messages on the status of the printing environment. Messages appearing on the left side of the status bar pertain to the printer. Messages on the right pertain to the document. Printer messages include the following:

Message	Description
Printing	The printer is printing a document.
Paused	The printer is paused.
Idle	The printer is ready and isn't printing any documents.
Error	An error condition (such as printer off-line or out of paper) has taken place.

The Toolbar

The Print Manager toolbar, unique to Windows for Workgroups, consists of 12 buttons that you can use rather than the Print Manager menus. These buttons make Print Manager easier to use. You use the first 7 buttons to manage the printers and the last 5 to manage the documents being printed.

Table 4.2 shows each button, provides the equivalent Print Manager menu command, lists the type of user that can use the button, and explains how that button is used.

Table 4.2 Print Manager's Toolbar Buttons

Button	Equivalent Command	User Type	Description
	Printer Connect Network Printer	Any	Connects you to a shared printer
	Printer Disconnect Network Printer	Any	Disconnects you from a shared printer
	Printer Share Printer As	Local	Turns a local printer into a shared printer
	Printer Stop Sharing Printer	Local	Turns a shared printer on your computer into a local printer
	Printer Pause Printer	Local	Stops the printer from printing

Button	Equivalent Command	User Type	Description
	Printer Resume Printer	Local	Enables the printer to continue printing
	Printer Set Default Printer	Any	Sets selected printer as your default printer
	Document Pause Printing Document	Local or job owner	Stops selected document from printing
	Document Resume Printing Document	Local or job owner	Enables the selected document to continue printing
	Document Delete Document	Local or job owner	Removes the document from the print queue
	Document Move Document Up	Local or job owner	Gives document higher priority so that it prints before documents listed under it
	Document Move Document Down	Local or job owner	Gives document lower priority so that it prints after documents listed above it

4

The Printer List

The printer list shows you the printers to which your computer is connected and the documents queued to be printed. The information in the printer list is displayed in four columns:

■ *Printer/Document Name.* Lists the printer's name. You also may see three types of printer icons to the left of the printer name. A plain printer indicates a local, unshared printer; a hand shown holding the printer indicates a shared printer; and a printer with a bent line under it indicates a network printer to which your computer is connected. A triangle pointing to the right indicates a document being printed.

Indented below a printer in use is a list of documents queued for that printer. A document icon is displayed beside the name of the document. Two bars indicate a paused document. No symbols indicate a document queued and ready to be printed.

■ *Status.* Displays the status of printers and documents. Idle indicates that the printer is inactive. Paused means the local user has put a hold on the printer. (Next to a document name, Paused means the local user or the job owner has placed a pause on his or her print job.) Printing means that this printer or document is printing. No entry in the Status column means that the document is ready to print but isn't at the top of the list.

■ *Size.* Lists the size of the files to be printed. Next to the printer name is a total number of jobs queued for that printer.

■ *Time.* Lists the time and date the document was sent to the Print Manager queue.

Figure 4.5 shows a Print Manager window with several different printers listed:

■ *Citizen 200GX.* This printer, attached to the local LPT2 port, isn't shared. Its status is Idle.

■ *HP DeskJet 500.* This shared printer is located on a computer named TANDY. Now printing, it has 2 documents in its queue (WFWSCRNS.DOC and WFWCHP05.DOC). The documents were originated by a user named DOUG, who is using Microsoft Word to print these documents. Both documents have been paused. The size of the documents and the date and time they printed also are indicated.

■ *HP LaserJet IIID.* This local printer is attached to the COM2 port. It's shared so that other network users can print to it under the name HP. It's currently idle.

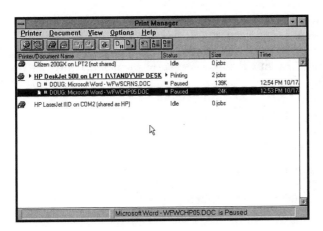

FIG. 4.5 *Print Manager's printer list.*

Using Print Manager

The following sections describe how to set up printers, share them, and manage the documents after they are queued to print. (Managing the queued documents consists of moving them up or down in the queue, pausing, resuming, and deleting them from the queue.) The following sections also cover how to place separator pages in front of each job, view other workgroup printer queues, bypass Print Manager on your computer, display printer error messages, and alter the appearance of Print Manager on your computer.

Managing Printers

If you have a printer attached to your computer, you can share your printer with the network. After the printer is installed, you can share it with your workgroups or revoke sharing rights. You also can pause and resume paused printers. The following sections show you how.

Setting Up Printers

You can set up the printer that you are going to share by using the Control Panel or Print Manager. This section focuses on the Print Manager. Appendix A, "Installing Windows for Workgroups," deals with setting up a printer using the Control Panel.

Before you can set up the printer, you must note the port in which the printer is plugged. You also need to know whether any extra font support is available for your printer and have those fonts available. Be sure that you also know the manufacturer and model of the printer(s) you plan to install. If the manufacturer provides a driver disk that works with Windows 3.1, have this disk on hand.

To set up a printer on Windows for Workgroups, first have the Windows for Workgroups installation disks 7 and 8 ready. Then follow these steps:

1. From Print Manager's **Options** menu, choose **P**rinter Setup. The Printers dialog appears, listing the currently installed printers and the default printer (if any exist).

2. Choose **Add.** A list of printers you can add appears at the bottom of the screen.

3. Select the desired printer from the list you see in the List of Printers scroll box (see fig. 4.6).

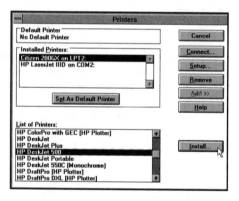

FIG. 4.6 *Adding a new printer from the List of Printers scroll box.*

> **TIP** You can type the first letter of the manufacturer's name to get to the name of your printer quickly.

If you don't find your printer on the list, Windows for Workgroups doesn't support your printer. You need to use the Windows 3.1-compatible driver disk supplied by the vendor and then select Install Unlisted or Updated Printer in the List of Printers scroll box. At the prompt, insert the vendor-provided disk in drive A (or type another drive letter if the disk is in another drive). Printer Setup reads the driver. Proceed to step 5.

4. From the Printers dialog, choose **Install**.

   When prompted, you need to supply Windows for Workgroups installation disks 7 and 8 or indicate the drive or directory containing the drivers for your printer. Your printer now appears on the Installed Printers list.

5. From the Printers dialog, choose **Setup**. A dialog like the one in figure 4.7 appears for the printer that you are installing.

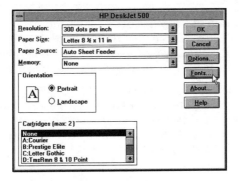

FIG. 4.7 *Installing an HP DeskJet 500 printer.*

You now can adjust any printer parameters as needed. The Options button enables you to change the quality of the print and print intensity. With the Fonts button, you can add fonts not normally included with Windows for Workgroups. Consult your printer manual for more information on any of the listed parameters that aren't clear.

After you finish making any changes to the printer's setup, choose OK to return to the Printers dialog.

6. Choose **Connect** to assign the new printer to a port. The Connect dialog appears.

   In the Connect dialog, your port choices should vary depending on whether you are setting up a printer that is directly attached to your computer or a network printer attached to another computer. If the printer to which you are connecting is attached to your computer, choose one of the ports listed: LPT1, LPT2, LPT3 (parallel ports), or COM1 or COM2 (serial ports). If you have an EISA or MCA bus computer, you also can select COM3 or COM4. You must have the ports physically available on your computer before you can select them.

> **NOTE**   If you are using a network in addition to Windows for Workgroups, you can print using the LPT1.DOS or LPT2.DOS ports. These phantom ports enable your print job to be redirected to the network print queue of another operating system.

If the printer to which you are connecting is a shared printer, choose **Network** from the Connect dialog. The Connect Network Printer dialog appears (see fig. 4.8). In this dialog, you can select a shared printer in one of two ways:

- In the **P**ath text box, type *computer**printer*, where *computer* is the name of the host computer and *printer* is the name of the shared printer. If you are connecting to a shared HP DeskJet printer on a computer named TANDY, for example, type **TANDY\HP DESKJET** in the Path text box.

- Select the desired computer in the **S**how Shared Printers On list box and the desired printer in the Sha**r**ed Printers On list box.

7. Put an X in the Reconne**c**t at Startup check box if you want this printer to be connected every time you run Windows for Workgroups on this computer.

In the Connect dialog, you may want to take note of two other options: Timeouts and Fast Printing Direct to Port. Timeouts notifies you in a set number of seconds whether a printing problem exists (**D**evice Not Selected). You also can specify the number of seconds the system retries printing before giving up (**T**ransmission Retry). Fast Printing Direct to Port is recommended only for local printers. This option bypasses normal DOS printer calls and accesses your parallel port directly from Windows. If you are defining a network

printer, Fast Printing Direct to Port may interfere with printing—
you aren't printing directly to your parallel port, you are printing
through the network.

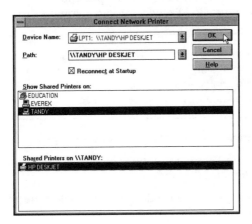

FIG. 4.8   *The Connect Network Printer dialog.*

Another option that you can select before you exit the Printers
dialog is to set a printer as the default printer, as explained in the
next section.

Choosing the Default Printer

After you define a number of printers, you can designate one as
your default. This printer then appears in the Default Printer section of the Printers dialog when you print from an application. In
the Print Manager printer list, the name of the default printer is
underlined.

You can choose the default printer in two ways:

■ From Print Manager, select the printer you want to set as the
default. Then click the Set Default Printer toolbar button or
choose Set Default Printer from the Printer menu.

■ From Print Manager's Options menu, choose Printer Setup.
In the Printers dialog, select the desired printer and then
choose the Set As Default Printer button. After the printer
you selected appears in the Default Printer section, choose
the Close button.

Removing an Installed Printer

If you change printers or remove an old printer, you also should remove the old printer from the list of printers defined for your computer (the Installed Printers list in the Printers dialog).

> **NOTE** Removing a printer from the list doesn't remove that printer's driver from disk. If you later want to reinstall the printer, you don't need your Windows for Workgroups floppy disks to do so.

To remove an installed printer, follow these steps:

1. From Print Manager's Options menu, choose Printer Setup. The Printers dialog appears.

2. From the Installed Printers scroll box, select the printer you want to remove.

3. Choose Remove. The printer no longer appears in the Installed Printers scroll box or Print Manager's printer list.

Sharing Your Printer

Any printer you want to make available to the network must be shared. Before you share your printer, be sure that it's installed. After you install and share the printer, its Print Manager icon changes to that of a printer held in the palm of a hand.

To share a printer, select it from Print Manager's printer list and then choose the Share Printer button on the toolbar or Share Printer As from the Printer menu. The Share Printer dialog appears (see fig. 4.9). In this dialog, type the appropriate information in each text box. (Table 4.3 lists the information needed for each option.) After you finish, choose OK.

	Share Printer	
Printer:	HP LaserJet IIID on COM2	OK
Share as:	HP IIID	Cancel
Comment:	Dual bin printer on Joe's desk	Help
Password:	SALES	☒ Re-share at Startup

FIG. 4.9 *The Share Printer dialog.*

Table 4.3 Share Printer Dialog Options

Option	Description
Printer	This text box should contain the name of the printer you selected.
Share As	In this text box, type a name for the shared printer that will appear on Print Manager's printer list.
Comment	Type any comments for your own reference.
Password	Type a password to secure the printer. Only users who know the password can access the printer. The password is optional.
Re-share at Startup	Check this option if you want the printer available when you restart your computer and run Windows for Workgroups, which is usually the case. This option is enabled by default. If you disable this option, the printer is available temporarily until you exit Windows for Workgroups.

Connecting to a Network Printer

After the printers are set up, users need to connect to the network printers. The best scenario is to arrange your users so that their computers connect to remote printers at start-up.

Problems may arise in the networking environment, however. Assume that Mary has a shared printer attached to her computer. John has no printer attached to his computer. Because John sits two cubicles down from Mary, you have set up his computer to connect to Mary's printer at start-up. One morning, John arrives at work before Mary. When John boots his computer and runs Windows for Workgroups, he cannot connect to Mary's printer because her computer isn't running. John doesn't notice this problem until he tries to print. John must turn on Mary's computer and reconnect to her printer.

In other cases, users may find that they need to connect to a printer temporarily. You can use Print Manager to handle this situation.

To connect to an existing shared printer, follow these steps:

1. In the Print Manager window, select the printer to which you want to connect.

2. Click the Connect Network Printer toolbar button or choose Connect Network Printer from the Printer menu. The Connect Network Printer dialog appears.

3. If you know the computer and shared printer name, type *computer**printer* in the Path text box, where *computer* is the name of the computer where the shared printer is located and *printer* is the shared printer name.

   If you don't know the computer and printer name, select the computer from the Show Shared Printers On list box and the printer from the Shared Printers On list box.

4. Choose OK.

You also can use these steps to connect to a new shared printer. You must have a printer on your Installed Printers list that matches the new printer to which you plan to connect. If the printers aren't the same, you must install the new printer as though it were a local printer. (See "Using Print Manager To Set Up a Printer" earlier in this chapter for directions on installing a new printer.)

Follow these steps to connect to the new shared printer:

1. From Print Manager's printer list, select the printer to which you want to connect.

2. Click the Connect Network Printer toolbar button or choose Connect Network Printer from the Printer menu.

3. In the Connect Network Printer dialog, choose an unused port (such as LPT2 or LPT3) from the Device Name drop-down list box.

4. Choose the printer to which you want to connect. If you know the computer and shared printer name, type *computer**printer* in the Path text box, where *computer* is the name of the computer where the shared printer is located and *printer* is the shared printer name.

   If you don't know the computer and printer name, select the computer from the Show Shared Printers On list and the printer from the Shared Printers On list.

5. Choose OK.

NOTE If the printer to which you want to connect doesn't appear on the list, it may be in another workgroup. If this situation happens, click the icon for that workgroup in the Show Shared Printers On list to expand the list of computers. Click each computer to discover which shared printers are available.

After you connect to a shared printer, you can make that connection permanent. In the Connect Network Printer dialog, enable the Reconnect at Startup option. If you don't enable this option, the connection will be temporary.

Pausing and Resuming Printers

At times, you may need to pause a printer. Only the local user can pause a printer. The following circumstances may make pausing necessary:

- The printer starts printing garbage (usually because a print job isn't properly defined for that printer).

- You need to service the printer (add paper or a toner cartridge, for instance).

- You need a different type of paper (such as a letterhead or forms).

When pausing, you first must select the printer to pause from Print Manager's printer list. Then, click the Pause Printer toolbar button or choose **Pause Printer** from the **Printer** menu. You see double bars on either side of the printer name, and the Status column reads Paused.

To resume a paused printer, you first must select the paused printer from the Print Manager—similar to what you do when pausing a printer. Then, click the Resume Printer toolbar button or choose **Resume Printer** from the **Printer** menu. The double bars disappear, and the Status column reads Printing or Idle, depending on whether a job is in the queue.

Managing Print Jobs

After you set up your printers, the function of the Print Manager changes. Now you mainly are concerned with managing the print jobs that are queued on a daily basis. Managing the print jobs in

the queue involves deleting jobs that are printing nonsense characters, moving jobs up or down in the queue, and pausing or resuming jobs. The following sections explain how to accomplish these
tasks.

Deleting a Job from a Print Queue

You may need to delete from the queue jobs that aren't printing
satisfactorily or jobs the user has accidentally (or unknowingly)
printed several times. The job owner can delete only his own print
job. The local user can delete any print job from the queue of the
printer to which his computer is attached.

To delete a print job, select the job to delete from Print Manager
and then press the Del key or click the Delete Document toolbar
button. Alternatively, you can choose Delete Document from the
Document menu to delete the selected print job. The listing for
this document disappears from the printer list.

NOTE	Deleting a document from the print queue doesn't delete the document from disk.

Changing a Job's Order in the Queue

Windows for Workgroups assigns each print job a priority. Normally, documents are assigned to the queue in the order in which
they arrive. Print jobs generated by the local user always receive
priority over any jobs already in the queue.

Users can change the order of their jobs in the print queue. You
can move jobs up or down in the queue. Remote users can reorga-
nize their jobs only below jobs sent by the local user.

To move the priority of a job up, first select the job in Print
Manager's printer list. Then choose the Move Up Document
toolbar button or choose Move Document Up from the Document
menu. The document then moves up one position in the queue.

To move the priority of a job down, first select the job in the
printer list. Then choose the Move Down Document toolbar button or Move Document Down from the Document menu. The
document then moves down one position in the queue.

> **TIP** An easier way to change the priority of a document is to drag the document to the new location. By using the mouse, you can move the priority of the document by more than one position at a time.

Using Separator Pages

Separator pages (also known as *banner pages*) separate one print job from another. A separator page enables you to identify quickly jobs that are printed on shared printers. Separator pages are especially useful when you have many users sharing one printer. Separator pages can include any or all the following information:

- File name of the document
- Logon name of the job owner
- Date and time

The local user controls the separator pages. Remote users can change their own separator page settings if the local user chooses not to use separator pages. In this case, the remote users get the separator pages they specify, but the local user gets no separator pages. If the local user chooses to use separator pages, the settings specified by the local user override any settings specified by a remote user.

To set up the separator pages, follow these steps:

1. From Print Manager's **O**ptions menu, choose Separator Pages. The Separator Pages dialog appears (see fig. 4.10).

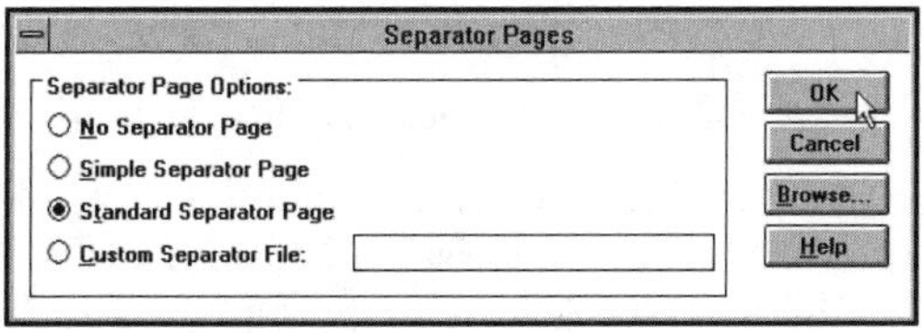

FIG. 4.10 *The Separator Pages dialog.*

2. From the Separator Pages dialog, choose one of four options:

Option	Description
No Separator Page	No separator pages are printed.
Simple Separator Page	The separator page prints in text mode.
Standard Separator Page	The separator page prints in graphics mode.
Custom Separator File	The user specifies a WMF (Windows Metafile format) file or a CLP (Clipboard) file containing the separator page picture. Aside from the Clipboard, no Windows for Workgroup standard utilities or accessories enable you to create this type of file.

TIP If you aren't sure what custom separator files are available, you can choose the **B**rowse button. Like the Browse feature found in other Windows applications, you can choose the file name (wild cards are acceptable for search purposes), drive, directory, and file type.

Pausing and Resuming Print Jobs

The process of pausing and resuming print jobs is similar to pausing and resuming printers, with two exceptions:

■ Pausing a document affects only the document you select.

■ Only the job owner or the local user can use this option.

When pausing a document, select the document you want to pause in Print Manager's printer list and click the Pause Printing Document toolbar button. Alternatively, from the **D**ocument menu choose P**a**use Printing Document to pause the selected print job.

If the document is printing, the printer prints what is now in its print buffer and then stops. Double bars appear on both sides of the document name in the printer list, and the Status column for that document reads Paused.

To resume printing a document, select the paused document and click the Resume Printing Document toolbar button or choose

Resume Printing Document from the Document menu. The document resumes printing on the printer.

Viewing Other Workgroup Printer Queues

When a network printer is busy, you may want to find a printer that has less activity. One way to find this printer is to view other printers in your workgroup to which you now aren't connected. To view other workgroup printer queues, follow these steps:

1. From Print Manager's View menu, choose Other Network Printer. The Other Network Printer dialog appears.

2. In the Network Printer text box, type *computer**printer*, where *computer* is the name of the other computer you want to view and *printer* is the shared name of the printer you want to see.

3. Choose the View button. A list of the documents waiting in the queue for that printer appears in the Other Network Printer dialog (see fig. 4.11).

FIG. 4.11 *The Other Network Printer dialog.*

TIP	If you aren't sure of the computer or printer names, you can get a list of computer names and shared printers by clicking the Connect Network Printer toolbar button or choosing **C**onnect Network Printer from the **P**rinter menu. You see a list of computers and shared printers available on your network. Don't complete the operation: choose Cancel to exit this screen. Choose **O**ther Network Printer from the **V**iew menu again and then enter the *computer**printer* name you found using the **C**onnect Network Printer option.

Configuring Print Manager

You can change Print Manager's appearance to suit your needs. You can hide certain parts of the window, for example, to maximize the information you view in the print queues. In the following sections, you learn how to configure Print Manager's appearance and how to fine-tune Print Manager's performance by setting foreground/background priorities.

Displaying Printer Error Messages

Print Manager notifies you if problems exist when printing. Common problems include the shared printer being off-line or out of paper. You have three choices: display error messages as they occur, flash the Print Manager icon or title bar (default), or ignore all warnings. Follow these steps:

1. From Print Manager's Options menu, choose Background Printing. The Background Printing dialog appears (see fig. 4.12).

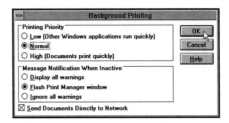

FIG. 4.12 *The Background Printing dialog.*

2. In the Message Notification When Inactive section, choose Display All Warnings or Flash Print Manager Window to display printer error messages. Choose Ignore All Warnings to ignore error messages.

If you choose to display error messages, when an error occurs you see ERROR in the Status column next to the shared printer name. The nature of the printing problem appears on the status bar at the bottom of the Print Manager window. If you choose to flash the Print Manager window, the Print Manager icon flashes when an error occurs if you have the Print Manager minimized. If you are in the Print Manager, its title bar will flash.

Changing the Print Manager Font

You can alter the font used in Print Manager to suit your tastes. From the Options menu choose Font. In the Font dialog, you can choose the font, the font style, and the font size (see fig. 4.13). At the bottom of the dialog, you see a preview of what the font looks like.

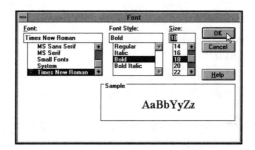

FIG. 4.13 *Changing Print Manager's font in the Font dialog.*

Altering the Print Manager Display

You can choose to display or hide the toolbar and the status bar. You also can control which columns you see in the printer list.

To change whether you view the toolbar or status bar, from the Options menu choose Toolbar or Status Bar. A check mark next to either option indicates that the respective bar appears on-screen. Remove the check mark to hide the bar.

You also can specify what information to display for each print job in the printer list. You can stop displaying the Time, Size, and Status columns. To do so, from the View menu choose Time/Date Sent to hide the Time column, Print File Size to hide the Size column, or Status Text to hide the Status column. A check mark next to one of the menu options indicates that the column displays information. Figure 4.14 shows Print Manager without any of the extra options.

Changing the Column Size

You can change the width of the columns displayed in the printer list. You can shorten the Status and Time columns, for example, to make more room for the Printer/Document name and Size columns. To adjust the column widths, follow these steps:

1. From Print Manager's Options menu, choose Set Column Widths. A resize arrow icon appears in the printer list area. This icon looks like a vertical bar with a left and right arrow on either side.

2. Press the right mouse button to move to the desired column or press Tab.

3. Move the mouse right or left to adjust the column, or use the right- and left-arrow keys.

4. Continue to adjust the width until all columns are set to the desired width. When finished, click or press Enter.

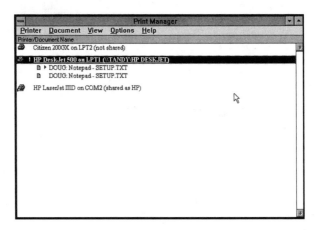

FIG. 4.14 *Print Manager without its information columns.*

Changing Print Manager's Priorities

You may decide to increase or decrease the priority given to print jobs printing to a printer directly attached to your computer. Setting the priority adjusts the amount of time given the printer at the cost of other application programs running on your computer. You can choose from low, normal, and high priority:

■ *Low.* Slows down printing but speeds up applications running on your computer. Users who have many applications running at once or applications that do many calculations (such as graphics applications like AutoCAD) should choose this setting.

- *Normal.* Balances the computer between printing and running applications. This default priority shouldn't be changed unless your users complain about how slow applications run on their computers.

- *High.* Tips the balance in favor of printing. This setting may be appropriate for the shared printer that sees frequent use. Realize, however, that the local user may complain because programs run slowly on his computer.

To change the printing priority, follow these steps:

1. From Print Manager's Options menu, choose Background Printing. The Background Printing dialog appears.

2. In the Printing Priority section, choose Low, Normal, or High. Click OK to save your change.

Bypassing Print Manager To Print Faster on the Network

You can print faster by bypassing Print Manager locally and printing directly to the network. Normally your print jobs are queued twice—once on your local computer by Print Manager and again in the queue managed by the host computer. To avoid queuing your jobs twice, you can have your printing go directly to the network.

NOTE	You don't have to disable Print Manager to print directly to the network. Although not the same as not using Print Manager, this option enables you to use Print Manager to manage jobs in the print queues. It stops Print Manager from queuing your job twice.

To print directly to the network, follow these steps:

1. From Print Manager, choose a shared printer in the printer list.

2. From the Options Menu, choose Background Printing. The Background Printing dialog appears.

3. Make sure that the Send Documents Directly to Network check box has an X in it.

Now, when you print to this shared printer, your jobs are queued only once.

Summary

This chapter explained how to use Print Manager in the work-group environment. Topics included setting up and managing shared printers and managing documents queued to be printed. You also learned how to pause or resume printers or documents, delete or move documents up or down in the queue, and print to a file. Finally, you learned how to alter Print Manager's appearance to suit your needs.

Chapter 5, "Using Mail," explains how to use Windows for Workgroups' electronic mail program.

FIVE

Using Mail

Electronic mail programs such as Microsoft Mail form the backbone of communications on your Windows for Workgroups network. An understanding of how Mail works, its features, and how to accomplish various actions is critical to the success of your network.

Microsoft Mail provides basic electronic mail capabilities for your workgroup and has many features found on high-end network mail packages. You can send and receive mail messages; attach files to your messages; and create, delete, and manage folders. Mail also enables you to do the following:

- Address a personal group of mail users
- Set priority levels
- Send return receipts
- Send carbon copies

This chapter gives you a thorough overview of the key elements of Mail. Menu commands, the toolbar, and various dialogs and menus are covered. You learn how to set up Mail and how to send, receive, delete, reply to, and forward messages. You also learn how to use your address book, include files and objects with your messages, and work with folders.

Introducing Electronic Mail

Electronic mail, also called *E-mail*, enables users to exchange messages without using paper. The electronic mail system is maintained by one computer, which is designated as a *post office*. The post office manages a list of all the system users.

You maintain your own *personal address list*, a list of user log-on names to whom you send information on a regular basis.

When composing a message, you see a dialog that enables you to identify to whom you want to send the message. Each message must have a title, known as the *subject*. After you finish writing the message, you *send* it. This process queues the message in the *Outbox* until the message recipient logs on.

Incoming mail is stored in your *Inbox*. You can move incoming messages to *folders*, which you can create or delete at any time. You can copy mail messages into a folder and move the folder around at will.

The following sections provide a quick introduction to electronic mail's main features.

Understanding the Post Office

The post office is a workgroup computer that has been designated to collect and disperse electronic mail. This computer should stay on all the time. When users sign in, they are registering with the post office and get access to their mail. (Signing in at the post office also prevents other users from reading your messages or sending messages in your name.) When users don't sign in, the post office holds their mail.

> **NOTE** The post office computer also is referred to as the *mail server*. A mail server is a machine that shares mailbox directories with *mail clients*. You can consider a user sending mail a mail client.

Sending Mail

You can send mail several different ways. At first, you send messages you compose. As your electronic mail messages start to grow, however, you find yourself replying to messages instead of creating new messages and addressing them. The *reply* function is similar to creating a new message, except that the person who sent you the message automatically becomes the recipient.

You can send a message to more than one user by typing a number of user names, separated by semicolons, in the *To* box. You also can enter a list of users, known as a *personal group*. Mail also supports the *Cc* (carbon copy) function, in which you can send copies of mail messages to users other than the recipients.

Other functions include *forwarding* and *return receipts*. You can forward a message to another user after you read it. This option retains the message and enables you to make changes. The post office sends you a return receipt when the recipient reads the message.

You must send electronic mail messages over the LAN to the post office. The post office keeps the message stored in a directory under the master WGPO (workgroup post office) directory.

Receiving Mail

After you start receiving mail messages, you can read them. Different icons identify each message. An unread message, for example, has an icon of an unopened envelope. Messages with attached files have an icon that looks like a note paper-clipped to an envelope. After the message is read, the icon changes to an opened envelope.

If the message contains an attached file, you can click the icon to see the file within the message. If you created an *association* for that type of file, the program associated with the attached file opens along with the file. For more information about using associations in Mail, see the later section "Attaching a File."

You can *search* for messages by using a variety of criteria: sender's name, subject, recipient, message text, and the folder in which to look.

After you read a message, you can move it to any of the *folders* available in your mail area. One folder is for deleted mail. Any message placed in this folder normally is deleted when you exit Mail. You can change this default.

Illustrating Mail in Use

This section uses an insurance company as an example of using electronic mail. The supervisor, MaryJo, sends a message to a claims adjuster, Judy, asking her to examine a certain claimant's file. Judy pulls the file; using data in the file, she creates a Quattro Pro for Windows spreadsheet, calculating the amounts for a settlement with the claimant.

After Judy completes the worksheet, she sends MaryJo a message with the spreadsheet file attached. MaryJo reads the message and reviews the attached spreadsheet. The figures she sees alarm her. She forwards the message and the attached spreadsheet as an urgent priority message to her boss, Marty, with a return receipt requested.

After lunch, MaryJo looks at her mailbox and discovers that she has no return receipt from Marty. She calls Marty, who agrees to read the message immediately. Marty sends a reply to the message, with a Cc to Judy, telling MaryJo that he called the claimant and was able to arrange for a settlement conference.

This example gives you an idea of how you can use Mail in your office. Microsoft Mail contains many powerful features found only in electronic mail packages that cost 10 times as much. The next section introduces you to the features of Mail.

Understanding the Mail Window

Mail takes full advantage of the Windows environment. It consists of a series of document windows that enable you to view incoming and outgoing messages quickly as well as the folders you created for your system.

Mail also has a rich variety of menu commands available. You can find many of the same types of menus in other Windows for Workgroups programs: File, Edit, View, and Window. In addition to the standard menu commands, the Mail menu has options unique to electronic mail, including options to compose messages, use the address book, and work with personal groups.

> **NOTE** The menus and functions you see in Mail change, depending on what you are doing. When you are composing a message, for example, the **E**dit menu offers you choices such as Cu**t**, **C**opy, and **P**aste. When performing other actions, such as viewing the titles of your incoming messages, these options aren't visible.

The Mail window consists of the standard Windows elements such as the title bar, the menu bar, contents windows, and a status bar. Figure 5.1 shows the elements of the Mail window. The following sections briefly explain each part of the window.

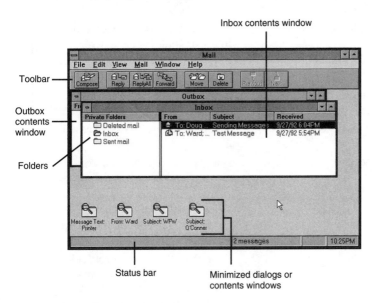

FIG. 5.1   *The Mail window.*

The Title Bar, Status Bar, and Menu Bar

The title bar has the standard Windows features, including the control box, the title of the utility (Mail), and the Minimize and Maximize buttons.

The status bar at the bottom of the window displays helpful messages pertaining to the status of your mailbox. At the bottom left of the status bar are informative messages that flash briefly during an operation. The middle section of the status bar displays a message telling you how many messages are displayed in the currently active contents window and how many of these messages haven't been read (if you are looking at the Inbox). At the far right of the status bar is the current time.

The menu bar under the title bar provides access to Mail menus: File, Edit, View, Mail, Window, and Help. Table 5.1 describes each Mail menu command and notes shortcut keys, where available.

Table 5.1 Mail Menu Commands

Menu Command	Description
File Open	Opens the selected message
File Move (Ctrl+M)	Moves a selected message from the Inbox or Outbox to a folder
File Copy	Copies the selected message(s) to a folder
File Delete (Ctrl+D)	Deletes the selected message(s)
File Save As	Saves the selected message as a text file
File Save Attachment	Separates an attached file from a message and saves it as a separate file
File Message Finder	Searches the folder(s) you specify for a message based on the criteria you enter
File New Folder	Creates a new folder or subfolder that you can designate as private or shared. You also can control the access level of users that open a shared folder.
File Folder Properties (Alt+Enter)	Enables you to view the properties of a folder (such as whether the folder is private or shared)
File Export Folder	Enables you to move one or more folders to another drive and directory. Subfolders are moved with the top-level folder.
File Import Folder	Enables you to move a folder from another drive and directory to your current drive and directory
File Print	Prints the selected message
File Print Setup	Enables you to change the currently selected printer

Menu Command	Description
File Exit	Enables you to exit Mail but doesn't sign you out of your mailbox. (Other programs, such as Schedule+, rely on you being signed into Mail to complete certain tasks.)
File Exit and Sign Out	Enables you to exit from Mail and sign out of your mailbox
Edit Undo (Ctrl+Z)	Undoes the last edit
Edit Cut (Ctrl+X)	Moves the selected text from your currently active screen to the Clipboard
Edit Copy (Ctrl+C)	Copies the selected text to the Clipboard
Edit Paste (Ctrl+V)	Inserts the contents of the Clipboard at the insertion point on the current editing screen
Edit Paste Special	Enables you to paste an object from the Clipboard into the mail message
Edit Delete (Del)	Deletes the currently selected text if you are in an editing screen. If you have a message selected, this option deletes the message.
Edit Select All	Selects all messages in the currently selected folder
Edit Object	Enables you to edit an embedded object. To do the editing, Mail calls the program that created the object.
Edit Insert Object	Opens the program you select and enables you to create an object to insert into your message
Edit Insert from File	Enables you to insert a file into your Mail message
View Private Folders	Lists your private folders in the contents window
View Shared Folders	Lists shared folders in the contents window

continues

Table 5.1 Continued

Menu Command	Description
View **N**ew Messages	Checks the post office for any new messages
View Sort by **S**ender	Sorts listed messages by sender
View Sort by Sub**j**ect	Sorts listed messages by subject
View by **D**ate	Sorts listed messages by date
View by Priority	Sorts listed messages by priority
View Open Inbox (Ctrl+G)	Moves the view back to the Inbox folder
View S**p**lit	Enables you to redefine the split point between portions of the contents listing window
View **T**ool Bar (Ctrl+T)	Toggles the toolbar on and off
View Status **B**ar	Toggles the status bar on and off
View **N**ext (Ctrl+>)	Enables you to switch to the next incoming mail message when reading your mail
View **P**rev (Ctrl+<)	Enables you to switch to the previous incoming mail message when reading your mail
View Change Font	Enables you to change the font that Mail uses
Mail Compose Note (Ctrl+N)	Enables you to create a new message
Mail **R**eply (Ctrl+R)	Enables you to reply to the sender of the message you have just read
Mail Reply to **A**ll (Ctrl+A)	Enables you to reply to all recipients of the message, including everyone in the To and Cc boxes
Mail **F**orward (Ctrl+F)	Forwards the selected message to the user to whom you address it

Menu Command	Description
Mail Address Book	Enables you to manage your address book. You can see names in your address book, add new user names, and add details about these users. You can look at the address list for your personal address book or for the post office.
Mail Personal Groups	Enables you to create, edit, and delete groups of users that you, not the post office administrator, manage
Mail Options	Enables you to customize your Mail environment
Mail Change Password	Enables you to change your Mail password
Mail Backup	Backs up the MSMAIL.MMF file, which contains all your mail messages. The file usually is stored in the Windows for Workgroups directory.
Mail Postoffice Manager	Administers the post office duties, which consist of adding, deleting, and editing mail-user information. This option is available only if the computer you are using hosts the post office.
Window New Window	Creates a new contents window (in addition to the default Inbox and Outbox windows) in which you can view any of your folders
Window Cascade	Cascades all currently active windows
Window Tile	Tiles all currently active windows
Window Arrange Icons	Neatly arranges any contents windows or Search windows minimized as icons
Window 1 Outbox	Takes you quickly to the Outbox

5

continues

Table 5.1 Continued

Menu Command	Description
Window 2 Inbox	Takes you quickly to the Inbox
Window X *xxx*	Takes you quickly to other windows or dialogs that you now have open, including Send Note dialogs, contents listing windows, and messages you are reading
Help	Provides Mail system help

The Toolbar

The toolbar consists of eight buttons that make Mail convenient to use. You can use these buttons rather than the Mail menus. Table 5.2 shows you each button, its equivalent menu command, and an explanation of how the button is used.

Table 5.2 The Mail Toolbar Buttons

Button	Equivalent Command	Description
Compose	Mail Compose Note	Creates a new message
Reply	Mail Reply	Replies to the sender of a mail message
ReplyAll	Mail Reply to All	Replies to all senders and carbon copy recipients of a message
Forward	Mail Forward	Forwards a message
Move	File Move	Moves a message into a folder
Delete	File Delete	Deletes a message
Previous	View Previous	Views the preceding message
Next	View Next	Views the next message

The Contents Windows

A *contents window* or *contents listing window* is a Mail window that lists the contents of a folder. The main contents windows in Mail are the Inbox and Outbox windows, as described in the following sections. Other contents windows include Search windows that you have set up and folders you want to display. Folders can include Deleted Mail, Sent Mail, and any other folder that you set up for your system.

You can tile and cascade contents windows much like you can the group windows found in Program Manager. You can adjust the width of each column in any contents window. To have fast access to a larger number of contents windows than you have room for on-screen, you can *minimize* the window to an icon.

The Inbox Window

The default contents window displayed when you first get into Mail is your Inbox window, which is a special folder containing messages you have received (see fig. 5.2). The Outbox window appears behind the Inbox window. The Inbox window consists of the following columns:

Column	Description
Private Folders	Lists all folders you have set up. Select a folder to access its contents. Click the heading for this column or choose Shared Folders from the View menu to see the contents of the Shared Folders.
Shared Folders	Uses the same column as Private Folders, but lists the Shared Folders set up on your system. Select a shared folder to access its contents.
From	Lists who the messages are from. If the message is one you are working on and haven't yet sent, the word To: precedes the name of the recipient.
Subject	Displays the title of the message
Received	Displays the date and time the message was received

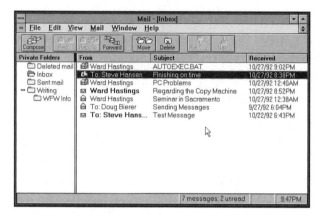

FIG. 5.2 *The Mail Inbox.*

In the From column, the icon next to each incoming message will change depending on what the sender has specified. The sender can specify low priority or high priority, or can attach a file to the message. When you read a message, the envelope icon changes from closed to opened. Figure 5.3 shows each type of icon.

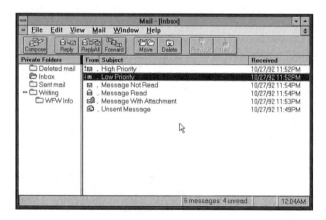

FIG. 5.3 *Incoming-mail icons.*

The Outbox Window

Information in the Outbox is similar to information in the Inbox, except that the Outbox contains only outbound messages. The

Outbox window contains three columns of information describing the waiting messages, as follows:

Column	Description
From	Lists who the messages were sent to. The word To: precedes the name of the recipient.
Subject	Displays the title of the message
Sent	Displays the date and time the message is received

Messages generally don't accumulate in your Outbox. As long as the post office computer in your workgroup is operating, messages that you send are transferred directly to whom they were addressed. Messages remain in the Outbox under one of two circumstances: you have many messages, and the post office is taking a long time to send them; or the post office computer isn't running or isn't available.

Using Microsoft Mail

The following sections focus on how to use Mail. First, you learn how to set up Mail. Set-up options covered include connecting to an existing post office or creating a new post office.

You also learn about a variety of display options that control what and how you see messages. You see how to send messages, use address books, manage received messages, attach files and objects to messages, and how to use folders. Finally, you learn how to use Mail off-line.

Setting Up a Post Office

Before you can use Mail, you must create a post office. When you first start Mail on your computer, you see a message like the one shown in figure 5.4. You start Mail by choosing its icon from Program Manager's Main group.

Notice the two options on-screen: Connect to an Existing Post-office or Create a New Workgroup Postoffice. The first option enables you to browse through a listing of other computers on the network and select the name of the computer containing the post office.

FIG. 5.4 *The Welcome to Mail message.*

If you want your computer to become the post office for the workgroup, choose Create a New Workgroup Postoffice. After you have the post office set up, your computer should remain turned on and running Windows for Workgroups when other workgroup users are using their computers. That way, users can receive mail and scheduling information any time they are working.

Creating a New Post Office

You should have only one post office per workgroup. This arrangement keeps your mail from dividing and going to two different post offices. If a split occurs, you may not have all your mail delivered correctly.

To create a post office, follow these steps:

1. From the initial Mail welcome screen, choose Create a New Workgroup Postoffice and then OK. A message box appears, telling you to connect to a preexisting post office (if one exists) rather than create a new one. At the bottom of this screen is a question, Do you want to create a new post office?

2. Choose **Yes**. The Create Workgroup Postoffice dialog appears.

3. Select the directory in which you want the post office directories and files kept. The default is your Windows for Workgroups directory. You can choose the default or create a directory (such as C:\WGPO, for example) somewhere on your hard drive.

4. After you choose a directory to contain WGPO (workgroup post office) and its subdirectories, choose OK. The Enter Your Administrator Account Details dialog appears (see fig. 5.5).

FIG. 5.5 *The Enter Your Administrator Account Details dialog.*

5. Enter the details for your administrator account. Each detail option is described as follows:

Option	Description
Name	Your first and last names
Mailbox	The name of your mailbox
Password	Your Mail password
Phone #1	Primary office phone number
Phone #2	Secondary phone number where you can be reached
Office	The name or location of your office
Department	The name of your department
Notes	Any additional comments you want to add

6. After you complete the administrator account information, choose OK. As the mail administrator, you have full access rights in Microsoft Mail.

7. The final message tells you that the post office has been created. Choose OK.

Assigning Full Rights to the Post Office Directory

After you create your workgroup post office, you must assign full security access rights. If you don't, users in your workgroup will not be able to access the post office and send or receive mail. You find this fact out quickly when installing mail for a new user. When you go to connect the new user to the directory containing the post office files (the WGPO directory), access is denied to you, and the installation fails.

To assign full access rights to your workgroup post office, follow these steps:

1. From File Manager, select the WGPO directory (probably C:\WINDOWS\WGPO).

2. Choose the Share Directory toolbar button or choose Share As from the Disk menu. The Share Directory dialog appears.

3. In the Share Directory dialog, complete the following information:

   ■ *Share Name.* Type the name of the shared directory. The default is WGPO.

   ■ *Path.* Type the path to the shared WGPO directory.

   ■ *Comment.* Type **Post Office** so that users recognize this directory as the post office.

   ■ *Re-share at Startup.* You should check this box; otherwise, you must return to File Manager every day so that users have access to the post office.

   ■ *Full Access Type.* Choose this option to enable users to read their mail and send mail to other users' mailboxes.

   ■ *Full Access Password.* Don't include a password for the post office directory. Although users can be assigned a password when they sign in to Mail, you don't need to assign an additional password for access to the post office directory.

4. After you enter all the information, choose OK to return to File Manager. Now you can exit File Manager and switch back to Mail.

Connecting to an Existing Post Office

The first time you run Mail, you can connect to an existing post office or create a new post office. Creating a new post office is discussed in the preceding section. If you already have a post office for your workgroup, you should connect to it rather than create a new post office. Follow these steps:

1. From the initial Mail welcome screen, select Connect to an Existing Postoffice. The Network Disk Resources dialog appears (see fig. 5.6).

FIG. 5.6 *The Network Disk Resources dialog.*

2. Select the computer and shared directory used for the post office and then choose OK.

3. Mail asks whether you have an account at the post office (see fig. 5.7). If you already have an account, choose **Yes** and ignore the next step. Mail prompts you for your password.

   If an account hasn't been set up for you, choose **No**. The Enter Your Account Details dialog appears.

FIG. 5.7 *The dialog asking whether you have a post office account.*

4. Fill out the Enter Your Account Details dialog to create a new account for yourself. The dialog asks for the following information:

■ *Name.* Type the name you want people to use when sending you mail. The user name you enter must be unique. If a duplicate name exists, a message box appears, warning you to enter another user name.

■ *Mailbox.* Type the name of the mailbox that you want to sign into each time you get into Mail or Schedule+ in Windows for Workgroups.

■ *Password.* Type your mail password.

■ *Phone #1.* Type your first phone number.

■ *Phone #2.* Type your second phone number.

■ *Office.* Type your office name.

■ *Department.* Type your department name.

■ *Notes.* Type any notes that may be appropriate.

After you complete the Enter Your Account Details dialog and choose OK, Mail checks the post office and updates the mailing list.

If the post office has gone down by this time or you have accidentally tried to sign up with another workgroup's post office, you get a warning message box. If this box appears, press OK and wait until your post office is available or connect with the post office in your workgroup.

Managing the Post Office Address List

The user who works at the computer with the post office is the *mail administrator*. As the mail administrator, you can manage the list of names available to all users in the workgroup.

The mail administrator is the only person in the workgroup with the Postoffice Manager option on the Mail menu. Selecting this menu option displays the Postoffice Manager dialog.

| **NOTE** | If you don't see the Postoffice Manager option on your menu, you aren't sitting at the computer that has the post office, or you don't have the post office set up. |

The *mail address list* or *post office address list* is a master list available to all users of the mail system in your workgroup. You can view this list from the Postoffice Manager dialog. From this dialog you can add, remove, or change the details of a user. You also can use the Postoffice Manager dialog to view information on the shared folders in your mail system (see fig. 5.8).

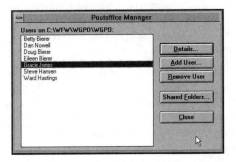

FIG. 5.8 *The Postoffice Manager dialog.*

Choose the **Add User** button from the Postoffice Manager dialog to add another user name to the master post office address list. You use this option when new people become workgroup members.

In the Add User dialog that appears, type all the information pertaining to the new user (see fig. 5.9). Information includes name, mailbox, password, phones numbers, office, department, and notes.

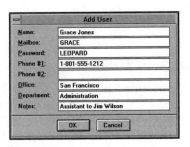

FIG. 5.9 *The Add User dialog.*

You also can remove a user from the list, when someone leaves the workgroup for one reason or another. To remove a user from the list, select the name of the user to be removed. Choose the

Remove User button from the Postoffice Manager dialog. A message appears asking you whether you are sure that you want to remove this user; choose **Yes**.

Through the Postoffice Manager dialog, you can change the details of a current mail user. To change the user's information, choose the **Details** button. In the Details dialog, change the appropriate user details. Use this option to update user information maintained by Mail, such as phone numbers or department. (Note that the title bar of the Details dialog changes according to the mailbox name of the user.)

Because you have folders that you can share on the network, you can display statistics about the shared folders. The statistics include the number of folders, the total number of messages in the folders, the total bytes used by the messages, and the number of recoverable bytes in the folders (you can recover bytes by compressing messages).

To view the statistics of the shared folders, choose the Shared Folders button. A dialog appears with statistics about your shared folders (see fig. 5.10).

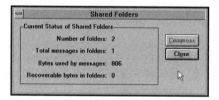

FIG. 5.10   *The Shared Folders dialog.*

Deleting Your Post Office

You may run into a situation where you want to relocate or reinstall the post office. The computer that hosts the post office can become very busy when many users are accessing their mail. Such a situation is inconvenient for the user using that computer. One solution is to change computers with another user. Use the Control Panel's Networks option to change the logon name of the users (refer to Chapter 8, "Configuring Windows for Workgroups," for more information). The other solution is to delete the post office and reinstall it on another computer.

To delete your post office and start over again, follow these steps:

1. From File Manager, select the WGPO directory (probably C:\WINDOWS\WGPO).

2. Choose the Stop Sharing toolbar button or choose Stop Sharing from the Disk menu. The Stop Sharing Directory dialog appears.

3. Select your Windows for Workgroup post office directory and then choose OK.

4. From the File Manager directory window, select the MSMAIL.MMF file. This file resides in the directory that contains the Windows for Workgroups application files. Press Del to delete this file.

5. Select the WGPO (workgroup post office) directory and delete it.

6. Select and delete the MSMAIL.INI file.

The next time you enter Mail, you again get the initial Welcome to Mail dialog.

Composing and Sending Messages

One of the earliest tasks you must master is sending a message to a user. You can send a message in many ways. You can send a message to a single user or to a number of users. You can send a copy of any message to another user at the same time you send the original to the addressee.

Sending a message really involves two processes: creating (or *composing*) the message and sending the message. The following steps explain how to compose a basic message:

1. Choose the Compose toolbar button, choose Compose Note from the Mail menu, or press Ctrl+N. The Send Note composition window appears.

2. In the To text box, type the name of the user to whom you want to send the message. Press Tab.

> **TIP** If you want to send a message to more than one
> user, you can use the post office address book
> or your personal address book. (See "Using the
> Post Office Address List when Sending Mes-
> sages" and "Using Personal Groups" later for
> more details.) To send a message to users that
> aren't in an address book, however, you must
> address those users specifically by typing all
> their names in the **T**o text box. Separate each
> user's name with a semicolon.

3. In the **Cc** text box, type the name of the user to whom you
   want to send a copy of the message, if applicable. If you
   don't send a copy of the message, leave the **Cc** text box
   blank. Press Tab.

> **NOTE** Carbon-copy messages usually are viewed as
> less important than messages that have the
> recipient's name in the **T**o text box.

4. In the Subject text box, type the title of the message. Press
   Tab. The title of the Send Note window changes to that of
   the subject.

5. Type the message that you want to send.

   Figure 5.11 shows the Send Note window filled out for a
   single recipient.

6. After you finish creating the message, choose the **S**end
   button to send the message.

After you finish typing and sending your message, the message
temporarily appears in the Outbox until it is processed by the post
office. Before sending the message, the post office checks the recipients names to see whether they are valid. If any problems exist,
you see an error message identifying the problem.

Creating a message is very similar to creating documents in a word
processor. You can type, edit, move, and delete information. You
also can work on more than one message at a time and transfer
information from one message to another. Use the same editing
operations as you use in Windows Notepad or most other word
processors. Other options that you have available include creating

and using a message template. The next few sections address some of the options you have when sending messages.

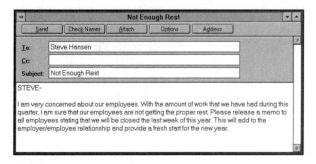

FIG. 5.11   *The Send Note composition window.*

Checking the Spelling of a Name

If you aren't sure how to spell the name of the user to whom you want to send a message, you can use the Check Names option in the Send Note window (refer to fig. 5.11).

To use the Check Names option, type a user's name in the To text box and then choose Check Names. If the spelling isn't correct, you see a message box warning you that the spelling doesn't check out. If the spelling is correct, however, the name appears underlined.

Setting Message Options

The Options button in the Send Note window provides message options that control how the message travels through the mail system after you send it.

To set message options, choose the Options button in the Send Note window. The Options dialog appears (see fig. 5.12). Table 5.3 describes each option in this dialog. After you set all the appropriate options, choose OK.

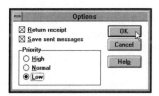

FIG. 5.12   *The Options dialog.*

Table 5.3 Message Options

Option	Description
Return Receipt	Tells the post office to send you a confirmation after the recipient reads the message
Save Sent Messages	Dumps a copy of this message into the Sent Mail folder. Use this option to save messages so that you can review them later.
High Priority	Tells the Mail server to expedite the message. The message appears in the receiver's Inbox with an exclamation point next to it.
Normal Priority	Gives the message no special treatment (default)
Low Priority	Causes a downward-pointing triangle to appear next to the subject in the recipient's Inbox

Saving Unsent Messages

Sometimes when you are working on a message but are called away from your desk, you need to save the incomplete message and come back to it later. To save a message that you haven't sent yet, press Esc or Ctrl+F4. You see a dialog that says, Do you want to save changes to "Unsent Message" in the Inbox? If you choose **Yes**, the message is saved in your Inbox. Note that the message's icon in your Inbox appears as an envelope that needs to be addressed with a document that is waiting to be inserted.

Using Message Templates

A message template is an unsent message with no text that sits in your Inbox. Templates are useful if you must send a regular message. If you send a report to three different managers each week, for example, you can save the report form in a message addressed to these three managers. Each week, select the message for forwarding, complete the form, and send it.

To create a message template, create a message and save it as unsent following the instructions in the preceding section. Be sure to address the message to those people to whom you plan to send the message on a regular basis. In the body of the message, type any information you send regularly.

To use the template, select the message in the Inbox. Then, choose the Forward toolbar button, press Ctrl+F, or from the Mail menu choose Forward. Make any changes necessary to the message. Choose the Send button from the Send Note window to send the message. The message is forwarded to the people you designated when you first created the message. The original message is still in your Inbox, waiting for the next use.

Using the Address Book

The address book enables you to keep a database of user names for the purposes of electronic mail. The next sections show you how to manage your address book and get information about users listed in the address book. The section "Using Personal Groups" explains how to create and manage a personal address book, enabling you to view only users to whom you regularly send mail.

Using the Address Book Toolbar

The address book has its own toolbar. Table 5.4 describes each icon.

Table 5.4 The Address Book Toolbar

Button	Button Name	Description
	Directory	Takes you to an index of address lists, including the post office list and your personal address book
	Personal Address Book	Takes you directly to your personal address book
	Name Finder	Enables you to specify a name pattern for which to search
	New Name	Enables you to add a name to the post office
	Add Names	Adds the currently selected name in the post office to your personal address book

Updating Your Personal Address Book

You can add names from the post office list to your personal address book. To add a user to your personal address book, first choose Address Book from the Mail menu. Then, make sure that the post office list is displayed in the Address Book dialog. Select the name of the user to add to your address book. Choose the Add Names toolbar button. The selected name is added to your personal address book.

You can use the New Name toolbar button to add a custom address to your address book. To add a user who is in another workgroup or post office, you need to enter his name, E-mail address, and E-mail type. (You need to ask the user for this information.) The user's name is the name on his post office. The E-mail address has this format:

> *nnn*(MS:*www\ccc\ppp*)

In this format, *nnn* represents the user's Mail name, MS represents Microsoft Mail, *www* stands for the user's workgroup name, *ccc* is the user's computer name, and *ppp* is the user's post office name. The E-mail type should be Microsoft Mail.

> **NOTE** You may not be able to send mail to this name without additional third-party software that supports this feature.

You also can change a name in your personal address book. To do so, select the user's name in the Address Book dialog. Choose the Details button. In the User Details dialog, edit the user's name and then choose OK.

In addition to the post office account name, you can enter in a nickname or alias for this person. This name can be a shortened or familiar name you use to identify the user. You then can address this person by his or her nickname rather than specify the Mail name. The alias doesn't appear when you send mail; it is strictly for your own convenience.

NOTE Only you can see the nickname or alias. The person to whom you have assigned the name has no idea how you address him or her. After the message is sent, you see it under your personal name in your Outbox. After the post office files the message, Mail substitutes the user's post office name.

Using the Post Office Address List When Sending Messages

You can use the post office address list when sending messages. This feature enables you to choose from the names of users in your workgroup and is helpful if you don't remember the correct spelling of a user's name.

To use the post office address list when sending messages, follow these steps:

1. Open the Send Note window by choosing the Compose toolbar button, choosing Compose Note from the Mail menu, or pressing Ctrl+N.

2. Select the To text box.

3. Choose the Address button. The Address dialog appears (see fig. 5.13). The post office address list appears by default.

FIG. 5.13 *The Address dialog.*

4. Select the name of the addressee. To place this user name in the To text box, choose the To button. To place this user name in the Cc text box, choose the Cc button.

5. Continue to add users until you finish addressing the message. Choose OK when finished.

6. Complete and send the message.

Finding User Names

You can use the address book to find a user's name by following these steps:

1. From the Mail menu, select Address Book. The Address Book dialog appears, listing user names (see fig. 5.14).

FIG. 5.14   *The Address Book dialog.*

2. Choose the Name Finder toolbar button (which looks like a magnifying glass). The Name Finder dialog appears (see fig. 5.15).

3. Type as much of the user's name as you can recall and press Enter or choose Find. A list of user names matching what you typed appears in the Address Book dialog.

FIG. 5.15   *The Name Finder dialog.*

> **TIP** You don't have to enter entire names. If you enter only a first name, you see a list of users with that first name. If you enter only a last name, you see a list of users with that last name. If you enter one or a few letters, Name Finder searches the first, middle, and last names starting with the first character. Name Finder doesn't find letters that occur in the middle of a name.

After you choose to find a user's name, you see only the matches for the name you typed. To see the entire list of names again, choose the Name Finder button, leave the Name Finder dialog blank, and choose the Find button. All user names return to the Address Book dialog.

Getting Details about a User

In addition to the user's mail name, you can find specific details about a user, such as the following:

- *Alias.* An alternative name the mail system recognizes.

- *Name.* The user's full name.

- *Type of Mail.* Microsoft Mail.

- *Mailbox Name.* The name assigned to the user's mailbox.

- *Post Office Computer.* The name of the computer to which this user logs on for mail.

- *Workgroup.* The name of the user's workgroup.

- *Phone Number.* The two phone numbers Mail keeps in its database.

- *Office.* The user's office.

- *Department.* The user's department.

- *Notes.* Any comments you want to add pertaining to the user.

To view details about a user, choose the **Details** button from the Address Book dialog. The User Details dialog appears. You can scroll through the dialog but cannot make changes to the post office address list. Only the mail administrator or the account holder can make changes. You can change the name and comments in your personal address book.

Using Personal Groups

A *personal group*, also called a personal address book, is a specific list of users that you can use for addressing mail. If you want to send mail regularly to a group of users, create a personal group. Then, rather than select several users, simply choose your personal group when you want to send mail. The following sections explain how to create and use personal groups.

Creating a Personal Group

To create a personal group, follow these steps:

1. From the Mail menu choose Personal Groups. A window appears, listing the current personal groups (see fig. 5.16).

FIG. 5.16   *The Personal Groups list window.*

2. From the Personal Groups list window, choose the New button. The New Group dialog appears.

3. Type the name of your new group in the New Group Name text box.

4. Choose the Create button. The Add Users dialog appears, listing post office users at the top and group members at the bottom.

5. From the top section of the Add Users dialog, begin selecting users to add to your personal group.

6. Choose the Add button to add the selected users to the group.

7. After you finish adding users, choose OK.

Editing a Personal Group

After you have created a personal group, you can make changes
to it. You can add or delete users from the personal group, for example.

To edit a personal group, select the appropriate personal group
from the Personal Groups list window and then choose the Edit
button. The Personal Groups dialog appears (see fig. 5.17).

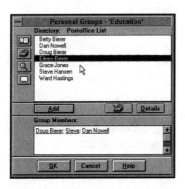

FIG. 5.17 *The Personal Groups dialog.*

To add a user to your group, select the new user's name from the
top part of the screen and choose the Add button. To remove a
user from your group, choose the user's name from the bottom of
the Personal Groups list window (the screen before the Personal
Groups dialog) and choose the Remove button. After you complete all changes to your personal group, choose OK and then
Close.

If you no longer need a personal group, you can remove the entire
group by selecting the appropriate group from the Personal
Groups list window and then choosing the Remove button.

Working with Messages You Have Received

You have many choices when dealing with received messages.
Usually, the first choice is to read the message. After you read
your messages, you can do one of the following:

■ Reply

■ Forward

■ Print

■ Save to a text file

■ Save in a folder

■ Delete

The following section explains how to perform these actions.

Reading a Message

Before you can read your message, you must have the Inbox window active. To activate your Inbox window, from the Window menu choose **2** Inbox. To read a message, select the appropriate message and press Enter or double-click the message.

You now see the text of the message. At the top of the message screen, you see who the message is from, the date it was sent, who the message is to, who received a carbon copy, and the subject. Figure 5.18 shows a message screen.

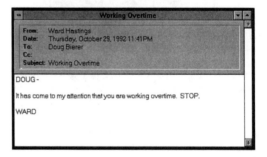

FIG. 5.18 *A message screen.*

Sending a Reply

You can send a message back to the sender immediately after reading the message. When you reply, your response can be only to the sender or to the sender and all users listed in the Cc text box.

Sending a reply is the same as composing a message, with these differences:

■ The sender's name is placed automatically in the To text box.

■ The same subject appears with RE: in front of it.

■ The original message appears in the message box so that you can delete it or add comments.

To reply to the sender, follow these steps:

1. In the Inbox, open or select the message.

2. Choose the Reply toolbar button or from the Mail menu choose **Reply**. A Compose Document window appears, with the **To** and Subject text boxes already filled out and the text of the original message at the bottom.

3. Delete, edit, or type over the text of the original message as you want. Leaving the original message in the box and typing your reply after the message, however, is preferable. The original message reminds the sender of why you are replying.

4. From the Compose Document window, choose the Send button.

When you send a reply, it goes only to the sender. Your reply doesn't go to any users who received carbon copies. The procedure for sending a reply to everyone who received the original message is the same as the preceding steps, except for step 2, in which you should choose the ReplyAll toolbar button, choose Reply to All from the Mail menu, or press Ctrl+A.

Forwarding a Message

Messages are forwarded when you want to retain the original text of the message and perhaps add some comments of your own. The process of forwarding a message is nearly identical to that of replying to a message. (See the preceding section.) The only difference is that you must fill in the name of the recipient in the **To** text box.

> **TIP** The Forward toolbar button also is used when you plan to use a message template (see the section "Using Message Templates" earlier in this chapter).

Printing a Message

To print one or more messages, follow these steps:

1. Select the message(s) to print or open a message to read.

2. From the File menu, choose Print. The Print dialog appears (see fig. 5.19).

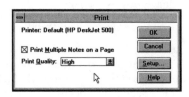

FIG. 5.19 *The Print dialog.*

3. In the Print dialog, you can change whatever settings you need to. You can select the printer by choosing the Setup button. The Print Quality drop-down list box enables you to choose between high, medium, low, or draft (very low) print qualities. If you want Mail to print more than one message on a page, mark the Print Multiple Notes on a Page check box.

4. After you make whatever changes you need, choose OK to start printing.

Saving a Message as a Text File

After reading a message, you may want to save the message in a separate text file. Later, you may want to incorporate the message into another document or delete the message from your Inbox but keep the text of the message on hand. To save a message as a text file, follow these steps:

1. Open the message or select it from the Inbox.

2. From the File menu, choose Save As. The Save As dialog appears.

3. Specify the file name, drive, and directory path.

4. Choose OK. If the file already exists, you have the following options:

   ■ *Append.* Enables you to add this message to the text already in the file

   ■ *Overwrite.* Overwrites the existing file with the new message

   ■ *Cancel.* Cancels the Save As operation

Deleting Selected Message

You can delete a selected message in several ways:

- Press the Del key.
- From the File menu choose **Delete**.
- Drag the file into the Deleted Mail folder.

When you delete a message, you don't remove the message for good. Mail moves the deleted message to the Deleted Mail folder, from which you can retrieve messages if necessary. The Deleted Mail folder is located under Private Folders.

NOTE If you notice that deleted messages constantly remain in the Deleted Mail folder, choose the **E**mpty Deleted Mail Folder When Exiting option in the dialog that appears when you choose **O**ptions from the **M**ail menu. When you check this option, messages in the deleted folder are deleted permanently when you exit Mail.

If you need to retrieve a deleted message, follow these steps:

1. From the Window menu choose Inbox.

2. Open the Deleted Mail folder by double-clicking the Deleted Mail icon. You now see the messages that haven't been deleted permanently.

3. Select the message that you want to keep.

4. Move the message to another folder by dragging the message using the mouse or by choosing Move from the File menu.

   If you choose Move from the File menu, the Move Message dialog appears. In the Move To list box, select the folder to which you want to move the message and then choose OK.

You successfully have restored the message.

TIP Rather than restore a deleted message, you can print the contents of the message or save the contents of the message to a text file.

Finding a Message

Mail provides a Message Finder feature that enables you to search for messages based on search criteria you enter, such as the name of the user who sent the message, the title or subject of the message, the message's receiver (including carbon-copy recipients), words or phrases inside the body of the message, and the folder or folders to search.

To find messages, follow these steps:

1. From the File menu choose Message Finder. The Message Finder dialog appears (see fig. 5.20).

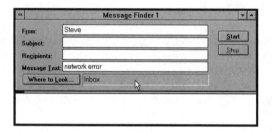

FIG. 5.20   *The Message Finder 1 dialog.*

2. Type information in one or all of the From, Subject, Recipients, and Message Text text boxes.

3. Choose the Where to Look button. The Where to Look dialog appears.

4. By using the Look In All Folders or the Look In option, you can specify the folder or folders to search. If you choose the Look In button, you must select one of the folders in the Look In list box.

5. Choose OK when you are finished with the Where to Look dialog. You return to the Message Finder dialog.

6. Choose Start to begin the search.

The Message Finder searches the folders you indicated for messages that match the criteria you provided. Matching messages that are found are listed at the bottom of the dialog. You can read, print, move, or delete messages that you find with the Message Finder.

> **TIP**
>
> For the purpose of speed, you can develop several Message Finder screens that are available at all times. First, fill out a Message Finder dialog by following the preceding steps. Rather than choose the **S**tart button in step 6, however, minimize the dialog. The dialog appears as an icon at the bottom of the Mail window with the title `Message Finder` *number*, where *number* represents the number of the icon. If you exit Mail completely and then return to Mail, the Message Finder icon displays an informational title rather than just a number.

Including Files and Objects in Messages

You may want to send files with the text of your message. Files may include word processing documents, spreadsheets, charts, graphics image files, and sound files. You can include files with Mail in three different ways:

- By copying the contents of the file into the text of the mail message

- By attaching the file to the message

- By embedding the file inside the message

The first option is useful when you have standard text you need to copy into your message on a regular basis. Messages containing boilerplate paragraphs are one example. *Boilerplates* are small text files that contain standard paragraphs—such as the paragraphs used regularly as a part of a contract. If you create contracts, you can include a series of boilerplate paragraphs in your message to build it up.

You attach a file when you want to give the recipient an easy way to detach the file for his own use. An attached file is like the luggage in a plane: you see your luggage only when you check into the airport from which you depart and check out of the airport to which you arrive. The recipient, after he reads the message, can copy the attached file to his system. To access or print the file, the recipient must have the application program that created the file available.

Embedding an object in a file makes the object part of the message. An *object* is an item in the format other than text. The advantage of embedding is that the recipient can see the object and all its original formatting in the message itself. The recipient cannot edit the object, however. Also, an embedded object prints without the recipient having to jump to the application program that created the object. Only certain applications work with this concept: Excel, Paintbrush, Package, and Sound.

Before working with files and objects, you must open the Send Note window (see the section "Composing and Sending Messages" earlier in the chapter).

Copying Information from a File

To copy information from a file, follow these steps:

1. From the Edit menu, choose Insert from File. The Insert from File dialog appears.

2. Select the file name, drive, and directory of the file you want to copy information from.

3. Choose OK.

The file must be in text format. If you plan to include a file in another format, use the attach or embed options (explained in the next two sections).

Attaching a File

To attach a file to your message, follow these steps:

1. From the Send Note window, choose the Attach button. The Attach dialog appears.

2. Select the file name, drive, and directory of the file.

3. Choose Attach.

   At the bottom left of the status bar you see a message telling you that Mail is attaching the file you selected. A bar appears next to this message. The bar indicates the amount of time it takes to perform the attach operation.

   The Attach dialog remains on-screen for you to attach additional files to the message.

4. After you finish attaching files to the message, choose Close.

You see the names of the attached files along with the icon of the program used to create them in the text of your message on the Send Note window.

Using Associations with Attached Files

You or your recipient can edit the attached file directly from Mail if you have access to the application that created the attachment and an association to that application. To associate documents with applications, follow these steps:

1. From File Manager, select the document you want to associate.

2. From the **F**ile menu choose **A**ssociate. The Associate dialog appears.

3. In the Associate dialog, note that the file extension appears in the **F**iles With Extension text box. Enter the file name of the application in the **A**ssociate With text box or choose the program name from the drop-down list box.

4. Choose OK. All files with this extension now are associated with the application program you specified.

Common associations include the following:

File Extension (Type)	Association
TXT	Notepad
WRI	Write
DOC	Word
XLS	Excel

For more information on associating files, see Chapter 3, "Using File Manager in a Workgroup."

5

Opening and Saving an Attachment

Figure 5.21 shows a message with two attached files. Each attachment has the icon of the program used to create it and the name of the attached file underneath. If you used Paintbrush to create the file, for example, the icon is the Paintbrush icon.

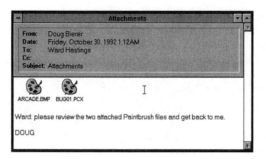

FIG. 5.21 *A message with attached files.*

When you receive a file with an attachment, you can work with the attachment from inside Mail or save the attachment and work with it later. To work with an attachment from inside Mail, open the message containing the attachment and then double-click the attachment icon. Windows for Workgroups loads the application and the attached file (if the application is available). From the application, you can work with the attachment as you want.

NOTE	You must have an association created for the file type before you can work with the attachment from inside Mail.

Rather than open the attachment immediately, you can save the attachment as a file and open it later. To save an attachment, follow these steps:

1. From the Inbox, open the message containing the attachment.

2. Locate and select the attachment icon.

3. From the **File** menu choose Save **Attachment**. The Save Attachment dialog appears (see fig. 5.22).

4. From the Save Attachment dialog, select the attached file to save from the **Attached Files** scroll box.

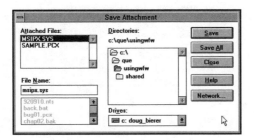

FIG. 5.22   *The Save Attachment dialog.*

5. You can save the attached files one at a time by choosing the Save button, or you can save all attached files at once by choosing the Save All button.

Embedding an Object in a Message

You can embed an object in a message in one of two ways: pasting or inserting. If the object is created already, you can paste it. If you are creating the object now, you can insert it. Before you paste or insert an object, you must be in the Send Note window, which use when you compose a message (see "Composing and Sending Messages" earlier in this chapter).

To paste an existing object into a message, follow these steps:

1. Start the application program containing the object and load the file, if necessary.

2. From the application program select the object and then choose Edit Copy to copy the object to the Clipboard.

3. Open Mail and compose a message. Ensure that the insertion point is in the message area of the Send Note window.

4. Paste the object to the note by choosing Paste Special from the Edit menu. In the Paste Special dialog, choose the data type and then choose the Paste button (see fig. 5.23). The object appears in its native format inside your message.

5. From the Send Note window, choose the Send button to send the message.

FIG. 5.23 *The Paste Special dialog.*

Rather than paste an object in a message, you can insert an object. This way, you can create the object with another application, such as Excel, and embed the object into the message while you are composing the message. Follow these steps to insert an object:

1. Compose a message in the Send Note window.

2. From the Edit menu, choose Insert Object. The Insert Object dialog appears.

3. Select the application to create the object and then choose OK. The application starts.

4. Within the application program, create the new object. While you are creating the object, Mail reserves a space for the new object by placing a shaded area in your message.

5. Exit the application and return to the Mail message.

6. A dialog appears, asking you whether you want to save changes to the Mail message. Choose Yes. You return to the Send Note window in Mail.

   The application program is now closed, and the new object immediately appears in your message.

7. From the Send Note window, choose the Send button.

Working with an Embedded Object

Certain objects in a message need to be activated. One such object is a Sound file. When you open a message with an embedded Sound file, you see the Sound icon. The Sound file doesn't play automatically. When you select the icon and press Enter (or double-click the icon), you can hear the Sound file.

Graphics images created in Excel or Paintbrush, on the other hand, display automatically when you open the message. You don't need to activate an embedded Excel or Paintbrush graphic image.

You also can edit an object. The object embedded in the message can be an Excel spreadsheet to which specific information must be supplied, for example. To edit an object, the recipient must have access to the application that created the object. If the object is the Excel spreadsheet, the recipient of the message must be able to start Excel.

To edit an object, follow these steps:

1. Open the message containing the object and select the object. You are now in the Send Note window for that message.

2. From the Edit menu, choose Edit *application* Object (where *application* is the name of the program that created the object). Mail takes you to the application that created the object and loads the object.

3. Edit the object and then save it.

4. Exit the application or switch back to Mail. You are now back in the Send Note window for that message, and the object is updated.

> **TIP**   An easy way to edit an embedded object is to double-click the object. Double-clicking starts the associated application and loads the object in the application for you to edit.

Using Folders

You can use folders to help you organize your incoming, outgoing, or already sent messages. Folders perform for mail messages what subdirectories perform for files. You can create or delete folders at will, like you can subdirectories. You can use other folders as subfolders. You can move messages in or out of folders or store them in a folder to be read at any time.

Folders can be *private* or *shared*. Only you can see a private folder. Anyone who has access to your mail system can see a shared folder. A shared folder is a good place to put messages that everyone in the workgroup may want to see.

Creating a Folder

To create a new folder, follow these steps:

1. From the File menu choose New Folder. The New Folder dialog appears.

2. In the Name text box, type the name of the folder to create.

3. From the Type options, choose Private or Shared.

4. Choose the Options button. The New Folder dialog expands to show other options (see fig. 5.24). Table 5.5 summarizes the other options available.

5. Choose OK.

FIG. 5.24   *The New Folder dialog.*

Table 5.5 Folder Options

Option	Description
Top Level Folder	Folder is at the top of the hierarchy
Subfolder Of	Folder is below another folder in the hierarchy
Read	Option is only for shared folders. Other users can read messages in this folder.
Write	Option is only for shared folders. Other users can save messages in this folder.

Option	Description
Delete	Option is only for shared folders. Other users can delete messages in this folder.
Comment	Descriptive information is for the benefit of other workgroup members

Making an Existing Folder a Subfolder

After you create a series of folders, you may need to rearrange the hierarchy of folders. By moving a folder and placing it inside another folder, you make that folder a subfolder. To do so, drag the folder onto the other folder. When you release the mouse button, the original folder becomes a subfolder of the folder on which it was placed.

Suppose that you originally created two top-level folders: International Sales and Domestic Sales. Several weeks later you decide to clean up your folders by putting both folders under another folder called Sales. To do so, drag International Sales onto the Sales folder, and likewise Domestic Sales. Now you have a top-level folder Sales, and two subfolders of Sales: International Sales and Domestic Sales.

Alternatively, you can move the folder by following these steps:

1. Select the appropriate folder.
2. Press Ctrl+M or choose the Move toolbar button. The Move Folder dialog appears.
3. In the Move Folder dialog, use the arrow keys to select the folder to which you want to move.
4. Choose OK.

Moving Messages between Folders

When a message comes to you, it is placed immediately in the Inbox folder. After you read the message in your Inbox, you may want to move it to a folder.

If you are using the mouse, moving a message is easy. Drag the message to the folder and release the mouse button.

Alternatively, you can follow these steps:

1. Select the message(s) to be moved.

2. From the File menu choose Move, press Ctrl+M, or choose the Move toolbar button. The Move Message dialog appears.

3. In the Move Message dialog, use the arrow keys to choose the folder to which you want to move the message.

4. Choose OK.

> **TIP**   Using the Move Message dialog has an advantage. You can use the dialog's **N**ew button to create a new folder to which to move the message.

Expanding and Collapsing Folders

Managing folders in Mail is similar to managing directories using File Manager. You can expand and collapse branches of folders, enabling you to view only top-level folders or also subfolders.

Like File Manager, Mail shows that subfolders are present by preceding the top folder with a plus sign. When the subfolders are displayed, the plus becomes a minus sign.

To expand a folder, click the plus sign to the left of the folder or select the folder using the arrow keys and press the plus key. To collapse the folder, click the minus sign with the mouse or select the folder using the arrow keys and press the minus key. You can expand or collapse down only one level from the level in which you are operating.

Deleting a Selected Folder

When you delete a selected folder, you also delete all messages and subfolders contained in that folder. You cannot delete shared folders and the Deleted Mail folder.

To delete a selected folder, press the Del key. A message appears, warning that all messages in the folder also will be deleted. Choose **Yes**.

Using Other Mail Options

Several other options are available when working with Mail. These
options control the process of sending messages and receiving
new mail. These options also control the status of the Deleted Mail
folder. To set the Mail options, choose Options from the Mail
menu to call up the Options dialog. The available Mail options are
summarized in table 5.6.

Table 5.6 Mail Options

Option	Description
Save Copy of Outgoing Messages in Sent Mail Folder	Copies all the messages you send to the Sent Mail folder. This way, you can retrieve the messages at any time and maintain an audit trail of messages sent. The disadvantage is that you use a good deal of disk space.
Add Recipients to Personal Address Book	Adds message recipients to your personal address book. Check this option to avoid adding these users manually.
Check for New Mail Every *x* Minutes	Forces Mail to check the post office for new mail at a time interval you specify. The setting depends on how often you receive mail. A lower setting slows down your computer, because the CPU takes time to do the checking, leaving less time for other activities.
Sound Chime	Causes your computer to beep when new mail arrives
Flash Envelope	Briefly turns the mouse pointer into an envelope icon when new mail arrives
Empty Deleted Mail Folder When Exiting	Erases the messages in the Deleted Mail folder every time you exit Mail

> **TIP** If you elect to save a copy of outgoing messages in the Sent Folder and to not empty the Deleted Mail folder when exiting Mail, the size of your mail file increases substantially. Eventually, you run out of disk space. You shouldn't save copies of sent messages. If you need a copy of a message, add yourself as a Cc user name.
>
> You should empty the Deleted Mail folder when exiting Mail. To save a message, don't delete it.

Working Off-Line

You can work in Mail off-line when you are away from the office working on your portable or when the LAN is down. If you are in either situation, a warning message appears when you first get into Mail. Choose the Yes button to continue working in Mail off-line.

When working off-line, you can create new messages, work with folders, or read existing messages. Because Mail cannot check with the post office during this time, however, no messages are sent or received. All messages you have "sent" are transferred to the post office when you reconnect to the LAN.

Backing Up and Restoring Your Message File

Your message file grows large over time. All messages, folders, and subfolders are kept in a large file named MSMAIL.MMF. This file is located in the Windows for Workgroups directory. If anything happens to this file, the mail system for your computer may become inaccessible. You may not be able to read messages, send new ones, or perform other Mail operations.

Mail provides a backup option that enables you to copy your mail file to another location for safekeeping. You also can back up your message file to a floppy disk or shared directory. To back up your message file, follow these steps:

1. From the Mail menu, choose Backup.

2. In the Backup dialog, indicate the file name, drive, and directory to which you want to back up.

3. Choose OK.

If you have a problem locating your message file (because it was deleted or became corrupted), you see an alert box with the words Unable to open message file. After you choose OK, you return to Program Manager. Mail cannot load if your MSMAIL.MMF file isn't accessible. To restore your message file, follow these steps:

1. Locate the floppy disk or directory on your hard disk containing the backup file. Copy the backup to your Windows for Workgroups directory. Now you can get into Mail.

2. Mail detects that the file is a backup file. You see a dialog that says, This message file is a backup file. Would you like to make it your primary message file? Choose Yes.

   Mail takes a few minutes to convert the backup file into the primary message file. After this process is completed, you see the main Mail window.

All further activity takes place against the newly converted file. You may have lost some messages, however. Mail acts on your messages from wherever the backup left off.

> **NOTE** If Mail cannot find your MSMAIL.MMF file, it will create a new one.

Summary

In this chapter, you learned about Windows for Workgroups' electronic mail feature, Microsoft Mail. This chapter discussed setting up Mail for a user and the post office. You also learned various ways to send messages, including replying and forwarding; and you learned how to insert and attach files and embed objects. Folder management was noted, including how to create, delete, and move folders. Finally, other Mail options were covered, such as backing up and restoring your Mail files.

Chapter 6's topic, Schedule+, closely relates to Mail. Schedule+ is a personal scheduler that uses Mail to assist in the group scheduling of events.

Using Schedule+

Schedule+ is a powerful scheduling tool that you can use not only as a personal calendar but also to coordinate schedules with other members of your workgroup. You can use Schedule+ to keep track of your personal meetings, schedule projects, and coordinate conference rooms. You also can work off-line with Schedule+. This chapter examines what Schedule+ can do for you and how you can use it.

Schedule+ depends on the Mail program to distribute and receive invitations to meetings. The mailing list also is used as the basis for workgroup scheduling. You need to run Mail first so that Schedule+ has a mailing list available for use.

Schedule+ also uses a memory-resident program, called Reminders, to remind you of upcoming appointments. If you are using another application, Reminders displays a window to remind you of an appointment. The Reminders program remains active and displays upcoming appointments even after you exit Schedule+.

The following section shows how to set up Schedule+ in Windows for Workgroups. Later sections explain the pertinent parts of the major windows (including the toolbar and the menus) and how to perform such Schedule+ functions as setting up your own schedule, working with other users' schedules, and configuring Schedule+ to suit your needs.

Setting Up Schedule+

The first time you use Schedule+, the program sets up files for you and asks for a password. You must run the Mail program once before you can use the workgroup features of

Schedule+. Until you run the Mail program, you can use only the personal scheduling features of Schedule+.

To set up Schedule+, follow these steps:

1. Run the Mail program to make sure that it is set up.

> **NOTE** If you haven't run Mail yet and run Schedule+ for the first time, a warning message appears telling you as much. To set up the Mail program for the first time, see Chapter 5, "Using Mail."

2. From Program Manager's Main group run Schedule+.

3. The Mail Sign In dialog appears. (To run Schedule+, you must sign into Mail.) Type your Mail user name and password, which were created when you set up your mail box in your workgroup post office. Choose OK.

4. The Confirm Password dialog appears. Confirm the password by retyping it and then choose OK. The main screen appears.

Schedule+ now creates two files: SCHDPLUS.INI and *NAME*.CAL, where *NAME* is your user name. SCHDPLUS.INI contains information telling Schedule+ your Mail name, the path to your calendar, and the location of the Schedule+ application. The *NAME*.CAL file is your personal appointment calendar.

Understanding the Schedule+ Window

As with any Windows application, the Schedule+ window contains the title bar with the Control menu button, the minimize and maximize buttons, the menu bar, and the status bar. The Schedule+ windows also contains a toolbar that's different than toolbars in other Windows for Workgroups programs.

When you first start Schedule+, you see also two subwindows—your schedule window and a messages window. The schedule window displays your scheduling information. The messages window displays any incoming messages pertaining to scheduling (for example, an invitation to a meeting). Figure 6.1 shows you a Schedule+ screen.

Windows for Workgroups comes with a wide array of features and tools designed to make access to information as easy as possible. These features are discussed in following sections.

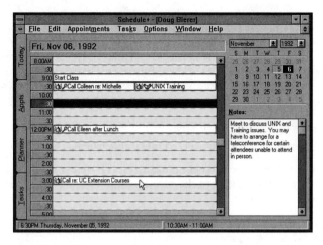

FIG. 6.1 *A Schedule+ screen.*

The Toolbar

Unlike toolbars found in other Windows for Workgroups utilities, the toolbar in Schedule+ goes down the left side of the screen and looks like manila folder tabs. (The toolbars in other Windows for Workgroups programs consist of buttons with icons across the top of the screen.) Information in the schedule window is organized around the four toolbar options, as follows:

Toolbar Tab	Description
Today	Displays today's appointments
Appts	Enables you to view the appointments for any day; display is like the one for Today
Planner	Displays one to three weeks (depending on the window's size) of the scheduled time in a spreadsheet format. Days are represented in columns and are blocked off into half-hour squares.
Tasks	Lists the projects (if this feature is enabled) and the various tasks

Clicking a toolbar tab moves you to that particular view of your schedule.

The Messages Window

The Messages window displays messages you have received from other users on the LAN. This window displays a list of all the meeting requests you have sent and responses you have received. You can view this window by choosing 1 Messages from the Window menu. You can choose from two buttons:

■ *Read.* Enables you to read incoming meeting requests.

■ *Delete.* Deletes the selected meeting request.

For each request, the following information is displayed: who sent the message, the subject of the message, and the date and time the message was sent.

The Status Bar

The status bar at the bottom of the screen is divided between two types of messages. The left side displays the current time, the day, and the date. The right side displays various messages, including the option being viewed (for example, Active Tasks or All Tasks) and the duration of the selected event (for example, 1:30PM - 2:00PM).

The Menu Bar

Schedule+ includes a menu bar that enables you to manage files, edit schedule information, create and manage appointments and tasks, and control the way Schedule+ appears. Table 6.1 lists all menu commands in Schedule+. Speed keys are shown in parentheses after the menu command. The commands are discussed in detail throughout the chapter.

Table 6.1 Schedule+ Menu Commands

Menu	Command	Description
File	Turn Off Reminders	Toggles off Reminders until you exit and restart Schedule+ or Windows for Workgroups

Menu	Command	Description
File	Turn On Reminders	Turns Reminders on. You see this option only if Reminders already is turned off.
	Work Offline	Enables you to work with your schedule outside the work-group environment
	Work Online	Enables you to work on-line with your schedule
	Move Local File	Enables you to move a local Schedule+ file to another computer, drive, and directory
	Open Other's Appt Book	Enables you to view the appointments for another user in your workgroup
	Export Appointments	Enables you to export your schedule to another system, using a range of dates
	Import Appointments	Enables you to bring in appointments from Schedule+, Windows Calendar, and Word-Perfect Office
	Create Archive	Enables you to archive dates before a speci-fied cutoff date
	Open Archive	Enables you to browse through archived files
	Print (Ctrl+P)	Prints your schedule for a specified range of dates. You can print daily, weekly, or monthly views, text, or your task list.

continues

Table 6.1 Continued

Menu	Command	Description
File	Print Setup	Enables you to change the printer and the printer setup
	Exit (Alt+F4)	Closes and exits Schedule+ but not Mail and Reminders. Reminder windows still appear if you use this option.
	Exit and Sign Out	Takes you out of Schedule+, Reminders, and Mail
Edit	Undo *action* (Ctrl+Z)	Undoes your last edit. The *action* is the last edit you performed (for example, delete or modify).
	Cut (Ctrl+X)	Cuts and pastes selected text in the Clipboard
	Copy (Ctrl+C)	Copies selected text and places it in the Clipboard
	Paste (Ctrl+V)	Inserts the contents of the Clipboard at the insertion point
	Edit Appt/Task/Project (Ctrl+E)	Enables you to edit the selected appointment, task, or project, depending on whether you are viewing the Appointments screen or the Tasks screen
	Copy Appt (Ctrl+Y)	Copies an appointment to another day, time slot, or both. The

Menu	Command	Description
		option is most useful for an appointment that repeats once or twice. Use the New Recurring Appt option on the Appointments menu for appointments that repeat more than twice.
	Move Appt (Ctrl+O)	Moves an appointment to another day, time, or both
	Delete Appt/Task/Project (Ctrl+D)	Deletes the selected appointment, task, or project
	Find (Ctrl+F)	Searches the schedule for the text you specify
	Go To Date (Ctrl+G)	Moves forward or backward to the date you specify. You also can move the date indicator on the appointment calendar at the top right of the screen.
Appointments	New Appointment (Ctrl+N)	Creates a new appointment
	Auto-Pick (Ctrl+A)	Selects the next available time slot for you to schedule an event. This command works only from the Planner window.
	New Recurring Appt (Ctrl+R)	Sets up an appointment that takes place on a regular basis

continues

Table 6.1 Continued

Menu	Command	Description
Appointments	Edit Recurring Appts	Enables you to edit recurring appointments
	Tentative (Ctrl+Shift+T)	Marks an appointment as tentative so that it appears in gray rather than in black. Other users looking at your calendar will see the time as free.
	Private (Ctrl+Shift+P)	Marks an appointment as private so that other users who look at your calendar cannot see it
	Set Reminder (Ctrl+Shift+R)	If checked, reminds you when the selected appointment comes up
	Re-Send Mail	Retransmits the mail messages that invited people to a meeting. This option is available only from the Appts screen when a meeting is selected.
Tasks	New Task (Ctrl+T)	Adds a new task to your list
	New Project	Enables you to group tasks under a project
	New Recurring Task	Enables you to schedule the due date for a task that takes place on a regular basis
	Edit Recurring Tasks	Enables you to edit a list of recurring tasks

Menu	Command	Description
Tasks	**View by Project/Task (Ctrl+Shift+V)**	Groups tasks by project or task. If selected, this option displays project headings and changes the primary sort to Project. If other Sort options are selected, tasks first are sorted by project, then by the secondary sort. If this option isn't selected, tasks are listed without the project names and aren't sorted by project.
	Sort by **Priority**	Sorts tasks by priority
	Sort **by** Due Date	Sorts tasks by due date
	Sort by **Description**	Sorts tasks by description
	Show **Active/All** Tasks	Hides tasks not in the start task/due by time window for today's date (Active), or displays all tasks
Options	**Change Password**	Enables you to change your Schedule+ and Mail password. (Both programs use the same password.)
	Set Access Privileges	Determines who can access your schedule and what that user can do with your schedule. Access privileges consist of no access, view free/ busy times, and read,

continues

Table 6.1 Continued

Menu	Command	Description
		create, or modify appointments and tasks. You also can designate rights by user and assign an assistant.
	Display	Enables you to adjust foreground and background colors and font size
	General Options	Enables you to adjust general options such as reminder on/off options and the default begin and end dates for the calendar
	Status Bar	When checked, displays the status bar at the bottom of the Schedule+ screen
Window	Cascade (Shift+F5)	Cascades the message, appointment/task, and schedule windows
	Tile (Shift+F4)	Tiles the message, appointment/task, and schedule windows
	Arrange Icons	Arranges icons so that you can have a less cluttered screen
	1 Messages	Moves you to the Messages window to view incoming messages
	n *XYZ*	Enables you to move immediately to window *n*. *XYZ* is the name of the user whose schedule

Menu	Command	Description
		appears in window *n*, or the incoming or outgoing meeting request window
Help		Displays the Schedule+ program's help screen

Understanding Personal, Workgroup, and Off-line Scheduling

You can use Schedule+ to schedule your personal time and the time you will spend with the workgroup. You also can do the following:

■ Assign an assistant to manage your schedule

> **NOTE**   An *assistant* is a workgroup member who manages the schedule for another account. A secretary, for example, can manage the schedule of his or her boss. An assistant can manage the complete schedule of another account with-out having to exit Schedule+ and sign back in.

■ Schedule the use of resources, such as a conference room or audio-visual equipment

■ Schedule meetings that involve other workgroup members

■ View and change the schedules of other workgroup members (depending on your access privileges)

■ Work off-line

Schedule+ refers to working with your own schedule as *personal scheduling*. Working with other workgroup members, having an assistant do your scheduling, or scheduling meetings is referred to as *workgroup scheduling*.

Schedule+ also enables you to work off-line, a feature designed for workgroup members who may not be connected to the network at all times—for example, a company's sales representatives, who have their own notebook computers. In the office, the representatives can connect to the LAN and do workgroup scheduling. On the road, they work off-line.

Scheduling Personal Appointments

Basic scheduling operations center on appointments. An *appointment* is an event scheduled for a certain date and time. A *recurring appointment* is an event that takes place at the same time every day, week, month, and so on. An example of a recurring event is a monthly staff meeting or a class that meets twice a week.

Scheduled days (and days with notes) appear in boldface in your calendar. Schedule+ starts your schedule with appointments set up on the half hour, with one appointment per half-hour period. Because appointments can take place at any time of day, however, you can have any of the following:

- Two or more appointments during the same time period

- Appointments that last for any amount of time

- Overlapping appointments

To set an appointment, you first must change to the appointment date, a process similar to flipping through pages in a desk calendar. After the desired date is selected, select the time for the appointment and type it. The following sections walk you through the basics of scheduling your personal calendar.

Changing the Date in the Appointment Book

To schedule an appointment, you first must move to the right date in your appointment book. If you need to schedule an appointment for today, make sure the Today window is on-screen by clicking the Today toolbar tab. To go to another date, you can choose the appropriate month and year from drop-down boxes in the upper right corner of the main Schedule+ screen. Then, click the appropriate day in the calendar that appears under the boxes.

You also can go to a date by choosing Go To Date from the Edit menu (or pressing Ctrl+G). In the Go To Date dialog, select the correct date (see fig. 6.2). Alternatively, type the correct date in the Go To text box and choose OK.

FIG. 6.2 *The Go To Date dialog.*

Scheduling an Appointment

You can schedule an appointment in two ways. You can select the appointment book date and type the appointment, or you can use the New Appointment option on the Appointments menu.

To schedule an appointment using the New Appointment option, from the Appointments menu choose New Appointment, or press Ctrl+N. In the Appointment dialog, use the scroll boxes and buttons to select the correct date and time, and use the Description box to enter the appointment description (see fig. 6.3). The options in the Appointment dialog are described as follows:

- *Start.* In the boxes provided, enter the time and date the appointment starts. You also can choose a time and date from the drop-down list accessed by clicking the arrow buttons.

- *End.* In the boxes provided, enter the time and date the appointment ends. You also can choose a time and date from the drop-down list accessed by clicking the arrow buttons.

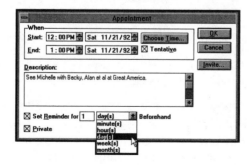

FIG. 6.3 *The Appointment dialog.*

TIP The times in the **S**tart and **E**nd drop-down list boxes are listed in half-hour increments. You can change the hour, minutes, or seconds that are displayed in the box by selecting the particular time element and changing it.

■ *Choose Time.* This option displays the Choose Time dialog (see fig. 6.4). In this dialog, you can select the block of time from a grid, or choose the Auto-Pick button to have Schedule+ select the next available time slot. (If you choose Auto-Pick, Schedule+ doesn't schedule appointments in already scheduled time slots and gray areas.) The selected time appears as a solid black bar on the grid. If the time is acceptable, choose OK to return to the Appointments dialog.

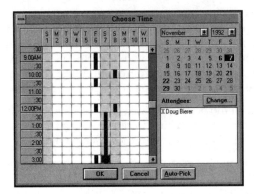

FIG. 6.4 *The Choose Time dialog.*

■ *Tentative.* If you select this check box, an appointment time in your book doesn't appear as busy when other users view your schedule. When you view your schedule, a tentative appointment appears in gray rather than black.

■ *Description.* You can type a description of the appointment.

■ *Set Reminder for ... Beforehand.* This option enables you to indicate how long before the appointment you want Schedule+ to remind you of the impending appointment. At the designated time and day, Schedule+ displays a pop-up screen as an appointment reminder (and beeps, if you have configured Reminders to do so).

- *Private.* When you select this option, the appointment doesn't appear when other workgroup members view your appointment calendar. The time slot that you use for this appointment is shown as taken, however, so that users cannot schedule another appointment in its place.

- *Invite.* With this button, you can invite other users to attend the appointment. You then are prompted to send a message out to the invited users asking for a response. (See the section "Scheduling a Group Appointment" later in this chapter for more details.)

After you are finished with the Appointment dialog, choose OK. The appointment is saved in your appointment book.

You can use the Appointment dialog to set two appointments for the same time. You may want to set two appointments for the same time if you have two activities that must be done within the same time period and you want two separate reminders for them.

Schedule+ enables you to set up gray times, in which you don't want to schedule appointments (for example, evenings and weekends). You easily can set up gray times by scheduling all these various times as tentative recurring appointments.

Schedule+ also enables you to schedule overlapping appointments. To do so, use the Appointment dialog to add your two appointments with overlapping times. Schedule+ displays both appointments side by side, as shown in figure 6.5.

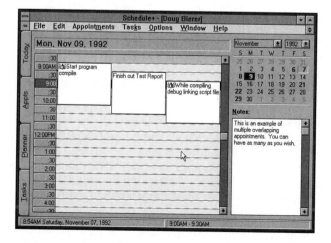

FIG. 6.5 *Overlapping appointments.*

Changing an Appointment

You easily can change appointments. To change an appointment, you first must select the appointment to change. Then, you can begin typing to change the description, if the description needs to be changed. To change other settings for the appointment, double-click the appointment, from the Edit menu choose Edit Appt, or press Ctrl+E. The Appointment dialog appears. Make any desired changes and then choose OK.

If you want to change only the time of the appointment, select the appointment and then from the Edit menu choose Move Appt (or press Ctrl+O). Use the Move Appointment dialog to select the new time and then choose OK.

TIP	To change the time of an appointment with the mouse, you can drag the appointment to the new time. This technique is useful only if you want to change the appointment to a different time during the same day.

Deleting an Appointment

To delete an appointment, choose the appointment to delete and then from the Edit menu choose Delete Appt (or press Ctrl+D). The appointment disappears from the schedule window.

Scheduling a Recurring Appointment

A *recurring* appointment is one that takes place on a regular basis, such as loan payments or weekly staff meetings. To schedule a recurring appointment, from the Appointments menu choose New Recurring Appt or press Ctrl+R. The Recurring Appointment dialog appears (see fig. 6.6).

The options in the Recurring Appointment dialog are similar to the ones in the Appointment dialog: Start, End, Tentative, Description, Set Reminder for ... Beforehand, and Private. (See the earlier section "Scheduling an Appointment" for descriptions of these options.) The day and time now selected in the appointment schedule is the default starting day and time for the recurring event.

To change the recurring appointment, choose the Change button. The Change Recurrence dialog appears (see fig. 6.7).

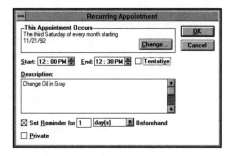

FIG. 6.6 *The Recurring Appointment dialog.*

FIG. 6.7 *The Change Recurrence dialog.*

In the Change Recurrence dialog, your choice in the This Occurs section determines the settings available in the section to the right. The settings are described as follows:

- *Daily.* If you choose this option in the This Occurs section, you can choose between Every Day and Every Weekday in the box to the right. Choose Every Day if you want the appointment scheduled for every day. Choose Every Weekday if you want the appointment scheduled for every day except Saturday and Sunday.

- *Weekly.* The Every Week On section lists the seven days of the week (refer to fig. 6.7). Select each day in which you want this recurring event scheduled.

- *Bi-Weekly.* The Every Other Week On section lists the seven weekdays. Select each day in which you want this event scheduled.

- *Monthly.* Choose this option if you want the appointment to take place on a certain number day of every month. Then you have two options, as follows:

Option	Description
The ... of every month	In the first box, enter **first**, **second**, and so on up to **last**. In the second box, enter **day**, **weekday**, **weekend day**, or **Sunday** through **Saturday**. In the last box, enter a month, such as **March**. When you are finished, you should have something like The third Thursday of every month.
Day...of every month	Use this option if the appointment takes place on a day number rather than on a say of week. After you finish, you have something like Day 10 of every month.

■ *Yearly.* If you choose this option, the following settings become available:

Option	Description
Every year on...	Enter the month and day number
The...of...	In the first box, enter **first**, **second**, and so on up to the **last**. In the second box, enter **day**, **weekday**, **weekend day**, or **Sunday** through **Saturday**. In the last box, enter a month, such as **March**. When you are finished, you should have something like The third Thursday of March.

In the Change Recurrence dialog, the options in the Duration section enable you to set the starting date and the ending date for this scheduled item. If you don't know how long the scheduled event will go, you can choose **No** End Date. This way, Schedule+ always will consider the time period you have selected as having been scheduled. After you determine an event ending date, you can choose the E**n**ds radio button and enter the ending date.

After you finish making selections in the Change Recurrence dialog, choose OK, and then choose OK from the Recurring Appointment dialog.

Editing a Recurring Appointment

Changing a recurring appointment is different than changing a regular appointment. You don't select the recurring appointment first. Instead, from the Appointments menu you choose Edit Recurring Appointments. The Edit Recurring Appointments dialog appears, with the following options:

- *Occurs.* The cycle of the appointment, such as daily, weekly, or monthly
- *Next.* The next occurrence of this appointment
- *Description.* The text of the appointment

From the dialog, select the appointment you want to edit and then choose the Edit button. Enter the new information in the Recurring Appointment dialog and choose OK. When you return to the Edit Recurring Appointments dialog, choose Close.

Deleting a Recurring Appointment

Deleting a recurring appointment is different than deleting a one-time appointment. You don't need to select the appointment you want delete first.

To delete a recurring appointment, from the Appointments menu choose Edit Recurring Appointments. In the Edit Recurring Appointments dialog, select the recurring appointment to delete and then choose the Delete button. Schedule+ asks whether you want to leave past occurrences of this appointment in the schedule. Choose Yes to leave them in the schedule, No to delete them, or Cancel to ignore the deletion.

Setting Appointment Reminders

A *reminder* is an optional feature you can set for any appointment that hasn't taken place yet. A ringing bell icon appears next to the text of an appointment that has a reminder set.

You can adjust the amount of advance warning you want for any reminder. When the reminder time comes up, a message appears and a tone sounds, depending on the options you set (see

"Setting Schedule+ Preferences" later in the chapter). One option is to have reminders set automatically whenever you set an appointment.

> **NOTE** You cannot set a reminder for an event that already has taken place. When the pop-up message appears, however, you can continue the notification even though the event time already may have passed. Suppose that you have scheduled time to go buy a present but have been delayed from going. By continuing the reminder, you can remember to go buy that present at a later time.

To set a reminder, first select the appointment. Then from the Appointments menu choose Set Reminder (or press Ctrl+Shift+R). An image of a bell appears to the left of the appointment's description. If a reminder already has been set for the appointment, the original reminder is removed.

When the time comes for the reminder, the Reminder dialog appears, as shown in figure 6.8. You can choose from the following options:

Notify Me Again in ...

Don't Notify Me Again

If you select Notify Me Again in ..., you can choose the length of time to the next reminder in minutes, hours, days, weeks, or months. After you make your selection, choose OK.

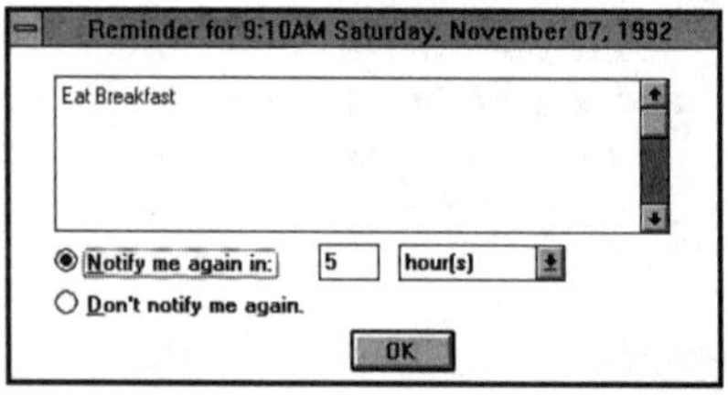

FIG. 6.8 *The Reminder dialog.*

Adding a Daily Note in the Appointment Book

You can enter notes for any day by entering text in the Notes section, which is in the lower right corner of the schedule window. After you enter text in the Notes section, a pop-up screen displays the notes for the day when you start Schedule+.

Finding Text in the Appointment Book

Schedule+ enables you to search for text in your schedule in three ways:

Forward from today

Backward from today

The whole schedule

To search for text, from the Edit menu choose Find, or press Ctrl+F. Enter the text to search for in the Search For text box in the Find dialog (see fig. 6.9). Then choose an option button: Forward from Today, Backward from Today, or Whole Schedule. Next, choose the Start Search button. Schedule+ locates—one at a time—each schedule window that contains the text. To continue searching, choose the Find Next button. To stop searching, press Esc or choose the Cancel button.

FIG. 6.9 *The Find dialog.*

Archiving Your Schedule

After a while your schedule file will grow large. You should *archive* your schedule on a regular basis. The more appointments you schedule, the more often you should archive your schedule.

The archive process reduces the size of your main schedule file but retains current schedule information. Place the archived file on a floppy disk or a shared directory.

> **NOTE** When you archive data, the data in your schedule before the cutoff date is removed from your main schedule file. To see appointments before the cutoff date, you need to view the archived file.

To archive your schedule, from the File menu choose Create Archive. In the Create Archive dialog, choose the drive, directory, and file name for the archive file. Enter the last date that you want archived in the Archive Before text box and then choose OK. Schedule+ displays a message warning you that information before this date will be removed from your schedule file and placed in the archive file. Choose OK. Schedule+ creates the archive file and moves data into it.

To review appointments in the archived file, first make sure that the floppy disk or the shared directory with the archived file is accessible. Next, from the File menu choose Open Archive. The Open Archive dialog appears. Select the drive, directory, and file name of the archived file, and then choose OK. Schedule+ opens a new schedule window containing the archived file. You can move around and view appointments just as though you were working with your current schedule.

Working with Your Task List

You may want to schedule events pertaining to projects. Schedule+ can keep track of projects and tasks associated with the project. You can place tasks at any time into your schedule and can prioritize tasks. You also can view projects and their associated tasks in different sort orders.

Projects consist of tasks to be performed. After you set up a project, you create the various tasks that belong to this project.

The easiest way to work with tasks is to move to the Tasks window by clicking the Tasks toolbar button. The following section discusses the Tasks window in detail. Later sections show you how to work with projects and tasks in Schedule+.

Understanding the Tasks Window

The Tasks window, shown in figure 6.10, displays projects and tasks you have created. The window contains three columns of information. You can use the buttons at the top of the columns to sort the projects and tasks, as follows:

Button	Description
Priority	Displays the importance of the task. You can have priority range from 1 to 9 and A to Z, with 1 the highest priority, and Z the lowest.
Due By	Lists the date the task is due
Description	Displays a description of the task

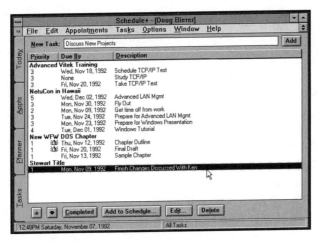

FIG. 6.10 *The Tasks window.*

At the top of the window is a box that enables you to add new tasks quickly for the currently selected project. You can control the order in which tasks are listed by selecting one of the options listed in the Tasks menu. At the bottom of the screen are the following buttons:

Button	Description
Up arrow	Moves to the preceding task or project on the list
Down arrow	Moves to the next task or project on the list

continues

Button	Description
Completed	Indicates that the task is completed
Add to Schedule	Schedules the task
Edit	Enables you to edit the selected task or project
Delete	Deletes the selected task or project

For more information on using these buttons, read "Working with Your Task List" later in this chapter.

Adding a Project

To add a new project, from the Tasks menu choose New Project. In the Project dialog that appears, enter the project name. If you don't want other workgroup members to see this project or associated tasks, select the Private check box. Then choose OK.

Adding a Task

Schedule+ enables you to add just the name of the task or complete task information. Before adding a task, select the project with which the task will be associated.

To add only a task name, from the Tasks menu choose New Task (or press Ctrl+T). In the Add Task dialog, type the name of the new task. Then choose Add or press Enter.

To add complete task information to a project, from the Tasks menu choose New Project (or press Ctrl+T). The Task dialog appears (see fig. 6.11). The Task dialog contains the following options:

- *Description.* In this text box, enter a description of the task.

- *Project.* This option shows which project this task is associated with. To change the association, type the name of the project or select from the drop-down list of project names to select.

- *Due Date.* You can choose None if the task has no due date. If you choose By, you must enter the date the task is due by.

- *Start Work ... Before Due.* In the first box, enter the number of days, weeks, or months before the due date that you should start the task. In the second box, select the unit of time (days, weeks, or months).

■ *Set Reminder.* If this check box is marked, a reminder box will appear.

■ *Priority.* Use this option to set the task's priority level, from 1 to 9 and A to Z (1 is the highest priority and Z is the lowest priority).

■ *Private.* Enable this option if you don't want other workgroup members to see this task scheduled.

After you make all the settings you need in the Task dialog, choose OK.

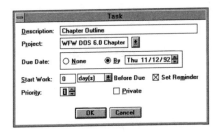

FIG. 6.11   *The Task dialog.*

Adding a Task to Your Appointment Book

To schedule tasks, select the task from the Tasks window. Choose the Add to Schedule button. In the Choose Time dialog, select the date and time to schedule the task. Choose OK. The task is added to your schedule, and you can view the task in the appointment window.

6

Adding a Recurring Task

A recurring task is similar to a recurring appointment, with two differences:

■ A recurring task has a due by date rather than a due date. The task can be accomplished any time up to the due by date.

■ A recurring task is assigned to a project and can be tracked along with that project.

To add a recurring task, from the Tasks menu choose New Recurring Task. The Recurring Task dialog appears (see fig. 6.12). Enter all appropriate information. Most options in the Recurring Task dialog are the same as in the Task dialog (discussed in the preceding section). The exception is the Change button in the dialog's Due By section.

FIG. 6.12   *The Recurring Task dialog.*

To change the recurring time period, choose the Change button. In the dialog that appears, enter the time cycle as in a recurring appointment (see "Scheduling a Recurring Appointment"). After you are finished, choose OK.

Then, after entering all other recurring task information, choose OK. The new task appears under its project with a recurring task icon next to the due date. The icon looks like two circular arrows.

Editing a Task or Project

To change a task, first select the task you want to work with. Then from the Edit menu choose Edit Task, press Ctrl+E, or choose the Edit button at the bottom of the Tasks window. In the Task dialog that appears, make any desired changes. Then choose OK.

Changing a project is similar to changing a task. First, select the project you want to work with. Then from the Edit menu choose Edit Project, press Ctrl+E, or choose the Edit button at the bottom of the window. In the Project dialog, change the name and then choose OK.

Deleting a Task or Project

To delete a task, first select the task. Then from the Edit menu choose **Delete Task**, press Ctrl+D, or choose the Delete button at the bottom of the window. The task disappears from the list.

To delete a project, first select the project in the schedule window. Then, from the Edit menu choose **Delete Project**, press Ctrl+D, or choose the Delete button at the bottom of the window. A warning message appears, telling you that all tasks for this project also will be deleted. Choose OK. The project and all associated tasks disappear from the list.

Sorting and Displaying Projects and Tasks

You can view your projects and tasks in different sort orders. You also can display different types of information, using the following options from the Tasks menu:

> View by Project (Ctrl+Shift+V)
>
> View by Task (Ctrl+Shift+V)
>
> Sort by Priority (Alt+I)
>
> Sort by Due Date (Alt+B)
>
> Sort by Description (Alt+D)
>
> Show All Tasks/Active Tasks

NOTE	An *active* task is a task in which today's date is between the scheduled start date of the task and the due date of the task.

Noting a Completed Task

You can mark a task completed by selecting the finished task from the Tasks window and then choose the Completed button.

Completed tasks don't appear in the Tasks window. A record of completed tasks appears in the Notes field of the Today window. Completed tasks have the word Done before the text of the completed task. The name of the project appears in parentheses afterward.

Tracking Appointments by Associated Projects

Schedule+ has no facility for keeping track of appointments associated with a particular project, other than the listing in the Tasks window. You can export your schedule to a text file, however, which then can be read into another program for sorting.

To export your schedule, from the File menu choose Export Appointments. In the Export Appointments dialog (see fig. 6.13), you can specify the following items and then choose OK:

- *File Format.* To export to Schedule+, choose Schedule+ format. To export to a program other than Schedule+, use the Text format.

- *Schedule Range.* To export a range of dates, you need to specify the first date in the From box and the last date in the To box. Choose All to export all dates in your schedule.

- *Include Daily Notes.* Enable this check box if you want the daily notes to be added to the export file.

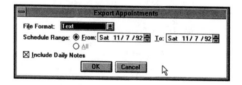

FIG. 6.13 *The Export Appointments dialog.*

After you choose OK in the Export Appointments dialog, you see a dialog asking you to supply the drive, directory, and file name for the export file. Enter the information as desired and choose OK. Schedule+ writes your schedule to an external file.

Printing Your Appointments and Tasks

This section shows you how to print your appointments and tasks. To access the Schedule+ print functions from any Schedule+ window, from the File menu choose Print (or press Ctrl+P). The Schedule+ Print dialog appears (see fig. 6.14).

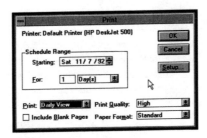

FIG. 6.14   *The Schedule+ Print dialog.*

The Schedule+ Print dialog contains the following options:

- *Schedule Range.* In the Starting box, indicate the date to start printing. In the For boxes, indicate the number of days, weeks, months, and so on to print.

- *Setup.* With this button (a standard button available in all Windows applications), you can set the printer for portrait, landscape, margins, and so on.

- *Print.* This option enables you to choose what to print. At the bottom left of each printout is the time and date of the printout. Recurring appointments print along with regular appointments. You can choose from the following options:

Option	Description
Daily View	Displays the information you see in the Today window, including your name, the date, the Notes field, and a miniature calendar of the month. A summary of your appointments also is presented.
Weekly View	Displays your appointments a week at a time, similar to that of the Planner window. The days of the week are displayed across the top. The times are displayed down the left. At the bottom of the page is a section titled More, which displays additional appointments when more than one appointment is scheduled per period. Below that section is a section titled Notes, which displays daily notes.

continues

Option	Description
Monthly View	Shows appointments a month at a time. The month is displayed in standard calendar format. Each day has as many appointments as can fit in the box for the day.
Text View	Lists your appointments without special formatting. The range of dates is displayed across the top. Your name appears at the top right. The day and date is at the left margin. The appointments are indented and displayed one after another in one column. The description of the appointment is in the next column. The notes for the day appear at the bottom of the listing.
Task List	Appears just as you see in the Tasks window in Schedule+. Projects are listed in boldface at the left margin. The priority, due date, and description of each task are indented underneath.

■ *Print Quality.* You can print your lists in a number of print qualities: High, Medium, Low, and Draft. The lower the quality, the faster the printing.

■ *Include Blank Pages.* If this option is enabled, a page prints, even if it has no appointments.

■ *Paper Format.* Schedule+ supports three types of paper formats: Standard (8 1/2 by 11 inches), Junior (4 1/2 by 7 1/4 inches), and Pocket (3 by 6 inches).

Using Schedule+ with Other Users

This section shows you how to use Schedule+ in the workgroup environment. Scheduling with other users is one of the most important features of Windows for Workgroups, one that makes this program stand out from other scheduling programs.

The two primary functions of group scheduling in Schedule+ are meetings and appointments. A *meeting* is an event scheduled at a location that a number of users in the workgroup are expected to attend. A *group appointment* is an appointment that other users are invited to attend. (A good example of a group appointment may be a weekly meeting of a manufacturing organization's production and assembly operations.) These scheduling options work with the Mail system and the post office.

The following sections discuss how to set up and manage meetings and group appointments. They also cover how to respond to a meeting request, how to reschedule, and how to cancel a meeting. You also see how to restrict or give others access to your schedule.

Setting Up a Meeting

To set up a meeting, follow these steps:

1. In the Planner window, select the Attendees list and then choose the Change button. In the dialog that appears, you see a list of potential attendees in the post office list. You can choose your Personal Address Book list, if desired.

2. To add an attendee, select the name and choose the Add button. Continue to add attendees in this manner.

3. After you finish, choose OK. The program returns to the Planner window.

4. Select the date and time for the meeting by moving to the desired week and selecting the block of time for the meeting.

5. Choose the Request Meeting button. The Send Request dialog appears (see fig. 6.15).

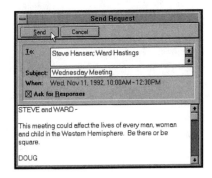

FIG. 6.15 *The Send Request dialog.*

You must provide the following information in the Send
Request dialog:

Option	Description
To	Enter the name or names of the user(s) to whom the meeting request message is addressed
Subject	Enter the subject of the meeting
When	Displays the block of time you outlined in the Planner window. You cannot change this option in this dialog.
Ask for Responses	Requests invited users for a return message indicating their response

Also, the text box at the bottom of the dialog is for the text
of the outgoing meeting request message. Enter any desired
information in this text box.

6. After you finish entering information, choose the Send
   button. Schedule+ notifies you of any schedule conflicts. If
   you have the necessary access to other users' schedules, you
   can book an overlapping meeting.

7. After everything is booked, you see a message saying so.
   Choose OK.

Responding to a Meeting Request

You can view incoming meeting requests in the Messages window.
To respond to a meeting request, from the Window menu choose
1 Messages. Select the message with the meeting request. Choose
the Read button or double-click the message, and the Meeting Request dialog appears, displaying the message (see fig. 6.16). You
can take any of the following actions: Accept, Decline, Tentative,
or View Schedule.

The procedures for accepting a request and tentatively accepting a
request are similar. To accept the request for a meeting, choose
the Accept button. To tentatively accept the request, choose the
Tentative button.

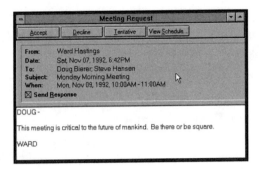

FIG. 6.16 *The Meeting Request dialog.*

> **NOTE** Schedule+ notifies you if a conflict exists. Choose OK if you want to book the meeting anyway.

When you see the Meeting was booked successfully message, choose OK. If Send **Response** is marked, you then are prompted to enter a response to the request. Enter any comments you want to make and then choose the **S**end button.

The meeting appears on your schedule with an icon of two hands shaking. A response from the meeting attendee message appears in your message list. A positive response (**A**ccept) appears with a check mark icon. An appointment for a tentative meeting appears in gray.

To decline the request for a meeting, choose the **D**ecline button. If the Send **R**esponse box is marked in the Meeting Request dialog, you are prompted to respond to the request. The words No, I won't attend are filled in for you. Add comments you want to make and then choose the **S**end button. The negative response message appears in your message list with an X icon.

To view your schedule, choose the View **S**chedule button. You see your schedule window with the proposed meeting time shaded. To switch back to the Meeting Request dialog, you can click it or choose Meeting Request from the **W**indow menu. Then choose **A**ccept, **D**ecline, or **T**entative, as explained earlier.

> **TIP** All meeting requests and responses are Mail messages. You can view them by going to the Mail program.

Rescheduling a Meeting

On occasion you may have to reschedule a meeting. To do so, select the meeting from your schedule window and then do one of the following:

- Drag it to the desired time slot.

- From the Edit menu, choose Move (or press Ctrl+O). From the Move Appointment dialog box that appears, select the new time and date for the meeting.

If you aren't the organizer of the meeting, you see a message stating that you may want the organizer of the meeting to know that you want to reschedule the meeting. If you are the organizer of the meeting, you see a message asking whether you want to notify the invited attendees of the change. Choose **Yes**.

Next, fill out the Send Request dialog and choose the **Send** button. You see a message, asking whether you want to schedule the meeting now. Choose the **Yes** button.

Canceling a Meeting

To cancel a meeting, select the meeting you want to cancel from your schedule window. Then, from the Edit menu choose **Delete** (or press Ctrl+D).

If you are organizing the meeting, you see a message asking whether you want to send out a cancellation notice to the invited attendees. Choose **Yes**. In the Cancel Meeting dialog, the subject is filled in already with the word Canceled, followed by the original subject, to which you can add more information. Choose the **Send** button. You see a message asking whether you want to remove this meeting from your schedule now. Choose **Yes**.

If you aren't organizing the meeting, you see a message telling you that you may want the meeting's organizer to know that you will not attend the meeting. Choose **Yes**. In the Send Response dialog, the words No I won't attend appear automatically. To these words add whatever you want and then choose the **Send** button. The meeting is removed from your schedule.

Scheduling a Group Appointment

In a *group appointment*, other workgroup members are invited to attend. A group appointment is the same as a meeting, except it is scheduled through your schedule window rather than the Planner window.

To schedule a group appointment, from the schedule window make a new appointment, as described earlier in the "Scheduling an Appointment" section. Fill in the Appointment dialog with all pertinent information. Then, choose the Invite button. In the Select Attendees dialog, use the post office list or your address book to add users to the list. After you are finished, choose OK. Schedule+ puts the appointment into each invited user's schedule and then updates the schedule window that contains the information about your new appointment.

In the schedule window, you see the users you selected in the Attendees box. Choose OK. In the Send Request dialog, enter any information you want invited attendees to see. After you are finished, choose the Send button.

If you are an assistant, you are asked whether you want to schedule the meeting for the people whose schedules you manage. Choose Yes.

A message indicates any conflicts in schedule times. If this conflict isn't a problem, choose Yes. (If you choose No, you must select a new time for this meeting.) The meeting appears in the schedule with an icon of two hands shaking.

Giving Others Access to Your Schedule

You can limit what other workgroup members can see of your schedule. The spectrum of rights runs from no access to full capability to add, change, or remove appointments. Even if you let others view your schedule, you still can designate an appointment as private. A private appointment doesn't appear on your schedule when viewed by workgroup members.

You need to manage user access to your directories in a timely manner so that you can be responsive to their needs. To facilitate access, you need to be able to set and change their access privileges, as discussed in the following sections.

Setting and Changing User Access Privileges

You can set or change access privileges for your schedule from the Schedule+ Options menu. First, from the Options menu choose Set Access Privileges. The Set Access Privileges dialog appears (see fig. 6.17).

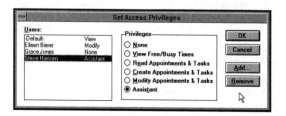

FIG. 6.17 *The Set Access Privileges dialog.*

You can choose the following rights:

- *None.* Provides no access to other users. You are the only person who can view or work with your schedule.

- *View Free/Busy Times.* Enables others to view your free and busy times when trying to schedule meetings. They cannot see what you have scheduled; they can see only that a particular time slot is free or busy.

- *Read Appointments & Tasks.* Enables other users to see what you have scheduled for any given time slot and view your task list. This access privilege is appropriate for peer-level coworkers. Only you can view private appointments.

- *Create Appointments & Tasks.* Enables other users to view your appointment and task lists and create appointments and tasks. Users with this level of access also can delete the appointments they create for you and can schedule you for a meeting. This access level is appropriate for a supervisor.

- *Modify Appointments & Tasks.* Enables other users to view and create appointments and tasks, and change or delete your appointments and tasks. This access level is appropriate for a secretary or an assistant. Only you can view and modify private appointments.

■ *Assistant.* Provides access at the Modify Appointments & Tasks level to an assistant, who also can receive and handle meeting requests and schedule meetings on your behalf. Any meeting that your assistant schedules is identified as such.

> **TIP** You can set access levels for all users (default) or for individual users. The access rights for different users can be different.

To alter the access rights for a user who isn't on the Users list of the Set Access Privileges dialog, choose the Add button in the Set Access Privileges dialog. From the Add Users dialog, use the Add button to choose the users who you want to give access rights other than the default. When finished, choose OK.

In the Users list of the Set Access Privileges dialog, select Default or the name of the user you want to work with and then select the access level for that user. Repeat this process until you adjust all the access rights. Finally, choose OK. After the rights are set, you can change them at any time by repeating this procedure.

Designating an Assistant for Your Schedule

To designate an assistant for your schedule, from the Options menu choose Set Access Privileges. In the Users list of the Set Access Privileges dialog, select the name of the user who will become your assistant and then choose the Assistant access level. Choose OK.

An assistant for a conference room or another resource is designated as an assistant is designated for a user. First, sign into Schedule+ as the resource. From the Options menu, choose Set Access Privileges. Choose the name of the user, give that person the access level of Assistant, and then choose OK.

> **NOTE** You can have only one assistant. If you already have an assistant, the Assistant option isn't available for anyone else on the Users list. To choose another assistant, you first must change the access level for the current assistant or remove the current assistant from the list. To remove an assistant, from the Options menu choose Set Access Privileges. In the Set Access Privileges dialog, select the assistant's name in the Users list box. Then choose the Assistant radio button (to toggle it off) and then choose OK.

To have meeting requests go only to your assistant, from the Options menu choose **General Options**. From the General Options dialog, enable the Send Meeting Messages Only to my Assistant option and then choose OK. Leave this option disabled if you want requests to go to you *and* your assistant.

Working with Other Users' Schedules

Depending on your access rights, you can view and update the schedule of any user in the workgroup. When you access someone else's schedule, a schedule window opens for that user. You can have several schedule windows open at one time.

When preparing for a meeting you want to schedule, previewing the appointment books for the people that are expected to attend the meeting often is necessary. The next section explains how to view other users' schedules.

Viewing Other Users' Appointment Books or Task Lists

To open another user's schedule from the schedule window, from the File menu choose Open Other's Appt Book. From the Open Other's Appt Book dialog, select the name of the user (or resource) you want to work with. Choose the Add button. Continue to add users until you list all users whose schedules you want to work with. Then choose OK. A new schedule window opens, showing the schedule of each user (or resource) you added in the dialog.

To view the appointment book for another user, first open the other user's schedule as outlined in the preceding paragraph. From the schedule window, select **Appts** or **Today**.

To view the tasks for another user, first open the other user's schedule as outlined. Then select the schedule window for the other user. From the schedule window, select **Tasks**.

Adding, Changing, or Deleting Other Users' Appointments or Tasks

To add, change, or delete another user's appointments or tasks, you must have at least Modify Appointments & Tasks access rights. (See "Giving Others Access to Your Schedule" earlier for more details.) If you have the appropriate rights, you first must open the other user's schedule, as outlined in the preceding section.

After the other appointment book or task list is open, select the appointment or task you want to work with, and perform the desired operation just as though it was your own.

Acting as an Assistant

An assistant manages the appointment book and task list for another user. An assistant is typically an office manager or secretary managing the schedules of one or more office workers. The assistant also can schedule meetings, send out meeting requests, and respond to meeting requests. If you designate an assistant, meeting requests can be sent only to your assistant, or sent to you and a copy to your assistant.

The responsibilities for a resource assistant are similar to those of a user's assistant. As a resource assistant you must manage the schedule for the resource by opening the appointment book of the resource. You may want to print the schedule for the resource for distribution around the office.

As resource assistant, you also must receive and respond to meeting requests involving the resource. You become the arbiter when overlapping meetings are scheduled for the resource. You can accept or decline meeting requests on behalf of the resource.

Scheduling a Conference Room or Other Resources

A *resource* is a room or equipment that must be scheduled with the people in the office. A conference room is a prime example of a resource. Other resources include overhead projectors, computer equipment, and audio-visual equipment.

When you schedule meetings, you must know whether the room you want to meet in is available. A perfect opportunity for workgroup scheduling is when employees are scheduling different events for the same room. The following sections explain.

Adding or Removing a Resource

Schedule+ treats the resource like one of the people in your workgroup. The resource must be given a name, a schedule, and an account at the post office.

To add a resource if you are in Schedule+, follow these steps:

1. From any window's File menu, choose Exit and Sign Out. You are now signed out of Schedule+ and Mail.

2. You or the post office administrator now must go into Mail and add a new account for the resource. (See Chapter 5, "Using Mail," for details.) You can add a user called "Conference Room 1" with a mailbox called ROOM1, for example.

3. Return to Schedule+. Sign in with the name of the mailbox for the new resource. Use ROOM1, for example, as the name with the password assigned to the resource mailbox.

4. Schedule+ displays a message indicating that the schedule file was found and this is the first time logging in as this "user." Choose the Yes button.

5. Schedule+ asks you to confirm the operation by retyping the password. Retype the password for the new resource and then choose OK.

   Schedule+ creates a new schedule file for the resource. To enable workgroup members to schedule this resource, you should assign full access rights.

6. From the Options menu, choose Set Access Privileges.

7. From the Set Access Privileges dialog, set the default access privilege to Create Appointments & Tasks. This way, all users can see and schedule the available times for the resource. If you want to limit the users' ability to schedule the resource, make sure that the default access is at least View Free/Busy Times.

8. From the schedule window you now must tell Schedule+ that this account is for a resource. From the Options menu choose General Options.

9. In the General Options dialog, enable the This Account is for a Resource check box and then choose OK. You are now ready to schedule and otherwise manage the resource.

Removing the resource is simple. Exit and sign out of Schedule+. You or the post office manager must get into Mail and remove the post office account for the resource. The resource now is removed.

Managing and Scheduling a Resource

To schedule a resource for a meeting, follow the instructions provided earlier in the section "Setting Up a Meeting" and include the resource on the Attendee list. Its name goes into the schedule along with other invited users.

To schedule the resource without involving other users, schedule a meeting with just you and the resource. When you request the meeting, you don't have to "ask for responses" from the resource. Not having to ask is possible only if you have enough access rights. Your minimum access right should be Create Appointments & Tasks.

Your access rights determine how much of the resource's schedule you can view. Most people scheduling resources only have the privilege of seeing the times that the resource already has scheduled or free. An assistant to the resource, on the other hand, can see the times that are scheduled as private meetings. To view the schedule of a resource from the schedule window, from the File menu choose Open Other's Appt Book. From the Open Other's Appt Book dialog, select the resource and then choose OK. A new schedule window opens, showing you the resource's schedule.

To manage the resource, you must know the password for that resource's Schedule+ file. Exit Schedule+ and sign out. Get back into Schedule+ but enter the name of the resource for the Mail name. Enter the password. You now are looking at the schedule for the resource and can enter appointments, change appointments, print the schedule, and so on.

The procedure for assigning an assistant to a resource is the same as assigning an assistant to a user. See the earlier section "Designating an Assistant for Your Schedule" for more details.

Working with Your Schedule Off-line

Even if the LAN is down or you are traveling, you don't have to stop using the scheduler. Schedule+ enables you to work off-line.

Schedule+ displays a warning message if you cannot access the network or the computer acting as the post office. Choose OK to continue to work off-line. Schedule+ functions as before, except workgroup features—such as printing to the network, accessing the schedules of other workgroup members, scheduling meetings, and creating or opening an archive file in a shared directory—are currently unavailable.

When working off-line, you can add appointments, tasks, and projects as usual. When you reconnect to the network, Schedule+ updates your post office, which is responsible for any scheduling that affects the workgroup.

You are working on-line if you start Schedule+ when connected to your network. The post office computer must be accessible. If you want to work off-line even when connected to the network and your post office, from the File menu choose Work Offline. To go back on-line, from the File menu choose Work Online.

TIP	You also can move your local schedule file to another computer or to a diskette. You then can work on your schedule from another computer. To move your local schedule file, from the File menu choose Move Local File. You see a dialog asking you to enter the drive, directory, and file name for the file and its new location. Schedule+ now accesses this drive, directory, and file name when you work off-line.

Sharing Information with Other Schedule Programs

Schedule+ has a limited capability for sharing its schedule files with other scheduling programs. You can export your schedule to other computers running Schedule+. You also can export using the text format. Import options include Schedule+, Windows Calendar, and WordPerfect Office. The following sections show you how to export and import your schedule.

Copying Information to Another Program

To copy information to another program, follow these steps:

1. From the File menu choose Export Appointments. The Export Appointments dialog appears.

2. Select the file format: Schedule+ or Text.

3. In the Export Appointments dialog, enter the range of dates to be exported from the following choices:

Dialog Item	What To Enter
Schedule Range From	The starting date
Schedule Range To	The ending date
Schedule Range All	All dates in your schedule

> **TIP** Enable the Include Daily Notes option if you want daily notes included in the export file.

4. After you finish entering information in the Export Appointments dialog, choose OK.

5. You now see a dialog asking you to supply the drive, directory, and file name for the export file. Fill in the information as desired and choose OK. Schedule+ writes your schedule to an external file.

Merging Information from Another Program

When you import a schedule from another program, Schedule+ combines the "foreign" appointments with your own. You are asked several questions regarding how you want the two files combined.

To merge information from another program, follow these steps:

1. From the File menu choose Import Appointments. The Import Appointments dialog appears.

2. Select the drive, directory, and file name of the file to be imported. If the file is located on another computer on the network, choose the Network button and browse the network.

3. Select the file type of the file to be imported. Schedule+ supports the following file types:

Extension	File Type
*.SCH	Schedule+ files
*.CAL	Windows Calendar files
*.FIL	WordPerfect Office files

4. Choose OK. The Import Format dialog appears (see fig. 6.18).

5. From the Import File From list box, select the program you are importing from.

6. After you finish selecting the options in the import format dialog, choose OK.

FIG. 6.18   *The Import Format dialog.*

Schedule+ proceeds to merge the two appointment files. If you enabled the Ask About Conflicting Appointments option, you must answer Yes or No to any conflicts. After Schedule+ completes the merge, you see your calendar with the additional appointments.

TIP	If you want to add all appointments and not have Schedule+ check for duplications, you also can choose Add All Appointments. Choose Do **N**ot Add Duplicate Appointments if you want Schedule+ to filter out duplicate appointments. Enable **A**sk About Conflicting Appointments if you want Schedule+ to stop and confirm an appointment that conflicts with an existing one.

Setting Schedule+ Preferences

Schedule+ preferences include the status of reminders, when a day starts and ends, and when the week starts. You also can work with color and font options. Schedule+ also enables you to re-move the status bar at the bottom of the window, as explained in the following sections.

Changing General Schedule+ Settings

Most general Schedule+ settings are in the Options menu. To access general options, from the Options menu choose General Options. The General Options dialog appears, with the following settings (see fig. 6.19):

- *Startup Offline.* Causes Schedule+ to default to off-line whenever you start the program.

- *Set Reminders for Notes.* Displays the daily notes when you start Schedule+.

- *Set Reminders Automatically.* Adds a reminder when you enter an appointment.

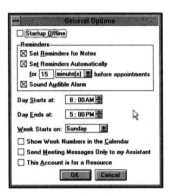

FIG. 6.19 *The General Options dialog.*

- *for ... before appointment.* Enables you to enter a default number of minutes, hours, days, weeks, or months to remind you before an appointment.

- *Sound Audible Alarm.* Triggers a sound when you get a reminder.

- *Day Starts At.* Sets the starting time for each day. The time before this setting appears in gray.

- *Day Ends At.* Sets the ending time for each day. The time after this setting appears in gray.

- *Week Starts On.* Sets the day you want for the first day of the week. In countries such as France, for example, the calendar week starts on Monday.

- *Show Week Numbers in the Calendar.* Displays the number of the week in the year.

- *Send Meeting Messages Only to my Assistant.* Diverts meeting messages to your assistant. By default, scheduling messages from other users appear in your Messages window.

- *This Account is for a Resource.* Tells Schedule+ that this "user" is a schedule for a resource (such as a conference room) rather than a person.

Displaying or Removing the Status Bar

You can turn off the display of the status bar from the Options menu to gain more viewing room in your schedule windows. To hide the status bar, from the Options menu choose Status Bar.

The Status Bar option acts as a toggle. When the option is check marked, the status bar appears at the bottom of the screen. When the option isn't check marked, the status bar isn't visible.

Turning Off Reminders

Some users may find the Reminder pop-up window disruptive while they are working. To turn off reminders, from the File menu choose Turn Off Reminders. To turn reminders back on, from the File menu choose Turn On Reminders.

Changing Colors and Fonts

Other display options enable you to control the color of various parts of the Schedule+ screen and to change the font size. To set display options, from the Options menu choose Display. A dialog appears with the following display options:

Option	Description
Appointment Book - Background	Enables you to control the background color of the appointment book screens
Planner - Background	Enables you to change the background color of the Planner window
Planner - User	Enables you to change the color of your scheduled events on the Planner window
Planner - Others	Enables you to change the color of other users' scheduled events on the Planner window

Option	Description
Page Background	Enables you to control the color of the background behind the current display
Font Size	Enables you to change the size of the fonts used in the Schedule+ screens. You can choose between 8 point or 10 point.

Summary

This chapter covered the many features available in Schedule+. You learned how to set up appointments and meetings, schedule projects, and assign prioritized tasks to projects. You also learned how Schedule+ manages resources, such as conference rooms. This chapter also showed you how to schedule meetings in relation to your workgroup.

Chapter 7 covers additional advanced Windows for Workgroups utilities: ClipBook Viewer, Chat, Net Watcher, and WinMeter.

Exploring Advanced Features of Windows for Workgroups

Windows for Workgroups sports many unique features. This chapter describes four of those features: ClipBook Viewer, Chat, Net Watcher, and WinMeter.

ClipBook Viewer provides you with the capability to share Clipboard pages with other users in your workgroup. The Chat program enables you to initiate a real-time, LAN-based electronic conversation with other users in your workgroup. With Net Watcher, you can manage the access of other users to your Windows for Workgroups computer. WinMeter enables you to monitor the relative use of your system by applications and the server.

Using ClipBook Viewer

The ClipBook Viewer enables you to view the contents of the Clipboard on your Windows for Workgroups station, save Clipboard pages to your Local ClipBook, and share ClipBook pages with others within your workgroup. The Clipboard stores information that you cut or copy from within an application. While within Microsoft Word for Windows, for example, you mark a block of text and then select the Scissors icon to move the information in the blocked area into the

Clipboard. After that block of text is on the Clipboard, you can use the ClipBook Viewer to share this text with other users within your workgroup.

You can access the ClipBook Viewer by choosing its icon from the Main group window.

The ClipBook Viewer window contains two smaller windows: the Local ClipBook and the Clipboard (see fig. 7.1). The Local Clip-Book contains the saved clippings (items that you have cut or copied) from applications that you want to save for future use. The Clipboard contains the current clipping that you just cut or copied from an application.

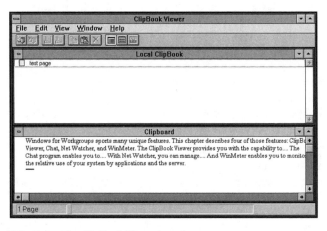

FIG. 7.1 *The ClipBook Viewer's main screen.*

The Clipboard temporarily stores information that you are transferring between documents. When you cut or copy information, it's moved to the Clipboard. You can paste that information into any document as often as you want. The Clipboard window in the ClipBook Viewer window shows the current contents of the Clipboard.

The ClipBook, on the other hand, permanently stores information that you want to save and share with others. You can save the current contents of the Clipboard permanently by copying it to your Local ClipBook. You can save several pieces of information (called *pages*) to the ClipBook and then copy the information back to the Clipboard when you want to paste it into a document.

You also can share your ClipBook information with other users in your workgroup. Each computer has its own ClipBook. You can connect to a ClipBook on another computer, and others can connect to a ClipBook on your computer. Through such connections, you and other users can exchange and use shared pages.

You now should have a good understanding of the function of the ClipBook Viewer. The following sections explain the ClipBook Viewer's various features and how to use them.

Using the Toolbar

You use the ClipBook Viewer's toolbar to move quickly from one option to another. The toolbar, located directly below the menu bar, provides you with the best performance and fastest access to the features of the ClipBook Viewer. Table 7.1 describes ClipBook Viewer's toolbar buttons.

Table 7.1 ClipBook Toolbar Buttons

Button	Name	Description
	Connect	Enables you to connect to a ClipBook on another computer
	Disconnect	Disconnects from a ClipBook on another computer
	Share	Enables you to share a ClipBook page
	Stop Sharing	Stops sharing a ClipBook page
	Copy	Copies the selected ClipBook page to the Clipboard
	Paste	Pastes the contents of the Clipboard to the ClipBook
	Delete	Deletes the contents of the Clipboard or selected ClipBook page
	Table of Contents	Displays titles of the pages saved to ClipBook
	Thumbnails	Displays small pictures (thumbnails) of each ClipBook page
	Full Page	Displays the contents of the selected ClipBook page

Managing the Clipboard

After you put information on the Clipboard, you can save the information, view it in other formats, or remove it from the Clipboard. You also can use the Clipboard to transfer information between applications. The method you use varies, depending on the type of application you are copying from and pasting to.

The following sections describe various methods of using the Clipboard for data transfer and manipulation. These methods include copying data from DOS-based applications to the Clipboard and pasting Clipboard contents to another document or application. Also covered are Windows-based techniques for data transfer and Clipboard procedures for viewing, saving, and clearing information.

Copying Information from a DOS-Based Program

When using a DOS-based application in a window, you can copy selected information, an image of the window, or an image of the desktop to the Clipboard. When using a DOS-based application in Standard mode, you can copy only an image of the entire screen to the Clipboard.

> **NOTE** To run a DOS-based application in a window, you must run Windows for Workgroups in Enhanced mode. DOS-based applications running under Windows in Standard mode can function only in a full screen. When you are operating Windows in Standard mode, you can copy only the contents of the entire screen into the Clipboard.

To copy selected information to the Clipboard, follow these steps:

1. From the application's Control menu, choose **Edit**.

2. From the submenu, choose **Mark**.

3. Within your document, select the information you want to copy.

4. From the Control menu, choose **Edit** again and then choose **Copy**.

> **TIP**
>
> To access the Control menu for a DOS-based application, press Alt+Enter. The application window will become a smaller, more graphical window with a control box in the upper left corner. Click that box or press Alt+space bar to pull down the Control menu.
>
> If your application uses Alt+space bar for another function, you cannot use that key combination to open the Control menu. Press Ctrl+Esc to switch to the Task List without quitting the application. The application then appears as an icon near the bottom of the Windows desktop. Click the icon to open the application's Control menu.

You also can use the Print Screen button on your keyboard to copy information to the Clipboard. To copy an image of the active window to the Clipboard, press Alt+Print Screen. To copy an image of the entire screen to the Clipboard, press Print Screen.

> **NOTE**
>
> The Alt+Print Screen or Print Screen procedure works only for DOS-based applications when they are running in Text mode. DOS-based graphics applications don't copy properly to the Clipboard.

Pasting Information into a DOS-Based Program

You can paste only text into DOS-based application files. You cannot paste graphics. To paste text into a full-screen application or a application running in a window, follow these steps:

1. Copy the information to the Clipboard from the source application, following the steps in the preceding section.

2. Switch to the DOS application into which you want to paste the information.

3. Open the file or document into which you want to paste the new information.

4. Position the insertion point at the location where you want the information to appear.

5. From the Control menu, choose Edit.

6. From the Edit submenu, choose Paste. The Clipboard's contents are pasted into the selected document.

> **NOTE** You can use the preceding process to copy/cut and paste information in DOS-based documents, between documents, and between different applications. Be careful when using the Clipboard and DOS-based applications, however. Word processing applications work well; other DOS-based applications, on the other hand, may not accept the information.

Transferring Information within a Windows Program

By using the Clipboard and the Cut, Copy, and Paste commands on the Edit menu found in most Windows-based applications, you can copy or move information within a document, between documents, or between applications. To transfer information by using the Clipboard, follow these steps:

1. Select the information you want to copy or move.

2. To place the information on your Clipboard, choose Copy or Cut from the application's Edit menu.

3. Switch to another document or application, if desired, or stay within the same document.

4. Position the insertion point at the location where you want the information pasted.

5. From the Edit menu for your application, choose Paste. The selected information is pasted into the document.

You also can use the Print Screen button on your keyboard to copy a window image or entire screen to the Clipboard. To copy an image of the active window to the Clipboard, press Alt+Print Screen. To copy an image of the entire screen to the Clipboard, press Print Screen. Using either keystroke, the information in the Clipboard is graphics information, not text.

Viewing the Clipboard's Contents

To view the Clipboard's contents, you choose the Clipboard icon from the ClipBook Viewer window.

The Clipboard stores information in multiple formats so that you can transfer information between applications that use different formats. Specifically, the Clipboard stores text in three formats:

- *Owner Display.* The character set of fonts you used when creating the text.

- *Text.* The character set usually used by Windows-based applications.

- *OEM Text.* The format used by DOS-based applications.

The View menu lists all the formats for the information now on the Clipboard. The current format has a check mark to the left of the format name. To view the Clipboard's contents in another format, choose a format name from the bottom of the View menu. To return to the initial format, choose **Default Format** from the View menu.

> **NOTE** Not all formats can be displayed. You cannot display dimmed options that appear on the menu.

Saving the Clipboard to a File

If you have cut or copied information that you want to use repeatedly, you should save the contents of the Clipboard into a Clipboard file. To do so, follow these steps:

1. Restore the Clipboard window if it's an icon, or select the Clipboard if it's already in window form.

2. From the File menu, choose Save **As**. The Save As dialog appears.

3. In the File **Name** text box, enter a file name. The default extension for a Clipboard file is CLP.

4. Choose OK. The Clipboard's contents are saved as a CLP file.

> **NOTE** You cannot share Clipboard files with other users unless you put the files in a shared directory on your system.

To open a Clipboard file, follow these steps:

1. Restore the Clipboard window if it's an icon, or select the Clipboard if it's already in window form.

2. Choose Open from the File menu. The Open dialog appears.

3. In the File Name text box, type the name of the CLP file or select the file you want to retrieve.

4. Click OK. The file opens.

Clearing the Contents of the Clipboard

The Clipboard stores information from many different applications. You can store different data pages on the Clipboard during normal operation. Applications, however, may need the memory used to store those pages. Clearing the Clipboard frees memory.

To clear the contents of the Clipboard, first select the Clipboard. Then click the Delete toolbar button, or from the Edit menu choose Delete.

Working with ClipBook Pages

The ClipBook Viewer enables you to share Clipboard information on your computer with others within your workgroup. Before you learn the major functions of the ClipBook Viewer, however, you need to understand how to work the basics, such as saving Clipboard files to a ClipBook page, viewing a ClipBook page in different formats, and copying a ClipBook page to the ClipBook. The following sections cover these basics.

Saving the Clipboard to a ClipBook Page

By saving Clipboard information into a ClipBook, you can share this information with others within your workgroup. Saving the information also enables you to create a card catalog of sorts for the ClipBook pages that you need to use many times.

To save the contents of the Clipboard on the Local ClipBook, follow these steps:

1. Select the Local ClipBook window.

2. Click the Paste toolbar button or choose Paste from the Edit menu. The Paste dialog appears (see fig. 7.2).

FIG. 7.2 *The Paste dialog.*

3. In the **Page** Name text box, type a descriptive name no more than 48 characters long for the page you are saving. Mark the Share Item Now check box to make the page available to all users on the network.

4. Choose OK.

If you marked the Share Item Now check box, the Share ClipBook Page dialog opens. Choose any other options you want and then choose OK. For more information on the Share ClipBook Page dialog, read "Sharing ClipBook Pages" later in this chapter.

Viewing a ClipBook Page in Different Formats

You can save in different formats the information that you save as a ClipBook page. Graphics formats include bit map and device-independent bit map (DIB). Text formats include Rich Text Format and Text format. Before you can view or change the format of the information on a ClipBook page, however, you must have the page selected and in full-page view.

> **NOTE** The type of display driver you are using determines whether you can view the page contents from another computer's ClipBook in bit-map format.

To choose full-page view, follow these steps:

1. Choose the Local ClipBook window.

2. Scroll to the page you want to view.

3. Choose the Full Page toolbar button, or from the View menu choose Full Page (see fig. 7.3). The page displays in full-page view.

FIG. 7.3 *Formats on the View menu.*

To view the contents of the ClipBook page in another format, choose the format name from the View menu. To return to the initial format, choose Default Format from the View menu.

Copying a ClipBook Page to the Clipboard

You must copy the ClipBook page back to the Clipboard before you can paste that page into another document.

 NOTE If you haven't copied any new information to the Clipboard, the information you want is already on the Clipboard—that is, the Clipboard's contents are the same as the selected ClipBook page.

To copy a ClipBook page to the Clipboard, follow these steps:

1. Open the ClipBook window.

2. From the Local ClipBook, select the page you want to transfer.

3. Click the Copy toolbar button, or from the Edit menu choose Copy. The page copies to the Clipboard.

Using the ClipBook To Share Information

When you store Clipboard information permanently in ClipBook pages, you can share that information with other users. Because each computer in your workgroup has a Local ClipBook, you can use information others have shared by connecting your Local ClipBook to the shared ClipBook pages from another computer.

NOTE Before you can paste information from any ClipBook page into a document, you first must copy the information back to the Clipboard.

The following sections explain how to share ClipBook pages and how to connect to and disconnect from another user's Local ClipBook.

Sharing ClipBook Pages

After you save information as a page on the Local ClipBook, you can share that information with other users. That way, other users can connect to your ClipBook and view or change the shared information, depending on the type of password protection you assign. The Shared icon appears next to each page being shared.

NOTE You can share pages only when Windows for Workgroups is running in 386 Enhanced mode.

To share a page on the Local ClipBook, follow these steps:

1. From the Local ClipBook window, select the ClipBook page you want to share.

2. From the File menu choose Share, or click the Share toolbar button. The Share ClipBook Page dialog appears (see fig. 7.4).

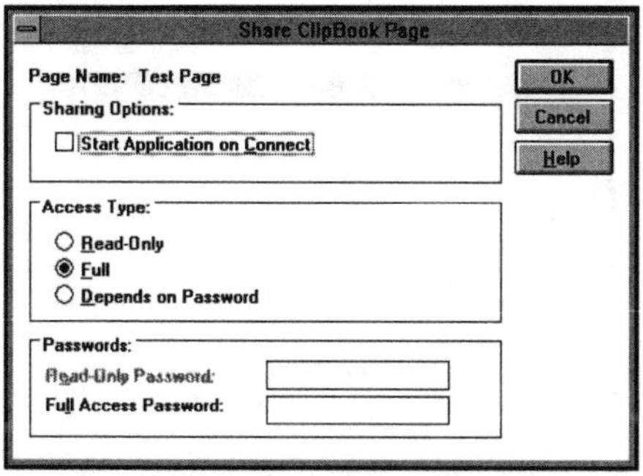

FIG. 7.4 *The Share ClipBook Page dialog.*

3. Choose from the following password-protection options:

   Read-Only. User can only view information.

   Full. User can view or edit information.

   Depends on Password. Access depends on user's password.

4. Type a password in the appropriate text box when appropriate.

5. Choose OK.

To stop sharing a page on the Local ClipBook, select the page to stop sharing. Then from the File menu choose Stop Sharing, or click the Stop Sharing toolbar button.

Connecting to and Disconnecting from a Shared ClipBook

Before you can use the shared pages on another computer, you must connect to its ClipBook Viewer. The user on that computer must share pages before you can access them.

To connect to a shared ClipBook, follow these steps:

1. Click the Connect toolbar button, or from the File menu choose Connect. The Select Computer dialog appears (see fig. 7.5).

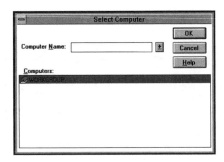

FIG. 7.5 *The Select Computer dialog.*

2. In the Computer Name text box, type the name of the computer that has the ClipBook you want to access, or select the computer from the Computers list. You also can choose a

computer by clicking the down arrow button next to the Computer Name box. From the list of computers that appears, select the computer to which you want to connect.

3. Choose OK.

A window opens, displaying the contents of the ClipBook to which you now are connected.

To disconnect from a shared ClipBook, first select the ClipBook window. Then choose the Disconnect button from the toolbar, or from the File menu choose **Disconnect**.

Embedding and Linking Objects by Using ClipBook Viewer

When you are embedding and linking objects, Windows temporarily stores the objects on the Clipboard while the objects are being transferred from the source document to the destination document. The source and destination documents can be on your computer, or you can embed or link an object from a source document on another computer. The following sections show you how.

> **NOTE** To embed or link an object, the application used to create the object must support this feature. Different applications may use different menu commands for these tasks. For more information, see the documentation supplied with the application.

Copying an Embedded Object

Embedding is very different from copying, cutting, and pasting. If you paste information into another document and then change the original information, you must copy the changes into the document with the copied information. If you embed an object, however, you can edit the object in a way that changes all copies of that object.

Suppose that you create a picture in Windows Paintbrush and used it in a Word for Windows document. If you embed the picture as an object, you can select it and then double-click to activate Paintbrush with the picture ready to be edited. After you make your the changes, the changed picture is returned into the Word document.

In Windows for Workgroups, you can copy an embedded object so that the copied object behaves the same as an embedded object. To copy an embedded object, follow these steps:

1. Open the source document.

2. Select the embedded object.

3. From the Edit menu, choose Copy. The object is copied to the Clipboard.

4. Switch to the destination document.

5. Position the insertion point in the document. From the Edit menu, choose Paste. The selected object is embedded at the insertion point in the destination document.

You also can copy an embedded object from a document on another computer. Such an object, however, first must be stored as a shared ClipBook page on the other computer. To copy an embedded object from another computer, follow these steps:

1. Click the Connect toolbar button, or from the File menu choose Connect. The Select Computer dialog appears.

2. In the Computer Name text box, type the name of the computer to which you want to connect, or choose the name from the Computers list box.

3. Choose OK. The ClipBook window shows the shared pages available on the other computer's ClipBook.

4. Select the page you want to embed in your document.

5. From the Edit menu, choose Copy. A copy of the object is placed on the Clipboard.

6. Open the document into which you want to embed the object.

7. From the Edit menu, choose Paste. The object is pasted into the document.

NOTE   You can edit an embedded object only when the application used to create the object is installed on your computer.

Linking an Object from Another Computer

You can create a link in a document on your computer with an object on another computer. The term *link* refers to the embedding of an object created on another computer into a document on your computer. To create a link, the object that you are linking to must be a shared page on the other computer's ClipBook.

> **NOTE** You cannot edit a linked object if its source document is on another computer and you aren't connected to the computer.

To create a link to an object from another computer, follow these steps:

1. Click the Connect toolbar button, or from the File menu choose Connect. The Select Computer dialog appears.

2. In the Computer Name text box, type the name of the computer to which you want to connect, or choose the name from the Computers list box.

3. Choose OK. The ClipBook window shows the shared pages available on the other computer's ClipBook.

4. Select the page you want to link to your document.

5. From the Edit menu, choose Copy. Windows for Workgroups copies the object to the Clipboard.

6. Open the destination document to which you want to link the object.

7. From the Edit menu, choose Paste Special.

8. From the dialog that appears, select the format you want to use, and then choose the Paste Link button.

> **NOTE** Depending on the type of display driver your computer uses, you may not be able to view the page contents from another computer's ClipBook in bit-map format.

7

Using Chat

The Windows for Workgroups Chat utility enables you to call another user within your workgroup and carry on a two-way electronic conservation. This utility is extremely useful if you need to
bring something immediately to the attention of a coworker.

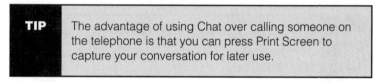

> **TIP** The advantage of using Chat over calling someone on
> the telephone is that you can press Print Screen to
> capture your conversation for later use.

The Chat window contains two smaller windows: your conversation and your partner's conversation (see fig. 7.6). The top
window is your conversation, and the bottom window is your
partner's.

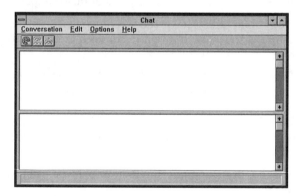

FIG. 7.6 *The Chat window.*

To establish an electronic conversation with another user, you
make a call over the network, selecting the computer name of the
user to whom you want to talk. Chat rings your partner's computer. When that person opens Chat, you are ready for an electronic conversation.

You can access Chat by choosing its icon from the Main program
group. The following sections explain how to use Chat.

Using the Chat Toolbar

You use Chat's toolbar to move quickly from one option to another. The toolbar provides you the best performance and fastest access to Chat's features. The toolbar, located directly below the menu bar, consists of the following buttons:

Button	Name	Description
![Call button]	Call	Enables you to request a Chat session with another computer
![Answer button]	Answer	Answers a call from another computer to your computer
![Hang Up button]	Hang Up	Disconnects from a conversation with another computer

Making a Call

You can use Chat to call another person in a workgroup and have an electronic conversation. To make a call, follow these steps:

1. Click the Dial toolbar button, or from the Conversation menu choose Dial. The Select Computer dialog appears (refer to fig. 7.5).

2. Specify the computer name of the user with whom you want to chat and then choose OK.

Chat dials the computer that you specified and waits for the person to answer. The computer that you are calling makes a ringing sound and displays a telephone icon.

If the other user selects the telephone icon, a connection is made automatically, and a message appears on your status bar to indicate that a connection has been made.

After the other person answers, you can type in the local Chat window at the top of the screen. In the bottom window, you see what the other person is typing.

If the other user doesn't answer, Chat indicates that no connection has been made. If the other person already is chatting with someone else, you see a message indicating that the connection is busy.

Answering a Call

When someone calls you, you need to answer the call to begin your conversation. If you already are in Chat, you will here a ringing sound (like a telephone) and see a message at the bottom of the window. If you are in Windows but in a different application, you hear a ringing sound and see a icon that looks like a telephone. When the ringing sound is heard, the telephone icon wiggles.

To answer a call when Chat is minimized, double-click the Chat icon to open it to a window. Then click the Answer toolbar button, or from the Conversation menu choose **Answer**. If Chat already is opened as a window, answer the call. After you answer the call, you can begin typing your conversation.

Hanging Up

After you finish your conversation, disconnect from your partner's computer by clicking the Hang Up toolbar button or by choosing Hang Up from the Conversation menu.

After you hang up, you cannot type in the Chat window. If your partner hangs up before you do, the message *USER* hung up appears in your status bar, where *USER* is the name of your Chat partner's computer.

> **NOTE** If you quit Chat, it hangs up for you. To quit Chat, from the **C**onversation menu choose E**x**it.

Configuring Chat

You can configure many parameters within Chat. You turn the sound on or off, you can change the font that is being used in your Chat session, you can change the background colors, and so on. The following sections discuss the options you can change to suit your needs.

Turning Sound On and Off

When you call another person or someone calls you, your computer emits a ringing sound. If you don't want to hear the sound, you can turn it off by choosing Sound from the Options menu. A check mark next to the Sound option means that sound is on.

If you have a sound card, such as SoundBlaster, you can change the sound of the incoming or outgoing ring. Choose the Sound icon in the Control Panel to assign a different sound to the Chat Incoming Ring and Chat Outgoing Ring sound events.

Changing the Font

You can change the color, style, and size of the font that you use in your conversation window. You can change the font through the Font dialog (see fig. 7.7), which you can access from the Options menu by choosing Font. The Font dialog enables you to do the following:

- To change the typeface, choose the name of the typeface you want to use from the Font list, or type the font's name in the Font text box. The default typeface is System.

- To change the font's style, choose the style you want to use from the Font Style list, or type the style name in the text box. The styles available vary from font to font. The default is Bold.

- You can change the font size from the Size list box, or you can type the new size in the text box. The default is 10 point.

- From the Effects options, you can choose Strikeout or Underline. By default, neither option is enabled.

- If you want to change the color of the text, select a color from the Color drop-down box. The default is Black.

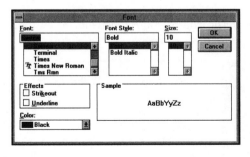

FIG. 7.7   *The Font dialog.*

After you finish setting the options you want in the Font dialog, choose OK. The changes you made take effect immediately.

Your partner's settings determine the font used to display the other end of the conversation. You can change this font by choosing **Preferences** from the **Options** menu. You can choose to view the other end of the conversation in the same font (and background color) that you are using. (See the section "Changing Window Preferences" for more details on the Preferences dialog.)

Changing the Background Color

By default, the background color of your Chat window is white. You can change the background color by following these steps:

1. From the **Options** menu, choose Background Color. The Color dialog appears (see fig. 7.8).

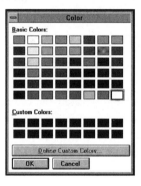

FIG. 7.8 *The Color dialog.*

2. Under **Basic Colors**, choose the color you want to use. You can choose from 48 system defined colors.

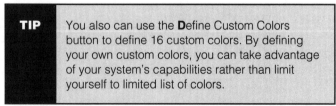

> **TIP** You also can use the **D**efine Custom Colors button to define 16 custom colors. By defining your own custom colors, you can take advantage of your system's capabilities rather than limit yourself to limited list of colors.

3. Choose OK. Your changes take effect immediately.

By default, your partner's window has the background color that your partner has selected. If you want to change this background color, use the **Preferences** command on the **Options** menu, as discussed in the next section.

Changing Window Preferences

You can display the two conversation windows side by side rather
than horizontally (see fig. 7.9). You also can choose whether you
want to receive messages in the font and background color that
you specify, or the font and background color that your partner
specifies. You make these changes in the Preferences dialog.

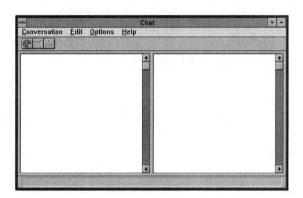

FIG. 7.9   *A different Chat window.*

To change your window preferences, follow these steps:

1. From the **Options** menu, choose **Preferences**. The Preferences dialog appears (see fig. 7.10).

FIG. 7.10   *The Preferences dialog.*

2. From the Window Style options, choose the layout you
   prefer. Choices include Top and Bottom, and Side by Side.

   From the Partner's Message options, choose between Use
   Partner's Font or Use **O**wn Font. If you use your partner's
   font, your partner's background color also is used.

3. Choose OK. Your changes take effect immediately.

Hiding or Displaying the Toolbar and Status Bar

If you want more room in the Chat window, you can hide the toolbar and status bar.

To display or hide the toolbar, choose **Toolbar** from the **Options** menu. You display or hide the status bar by choosing **Status Bar** from the **Options** menu. A check mark next to the **Toolbar** or **Status Bar** command means that the bar will display.

Using Net Watcher

If many users are accessing your system, the operation of your computer may become sluggish. To determine why performance has degraded, use Net Watcher. You can access Net Watcher by choosing the Net Watcher icon from the Main program group.

> **NOTE** Net Watcher can operate only on a Windows for Workgroup server. You must be running Windows for Workgroups in 386 Enhanced mode to be a server.

Net Watcher displays connection information on your computer system (see fig. 7.11). This utility enables you to find out who is connected to your computer and who is using which files in your shared directories. (The information you can monitor also includes shared ClipBook pages.) If you have a shared printer, you can monitor usage of this resource.

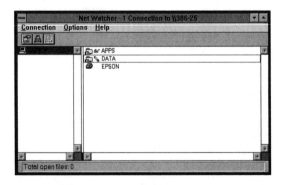

FIG. 7.11 *The Net Watcher window.*

The left side of the window displays the computer names of the users connected to your computer. When you select a computer name, the right side of the window displays the directories, printers, or ClipBook page the user is connected to and any of your shared files the user has open. A pencil icon next to a resource indicates that the user has full access. An eyeglasses icon indicates the user has read-only access.

You can select a computer name and use the toolbar or menu commands to find out more information about the connection or to disconnect the user from your computer. You also can select files being used by other people and close them. The following sections explain how.

Using the Net Watcher Toolbar and Status Bar

The Net Watcher toolbar gives you easy mouse access to the features you commonly use in Net Watcher. The status bar, located at the bottom of the Net Watcher window, displays information about the select item.

The following table provides the details on the toolbar buttons.

Button	Name	Description
	Properties	Displays the properties of the selected connection
	Disconnect	Disconnects a selected computer
	Close Files	Closes the selected file

You can display or hide the toolbar and the status bar to provide more room on the Net Watcher window. To display or hide the toolbar, choose Toolbar from the Options menu. To display or hide the status bar, choose Status Bar from the Options menu. A check mark next to either menu option means that the option is displayed.

Displaying Information about a Connection

The Net Watcher window shows connections to your computer and which of your shared resources those users are using. You can display more information about a particular connection, however, such as who's logged on, how long the connection to your computer has been active, or how long since the person used one of your shared resources.

To display this information, select the computer name about which you want more information in the left column. Then click the Properties toolbar button or choose Properties from the Connection menu.

NOTE   Make sure that you click the button on the far left of the toolbar rather than the middle button. The middle button disconnects computers from your PC.

Disconnecting a User

You can disconnect any user connected to your computer, such as a user connected to your system but not performing any function, or a user who is accessing your system without proper permission. To disconnect a user, follow these steps:

1. In the Net Watcher window, select the computer name for the user you want to disconnect.

2. Click the Disconnect toolbar button or choose Disconnect from the Connection menu. A message appears, asking you to confirm that you want to disconnect the user.

3. Choose Yes to disconnect the user; choose Cancel if you don't want to disconnect the user.

After you disconnect the user, that user receives an error message that your system is not available if he tries to access your system. The user may reconnect to your system, however. If you don't want that user to reconnect, you must change his access privileges.

CAUTION

Disconnecting a user from your computer may cause loss of any information that hasn't been saved. Asking the user to log out of your system is better than disconnecting the user.

Closing a File

You can close a file that another user has opened. You may want to close a file if the other user has gone to a meeting with the file left open on his computer screen. You need to access the file to make changes to it; however, rather than walk across the room to remove the file from his screen, you can use this feature to close the file. To close a file, follow these steps:

1. In the Net Watcher window, select the file you want to close.

2. Click the Close File toolbar button or choose Close File from the Connection menu. A message appears, asking you to confirm that you want to close the file.

3. Choose Yes. When the other user tries to save or access the file, he sees an error message indicating that you have closed the file.

> **NOTE** If you close a file, the person using it may lose any information that hasn't been saved. Contacting and then asking the user to close the file is better than using Close File. If the user has only read-only access, however, this procedure will cause no problem.

Updating Information in the Net Watcher Window

Every 20 seconds, Net Watcher checks to see who is connected to your computer and what resources are being used. The utility then updates the information displayed in the window. Anytime you want to update the information, you can do so by using the Refresh command on the Options menu.

Using WinMeter

WinMeter is a utility that monitors how much applications and the server are using the computer. (The *server* is the portion of Windows for Workgroups that manages connections over the LAN.) The longer you or others use the LAN, the more computer time the server uses. The more you do on your own computer, the more time applications use.

You can access WinMeter by clicking its icon in the Accessories program group.

WinMeter checks your computer's microprocessor every so often to determine what it's doing. The graph you see in the WinMeter display shows the percentage of how much the applications and the server use the microprocessor. Figure 7.12 shows a slice of time in which the computer is running several programs and a network user prints to a shared printer on your computer.

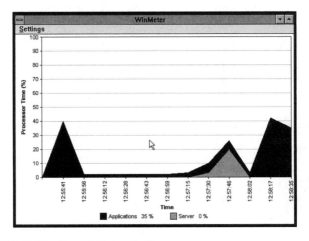

FIG. 7.12   *The WinMeter display.*

The options available in WinMeter enable you to adjust the time intervals, control what you see in the display, and alter the colors of the Applications and Server percentages. You control these options with commands on the Settings menu (see fig. 7.13).

FIG. 7.13   *The WinMeter Settings menu.*

Four options enable you to alter the WinMeter window: Show Legend, Hide Title Bar, Application Color, and Server Color. You also can adjust the time intervals at which WinMeter calculates average microprocessor usage. The following sections discuss the various WinMeter options.

Altering the Time Interval

The most critical setting in WinMeter is the time interval. During this interval, WinMeter calculates the average microprocessor usage.

If you want to run WinMeter for a long period of time, set this setting high (10-minute intervals). If you want to get an immediate snapshot of usage, set the setting low (5-second intervals). Notice that the scale at the bottom of the graph in the WinMeter window reflects the new time interval.

To alter the time interval, choose the desired interval from the Settings menu. You can choose from five intervals:

- 5 seconds
- 15 seconds
- 1 minute
- 5 minutes
- 10 minutes

WinMeter immediately begins updating each time interval you specify.

Changing Applications and Server Colors

The Application Color and Server Color options enable you to change the colors used in the legend to represent the percentage of usage by applications and by the server process. To change the colors for applications, follow these steps:

1. Choose Application Color from the Settings menu. The Color dialog appears.

2. Select the desired color from the Basic Colors section.

3. Choose OK. The color changes take effect, and the selected colors are recorded permanently in the WINMETER.INI file.

If you want to define a custom color, follow these steps:

1. Choose Application Color from the Settings menu. The Color dialog appears.

2. Choose Define Custom Colors.

3. From the Define Custom Color dialog, choose the appropriate values for the following:

   ■ Hue

   ■ Sat

   ■ Luminescence

   ■ Red

   ■ Green

   ■ Blue

4. After you have the desired color mix, choose Add to Custom Colors.

5. Select the custom color that you have mixed. Choose OK when done.

To change colors for the Server, follow the preceding steps, except choose Server Color from the Settings menu rather than Application Color.

Showing or Hiding the Legend and Title Bar

The WinMeter legend, at the bottom of the window, shows you the color and percentage of microprocessor usage for the applications and the server. Hiding the legend makes this display disappear from view. Hiding the title bar removes the WinMeter title bar and the menu bar.

To hide the legend, choose Show Legend from the Settings menu. When a check mark appears next to Show Legend, the legend displays. Choosing the command removes the check and hides the legend.

To hide the title bar, choose Hide Title Bar from the Settings menu.

CAUTION

If you hide the title bar, you cannot get it back from WinMeter because the menu bar also has been hidden. To restore the title bar, you need to edit the WINMETER.INI file using Notepad.

To restore the title bar, follow these steps:

1. Open Notepad.

2. From Notepad's **F**ile menu choose **O**pen.

3. In the Open dialog, type **WINMETER.INI** in the File Name text box. Choose OK to open the file. Your file may look like the following:

```
[Settings]
Position=32,14,617,439
Interval=15
ServerColor=0,255,255
AppColor=128,0,128
Options=0,0,0,1
```

4. From the editing window, locate the line that begins with the word Options. Delete this line.

5. Exit Notepad and save the WINMETER.INI file.

6. Close WinMeter if it's open and then reopen it. The title bar is restored.

Summary

This chapter covered additional advanced Windows for Workgroups utilities: ClipBook Viewer, Chat, Net Watcher, and WinMeter. ClipBook Viewer enables you to store in an organized fashion information pasted from applications. By using Chat, network users can converse with each other. You also learned how to use Net Watcher to monitor usage of your shared resources and how to use WinMeter to view the usage of resources on your computer.

Chapter 8, "Configuring Windows for Workgroups," shows you how to customize Windows for Workgroups.

Configuring Windows for Workgroups

You can customize Windows for Workgroups to modify the capabilities of your LAN. Having this capability is important because in any network, performance is always an issue.

You already have configured most aspects of your workgroup. When you use a Windows for Workgroups utility for the first time (including Windows for Workgroups itself), you specify various options. Think back to the options you already have specified:

- Your workgroup name
- The name of your computer
- The name of your mailbox
- The name and location of your mail server
- Shared printer names
- Shared directories

This chapter discusses where performance problems can occur in the network and how to deal with them. You then learn ways to adjust settings in your network software to improve performance.

In this chapter, you also learn how to add a non-Windows computer to your Windows for Workgroup network by using a separate product called Workgroup Connection. With Workgroup Connection, a computer that cannot or doesn't use Windows for Workgroups can access and use shared resources from a Windows for Workgroups network.

Understanding Network Bottlenecks

A *bottleneck* is a point in the LAN where performance is the slowest. Putting too many computers on the same cabling system, for example, can cause bottlenecks. In other cases, bridges or routers may cause LAN performance to bog down. All networks can have three types of bottlenecks: I/O bound, bus bound, and LAN bound.

If your hard disk cannot handle the amount of information it receives, the data backs up, and your computer is *I/O bound*. When this situation takes place, Windows for Workgroups must take time from other processes to wait for the information to be written successfully to disk.

When information moving over the computer's data bus cannot move fast enough, your computer is *bus bound*. Your computer may be bus bound, for example, if data arriving in your network adapter must wait for the processor to clear room in RAM.

If your network adapters cannot move information from one node to another fast enough, your information is *LAN bound*.

Solutions for each type of bottleneck are explained as follows:

Bottleneck	Solution
I/O bound	Buy a faster hard disk drive.
Bus bound	Buy a faster computer. If you have a 386 computer, consider moving to a 486 with an EISA bus. Balance your performance needs with costs.
LAN bound	Buy faster network adapters. Fiber-optic cards give you the fastest LAN transmission speed but are very expensive. Also, consider changing your cabling. You also can tweak some parameters in Windows for Workgroups.

Because any network always will have a slow point, at least one bottleneck always will exist. As the preceding table shows you, you can adjust your network to minimize this problem by changing hardware. You also can adjust many of the problems caused by

LAN-bound systems by tweaking your Windows for Workgroups computer configuration. (You cannot adjust parameters in Windows for Workgroups, however, to resolve I/O-bound and bus-bound problems.) The following section explores tweaking LAN performance.

> **TIP** As you proceed with configuring Windows for Workgroups, keeping a record of the settings, names, and passwords you have used is useful. Later, when you need to make changes or solve performance problems, this list will be invaluable.

Changing Your Workgroup Configuration

By using the Control Panel's Network option, you can change the way your Windows for Workgroups computer interacts with other workgroup computers and applications. Many changes you make to network settings in this section don't take effect until you restart your computer.

> **NOTE** You may want to make copies of your configuration files before you make any changes. (These files consist of AUTOEXEC.BAT, CONFIG.SYS, and all files with an INI extension. These files control the operation of your system.) This way, you can restore your system quickly and easily should a conflict or a mistake occur.

To make these changes, you use the Network Settings dialog, which you can access by choosing the Network icon from the Control Panel. In the Network Settings dialog, you can change the computer and workgroup names, add comments, enable sharing, and set performance priorities (see fig. 8.1).

> **NOTE** The options in the Network Settings dialog are specific to Windows for Workgroups. Additional options may appear if you are using additional networks.

8

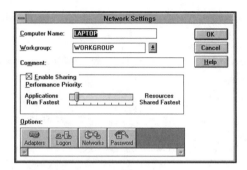

FIG. 8.1 *The Network Settings dialog.*

The buttons in the Options section of the Network Settings dialog open additional dialogs that enable you to configure more specific aspects of Windows for Workgroups. The buttons are described as follows:

■ The Adapters button opens the Network Adapters dialog, which enables you to add, remove, and configure settings for a network adapter driver.

■ The Logon button opens the Logon Settings dialog, which enables you to log off without exiting Windows, and to specify options for logging on when you start Windows for Workgroups.

■ The Networks button opens the Compatible Networks dialog, which enables you to select and set options for other networks you use with Windows for Workgroups. Other networks include Novell NetWare and Microsoft LAN Manager.

■ When you choose the Password button, Windows for Workgroups displays the Change Logon Password dialog, in which you can change your logon password.

Configuring a computer system often means paying close attention to the fine details of various options used in the configuration process. The next sections explain the options of the Network Settings dialog. In the sections, you learn how to change the workgroup name and description information, and how to speed up file sharing and information processing.

Changing Computer Name, Workgroup, and Description

In the Network Settings dialog, you can change the name assigned to your computer, the comment that the system uses to describe your computer, and the workgroup to which you belong. You also can create a new workgroup within this dialog.

To change these settings, first click the Network icon in the Control Panel. Then use the following options in the Network Settings dialog:

- *Computer Name.* Enables you to change the name assigned to your workgroup computer. The name of your computer must be unique; it cannot have the same name as any other computer or workgroup. To set the computer name, type the name for your computer in the text box. You can use up to 15 of the same characters used in DOS file names.

- *Workgroup.* Enables you to select a workgroup or create a new one. To change the workgroup to which your computer belongs, select a workgroup name from the drop-down list. To create a new workgroup, type a name for it in the text box. For the workgroup name, you can use up to 15 of the same characters used in DOS file names.

- *Comment.* Describes your computer. This description appears next to your computer name in the Connect Network Drive and Connect Network Printer dialogs. In the text box, type a comment that describes your computer completely. The comment can be up to 48 characters long but cannot contain any commas. If this computer is used mostly for desktop publishing, for example, you may want to state that fact in the description so that other users will be more aware of what they can and cannot expect from this computer.

After you change these settings, choose OK. A message appears, asking you to restart your computer so that the new computer and workgroup names take effect. To put your changes into effect, choose the Restart Computer button.

Running Applications or Sharing Resources Faster

By using the Performance Priority setting in the Network Settings dialog, you can adjust the speed at which your applications run or your resources are shared (refer to fig. 8.1). You also can disable

8

sharing of your directories, printers, and ClipBook pages by disabling the Enable Sharing check box.

When the Enable Sharing check box is selected, you can use the Performance Priority option to adjust the speed at which your applications run and your resources are shared. Move the slider toward the appropriate side to speed up the applications or shared resources.

Adjusting the Performance Priority setting involves three tradeoffs: faster applications but slower shared resources, equal time for applications and shared resources, or slower applications but faster shared resources.

If the main purpose of your computer is to process information, move the Performance Priority slider toward the Applications Run Fastest side. You also should move the slider closer to Applications Run Fastest if you use your computer primarily for your own work. Other users who connect to your computer, however, may notice a decrease in performance when they use your shared resources.

If your main goal is to share resources with others in your workgroup—for example, if your computer is used primarily as a server for others to gain access to your shared directories, printers, and ClipBook pages—move the slider closer to Resources Shared Fastest. That way, you decrease the speed of your applications but speed up users' ability to access your resources.

If your system is used for sharing resources *and* processing data, adjust the slider to a middle point of the scale. Because guessing the proper middle setting is difficult, choose a setting, and then operate your computer for some time. You can readjust the setting until you find the proper setting for this computer.

> **NOTE** The Performance Priority setting is in effect only if others are connected to your computer. If no other users share resources on your computer, Windows for Workgroups always runs in the Application Run Fastest mode, regardless of where the performance gauge is set.

After you finish adjusting the Performance Priority setting, choose OK. If you have changed the Enable Sharing setting, you see a message asking you to restart Windows for Workgroups. For that change to take effect, choose the Restart Windows button.

Setting Up a Network Adapter

If you installed a new network adapter in your computer, you need to add the driver for the adapter. You can change network adapter settings and add protocols while installing the driver, or at any time afterward. The following sections explain what to do.

> **NOTE** When you add, remove, or change settings for a network adapter, your changes don't take effect until you restart your computer. Be sure to make backup copies of your configuration files before you set up a network adapter.

Adding a Network Adapter

Sometimes you may want to use more than one network adapter. If, for example, you are using more that one type of network—such as token-ring and EtherNet networks—you need to install a network adapter for each network type. (Windows for Workgroups supports up to four network adapters in a single computer.) If you want to use more than four protocols, you need to install a second network adapter because each network adapter supports up to only four protocols.

After you install a network adapter, you need to add its driver. To add a network adapter driver, follow these steps:

1. From the Control Panel, choose the Network icon. In the Network Settings dialog, choose the Adapters button. The Network Adapters dialog appears (see fig. 8.2).

2. Choose Add. The Install New Network Adapter dialog appears, listing various adapters that are available.

3. From the list of network adapters, select the one you want to add and choose OK.

   If your network adapter isn't listed, select Unlisted or Update Network Adapter and then choose OK. The Install Driver dialog appears.

4. Insert the requested disk in drive A and then choose OK. Alternatively, you can type the drive letter and directory where the driver is located and then choose OK.

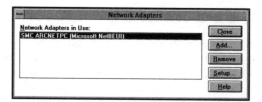

FIG. 8.2 *The Network Adapters dialog.*

If you selected Unlisted or Updated Network Adapter, a dialog appears, listing the supported network adapters on disk. Select the network adapter you use and then choose OK.

5. A dialog listing the settings for your adapter appears. Set the Interrupt, Base I/O Port, and Base Memory Address options to values that match the settings on your network adapter.

To change advanced settings or the protocols you want to use, choose the Advanced or Protocols button and then complete the dialogs. The next section discusses the advanced settings in more detail. For more information on protocols, see "Using Protocols" later in the chapter.

> **NOTE** In most cases, the default adapter settings should work, as long as they don't conflict with other devices, such as a mouse, sound card, or memory managers, installed on your system. See the manuals for your devices to determine the settings each device is using.

6. In the settings dialog for your adapter, choose OK. Choose OK again to close the Network Settings dialog. A message appears, prompting you to restart your computer. For your changes to take effect, choose the Restart Computer button.

Setting Network Adapter Options

You can set options for your network adapter while you add the network adapter driver, or at any time afterward. If on your network adapter you adjust a hardware switch that changes the interrupt setting, for example, specify what the new setting is in the settings dialog for the adapter.

The type of settings you can change depends on the type of network adapter you are using. Some network adapters require that you set basic options, such as base I/O port address or interrupt; other adapters require that you set more advanced options. On some adapters, all options are built into the adapter or determined by the driver and cannot be changed.

The following sections explain how to set the basic and advance settings for your adapter.

Setting Basic Options

To set basic options for your network adapter, follow these steps:

1. From the Control Panel, choose the Network icon to call up the Network Settings dialog. Then choose the Adapters button.

2. In the Network Adapters dialog, select the adapter with the settings you want to change, and then choose the Setup button. A Setup dialog appears, listing options specific to your adapter.

3. Set any options you want and then choose OK. These settings include interrupt, base I/O port, and base memory address. Change these settings from the default only if you are sure that the settings you will use are required.

> **NOTE** If an option is labeled `Automatic` or `Unused`, the setting for that option is built into the adapter, determined by the driver, or isn't needed by the adapter. You cannot change this setting.

4. In the Network Adapters dialog, choose the Close button. In the Network Settings dialog, choose OK.

5. A message box appears, asking you to restart your computer. To put your changes into effect, choose the Restart Computer button.

Setting Advanced Options

To set advanced options for your network adapter, follow these steps:

1. Call up the Network Settings dialog by choosing the Network icon in the Control Panel. Then choose the Adapters button.

2. In the Network Adapters dialog, select the adapter whose settings you want to change and then choose **Setup**.

3. A dialog listing setup options for your adapter appears. Choose the **Advanced** button. A dialog box appears with a description of the network adapter card in your computer.

> **NOTE** The Advanced button appears only if your network adapter includes advanced options that you can set.

4. In the Advanced Network-Adapter Settings list, select the setting you want to change, change its value, and then choose the **Set** button. To use the value you last specified, choose the **Revert** button.

   You can set the following settings: Maximum Requests, Maximum Transmits, Receive Buffer Size, Receive Buffers, and Receive Chain Entries. These settings require very specific technical knowledge about your adapter card and should not be changed from the default unless absolutely necessary. For information about the specific settings and the values they require, see the documentation for your network adapter.

> **NOTE** If you decide to use the default setting and the last saved setting isn't the default, you need to delete the network adapter driver from your hard disk and then add the driver again to restore the default settings.

5. After you finish setting options, choose OK to save the settings and close the dialog. Exit the other dialogs by choosing OK or Cancel.

6. A message appears, asking you to restart your computer. To put your changes into effect, choose **Restart Computer**.

Using Protocols

To communicate and exchange information with others over a network, you must specify a protocol for your network adapter. The SETUP program installed and configured the NetBEUI protocol when you set up Windows for Workgroups.

The NetBEUI protocol and its settings should work most of the time. You may need to add a protocol to communicate with a computer that doesn't use NetBEUI, however, or change protocol settings or remove a protocol. The following sections explain how.

Adding a Protocol

To communicate or exchange information with a computer that isn't using the NetBEUI protocol, you need to add a driver for the protocol that computer is using. To add a protocol driver, follow these steps:

1. Call up the Network Settings dialog by clicking the Network icon in the Control Panel. Then choose the Adapters button.

2. In the Network Adapters dialog, select the adapter for which you want to add a protocol and then choose the Setup button.

3. In the setup dialog for your adapter, choose the Protocols button. The Protocols Used dialog appears.

4. From the Available Protocols list, drag the name of the protocol you want to add to the Protocols in Use list. Alternatively, select the protocol and then choose the Add button.

   If the protocol you want to add doesn't appear on the list, drag or select Unlisted or Updated Protocols. A dialog appears, asking you to insert the floppy disk that contains the new protocol to be added to the system. This disk is supplied by the adaptor vendor.

5. Insert the disk in drive A and then choose OK. Alternatively, type the drive letter and directory where the protocol driver is located and then choose OK.

6. A dialog appears, listing the protocol drivers on the disk. Select the driver you want to use and then choose OK.

7. Choose OK or Cancel to exit the rest of the dialogs. A message appears, asking you to restart your computer. To put

your changes into effect, choose the **R**estart Computer button.

Changing Protocol Settings

You can set options for the protocols you are using. If you upgrade your adaptor card to a newer version, for example, you may need to set protocol options. To do so, follow these steps:

1. Open the Network Settings dialog by clicking the Network icon in the Control Panel. Then choose the Adapters button.

2. In the Network Adapters dialog, select the network for which you want to add a protocol and then choose **S**etup.

3. In the setup dialog for your adapter, choose the **P**rotocols button. The Protocols Used dialog appears.

4. In the Protocols in Use list, select the protocol with the settings you want to change, and then choose the **S**ettings button. A dialog box appears with the name of the protocol you chose.

5. In the **A**dvanced Protocol Settings list, select the protocol option with the setting you want to change.

6. Change the value for the setting, and then choose the **S**et button. To use the value you last specified, choose the **R**evert button.

7. After you finish, choose OK.

Removing a Protocol

Protocols take up memory. If you no longer are using a protocol, you can remove it to free memory for sharing resources and running applications. To remove a protocol, follow these steps:

1. Open the Network Settings dialog by clicking the Network icon in the Control Panel. Then choose the Adapters button.

2. In the Network Adapters dialog, select the network for which you want to add a protocol and then choose **S**etup.

3. In the setup dialog for your adapter, choose the **P**rotocols button. The Protocols Used dialog appears.

4. From the Protocols in Use list, drag the name of the protocol you want to remove to the Available Protocols list.

Alternatively, select the protocol and then choose the **Remove** button.

5. Choose OK to close the Protocols Used dialog.

6. Choose OK or Cancel to close the rest of the dialogs. A message appears, asking you to restart your computer. To put your changes into effect, choose the **Restart Computer** button.

Removing a Network Adapter

If you removed a network adapter from your computer, you also should remove the driver; otherwise, an error may result. Follow these steps:

1. From the Control Panel, choose the Network icon. In the Network Settings dialog, choose the Adapters button. The Network Adapters dialog appears.

2. In the **Network Adapters in Use** list box, select the network adapter driver with the driver you want to remove.

3. Choose the **Remove** button. A dialog appears, asking you to confirm your decision to remove the network adapter driver. Choose **Yes**.

4. In the Network Settings dialog, choose OK. A message appears, prompting you to restart your computer.

5. For your changes to take effect, choose the **Restart Computer** button.

> **NOTE** Removing the driver doesn't delete it from your hard disk. If you decide to use the network adapter later, you easily can add it again, as explained earlier in the section "Adding a Network Adapter."

Specifying Logon Options

When you start Windows for Workgroups, you can specify options for how you log on. By using the Logon Settings dialog, you can change the default logon name, for example, or you can choose not to log on at all. You also can log out of Windows for Workgroups without exiting Windows by using the Logon Settings dialog.

To specify logon options, follow these steps:

1. Call up the Network Settings dialog by clicking the Network icon in the Control Panel. Then choose the Logon button. The Logon Settings dialog appears (see fig. 8.3).

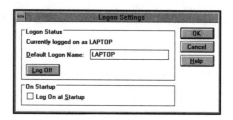

FIG. 8.3   *The Logon Settings dialog.*

2. To start Windows for Workgroups without logging on, disable the Log On at Startup check box option. To change the default logon name, type the name in the Default Logon Name text box.

3. Choose OK to save your changes and close the Logon Settings dialog. The new options take effect the next time you start Windows for Workgroups.

NOTE	If you choose not to log on at start-up, your previous connections will not be restored the next time you start Windows for Workgroups. If you want to make a new connection, you must log on first. Open the Logon Settings dialog to log on.

When you are logged on to Windows for Workgroups, you can share your resources. You also can browse and connect to resources that are being shared by others. When logged off, you still can use your own resources, but you cannot connect to resources shared by others nor gain access to your previous connections.

You may want to log off during a Windows for Workgroups session if others use your computer. That way, another user can log on to your computer to gain access to his own connections, which may be different from yours. You also may want to disconnect temporarily if you are working on sensitive data and don't want to risk having the file available to network users.

To log off without exiting Windows, follow these steps:

1. Call up the Network Settings dialog by clicking the Network icon in the Control Panel. Then choose the Logon button.

2. In the Logon Settings dialog, choose the Log Off button.

3. A dialog appears, warning you that logging off will break your connections to the network. To log off, choose Yes.

You can log back onto the network by following these steps:

1. Call up the Network Settings dialog by clicking the Network icon in the Control Panel. Then choose the Logon button.

2. In the Logon Settings dialog, choose the Logon button.

> **NOTE** The name of the Logon button changes to Log Off after you are logged on.

You see the Welcome to Windows for Workgroups dialog, in which you type your logon password. If you don't use a logon password, the dialog doesn't appear; you automatically are logged on.

3. Type your logon name and password in the appropriate boxes and then choose OK until all the dialog boxes are closed.

Using Additional Networks

Windows for Workgroups supports the use of LAN Manager and Novell NetWare. If you want to use additional network software with Windows for Workgroups, you can use the Networks button in the Network Settings dialog to add support for the network and then configure its settings. You also can remove support for a network that you no longer are using. The following sections explain how.

> **NOTE** When you add, remove, or change settings for an additional network, your changes don't take effect until you restart your computer. You may want to copy your configuration files before you change additional network settings.

8

Adding Support for an Additional Network

To use an additional network, you first need to install the Windows for Workgroup drivers for that network. Follow these steps:

1. From the Control Panel, click the Network icon to call up the Network Settings dialog. Choose the Networks button. The Compatible Networks dialog appears (see fig. 8.4).

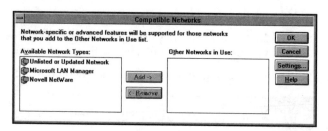

FIG. 8.4   *The Compatible Networks dialog.*

2. From the Available Network Types list box, drag the network type you want to use to the Other Networks in Use list box. Alternatively, select the network type and then choose the Add button.

   If your network type doesn't appear in the Available Network Types list, use the Unlisted or Updated Network option. A dialog appears, requesting you to insert a disk.

3. Insert the requested disk in drive A and then choose OK. Alternatively, type the drive letter and directory where the network driver is located and then choose OK. A dialog appears, listing the network drivers on the disk. Select the driver you want to use and then choose OK.

4. Choose OK twice to close the Compatible Networks and Network Settings dialogs. A message appears, asking you to restart your computer. To put your changes into effect, choose the **Restart Computer** button.

Setting Options for an Additional Network

After you add support for a network, you can configure its settings. These settings will vary, depending on the type of network you are using.

To set options for an additional network, follow these steps:

1. Open the Network Settings dialog by choosing the Network icon in the Control Panel. Then choose the Networks button.

2. In the Compatible Networks dialog, select the network you want to configure from the Other Networks in Use list box.

3. Choose the Settings button.

4. A dialog appears with options specific to the selected network. Complete the dialog for your network, and then choose OK to save your settings and close the dialog.

5. Choose OK twice to close the Compatible Networks and Network Settings dialogs. A message asking you to restart your computer appears. To put the changes into effect, choose the Restart Computer button.

Removing Support for an Additional Network

If you no longer are using an additional network, you can remove support for it. By removing support for the network, you save memory because the network drivers will not need to be loaded.

> **NOTE** Removing support for a network doesn't delete the network drivers from your hard disk. If you decide to use the network again, you can add it again.

To remove support for an additional network, follow these steps:

1. Open the Network Settings dialog by clicking the Control Panel's Network icon. Then choose the Networks button. The Compatible Networks dialog appears.

2. From the Other Networks in Use list box, drag the network type you want to remove into the Available Network Types list box, or select the network and then choose Remove.

3. Choose OK twice to close the Compatible Networks and Network Settings dialogs. A message asking you to restart your computer appears. To put your changes into effect, choose the Restart Computer button.

8

Changing Your Logon Password

To prevent unauthorized users from starting your computer and gaining access to your connections, you can use a logon password. You also should change your password periodically. To change your logon password, follow these steps:

1. From the Control Panel, choose Network. In the Network Settings dialog, choose the Password button. The Change Logon Password dialog appears (see fig. 8.5).

FIG. 8.5   *The Change Logon Password dialog.*

2. If your name doesn't appear in the Change Password for User text box, pull down the drop-down list and select your name, or type your logon name in the box.

3. In the Old Password text box, type your current password. Type the new password in the New Password text box. In the Confirm New Password text box, retype the new password.

4. Choose OK twice to close the Change Logon Password and Network Settings dialogs. Your new logon password takes effect immediately.

Using Workgroup Connection

You can obtain for your Windows for Workgroup network an optional product called Workgroup Connection. This Microsoft product enables a computer that isn't running Windows for Workgroups to access shared network resources. This set of utilities also includes a DOS-based version of Microsoft Mail.

Unlike a computer running Windows for Workgroup, which can be a server *and* a client, a computer running Workgroup Connection can be only a client. In other words, a computer running Workgroup Connection can use shared resources on computers running Windows for Workgroups but cannot share any of its own resources.

The following sections discuss installing Workgroup Connection, logging on and off a network, connecting to shared directories and shared printers, and sending and receiving Mail messages.

Installing Workgroup Connection

Before you begin installing Workgroup Connection on a computer, you need to have in front of you a few key pieces of information:

- The name of your network adapter

- The network adapter's interrupt request (IRQ)

- The network adapter's base address

- A name for the computer running Workgroup Connection

- The workgroup name that you plan to connect to

This information is key to installing Workgroup Connection successfully. The first three items, dealing with the network adapter, you can obtain as you are installing the network adapter. The fourth item, the computer name, you make up yourself. The fifth item, the workgroup name, was determined when the first copy of Windows for Workgroups was installed.

To install Workgroup Connection, insert the Workgroup Connection disk in your floppy drive and then proceed as follows:

1. At the DOS prompt, start the setup program by typing **A:WCSETUP**. You see the initial welcome screen, which gives you three choices:

    - Press F1 to get help.

    - Press F3 to quit WCSETUP.

    - Press Enter to continue with WCSETUP.

    If you press F3, you are given another prompt telling you to press Y to exit SETUP or to press any other key to return to SETUP.

2. Press Enter to continue. The directory path screen appears.

3. Type the directory path to which Workgroup Connection files will be copied (for example, **C:\WGC**) and then press Enter. SETUP begins examining your system files and then starts setting up your network drivers.

4. When prompted for a computer name, type a name of up to 15 characters long to identify the computer. (Notice on-screen the list of characters that you cannot use.) After you type the computer name, press Enter. The workgroup name screen appears.

5. When prompted for the workgroup name, type the name of the workgroup to attach the computer to. After you type the workgroup name, press Enter. The settings screen appears (see fig. 8.6).

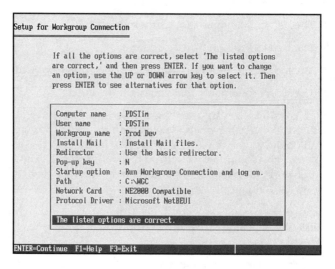

```
Setup for Workgroup Connection

        If all the options are correct, select 'The listed options
        are correct,' and then press ENTER. If you want to change
        an option, use the UP or DOWN arrow key to select it. Then
        press ENTER to see alternatives for that option.

        ┌──────────────────────────────────────────────────────────┐
        │ Computer name    : PDSTim                                 │
        │ User name        : PDSTim                                 │
        │ Workgroup name   : Prod Dev                              │
        │ Install Mail     : Install Mail files.                    │
        │ Redirector       : Use the basic redirector.             │
        │ Pop-up key       : N                                      │
        │ Startup option   : Run Workgroup Connection and log on.  │
        │ Path             : C:\WGC                                 │
        │ Network Card     : NE2000 Compatible                     │
        │ Protocol Driver  : Microsoft NetBEUI                     │
        │ ──────────────────────────────────────────────────────── │
        │ The listed options are correct.                          │
        └──────────────────────────────────────────────────────────┘

ENTER=Continue   F1=Help   F3=Exit
```

FIG. 8.6 *The Workgroup Connection settings screen.*

6. In the Workgroup Connection settings screen, make any changes you want by selecting the desired setting. Table 8.1 summarizes each setting that you can change.

7. After you review the settings, select The listed options are correct and press Enter. SETUP completes copying the Workgroup Connection files to the directory that you specified and sets up the network connections according to your settings by modifying your CONFIG.SYS and AUTOEXEC.BAT files. A final screen shows that you successfully completed setup.

8. To reboot your computer so that the Workgroup Connection drivers can load, press Enter.

   To quit WCSETUP without rebooting your computer, press F3. Quitting without rebooting doesn't affect your new setup. You can quit without rebooting if you want to return to the DOS prompt and not use Workgroup Connection at this point.

9. After the computer restarts, the network drivers are loaded into memory. If you selected to log on when you start the network, you will see a prompt asking you to enter your user name. The user name entered during setup is the default. If this name is correct, press Enter.

10. At the password prompt, you may type a password that only you will use to log into the computer. You do not have to use a password. If you decide to use a password, however, type the password and press Enter.

11. A prompt appears, asking you to confirm your password. If you typed a password, type it again. Then press Enter. You now are successfully logged onto the network. Remember the password you selected.

You can make changes to your setup at any time. To make changes, type **WCSETUP** and press Enter. WCSETUP resides in the directory selected to contain the Workgroup Connection files.

Table 8.1 Workgroup Connection Settings

Option	Description
Computer name	Shows the computer name you selected
User name	Initially shows the same as the computer name, but can be changed
Workgroup name	Shows the workgroup name you selected to attach to
Install Mail	Initially shows Install Mail Files. You can choose to install or not install mail files. Choose Install Mail Files if you want to send and receive mail through the network. If you are short on disk space, choose Do Not Install Mail Files. Mail files take approximately 270K of disk space.
Redirector	Offers two options: Basic or Full. The Basic redirector is a memory-resident program that provides standard

continues

Table 8.1 Continued

Option	Description
	workgroup functions, such as connecting network drives for directory sharing and printer sharing. The Full redirector provides more advanced connections for network-aware programs. You should choose this option if you are connecting to a network such as LAN Manager that uses an OS/2 program that makes use of features such as *named pipes*, which enable network programs to access resources on many distributed computers. The Full redirector requires more disk space than the Basic redirector.
Pop-up key	Enables you to choose which key to use with the Ctrl key when calling up the Workgroup Connection pop-up menu. The default is Ctrl+N. This menu enables you to access shared directories and printers without having to exit the current program you are running. Some programs use certain Ctrl+key combinations. If a program already uses Ctrl+N, you can choose another letter for the Workgroup Connection pop-up menu.
Startup option	Offers three start-up options: ■ *Run Workgroup Connection Only.* Activates Workgroup Connection but doesn't log you on automatically. When you choose this option, you must log on to the network manually to use shared resources. ■ *Run Workgroup Connection and Log On.* Runs Workgroup Connection and automatically logs you onto the network. ■ *Run Workgroup Connection, Log On, and Load Pop-up.* Connects you, logs you on, and loads the

Option	Description
	memory-resident Workgroup Connection menu.
Path	Shows the drive and directory you selected to contain the Workgroup Connection files.
Network Card	Shows the network adapter card SETUP selected. Examine this setting to ensure that SETUP selected the correct card and the correct settings for the card.
Protocol Driver	Shows the network communications protocol used in your Windows for Workgroup network (Microsoft's NetBEUI). Support for other protocols is limited.

Checking Your Network Card Settings

For Workgroup Connection to work properly, the settings for the Workgroup Connection network card driver must match the settings on the network card itself. You make these settings when using WCSETUP. The settings are as follows:

- The name of the card
- The interrupt request (IRQ)
- The base address

When you install the network card, write down the settings you made. When viewing the settings made during Workgroup Connection Setup (refer to fig. 8.6), select the Network Card option to call up a network drivers configuration screen. This screen contains three options:

- Change Driver for Network Card
- Edit Settings for Network Card Driver
- Driver Configuration Is Correct

If the name of the network card is incorrect, choose Change Driver for Network Card and press Enter. From the list of network cards that appears, select the correct name for your

continues

Checking Your Network Card Settings Continued

card and press Enter. You return to the network drivers configuration screen.

Choose the Edit Settings for Network Card Driver option and press Enter. You see a screen displaying Drivername, IOBASE, and INTERRUPT. If any of these settings are incorrect, select the option and press Enter. A new screen lists selections for the option. Make the correct selection and press Enter. After you select the correct driver name, IOBASE, and INTERRUPT, choose The Listed Options Are Correct and press Enter. You return to the network drivers configuration screen. Choose the option Driver Configuration Is Correct and press Enter. You return to the screen listing all the Workgroup Connection settings. Choose The Listed Options Are Correct and press Enter. Your workgroup connections now are set correctly.

If, when selecting the correct network adapter name, you don't see your adapter listed, you must supply the drivers on a disk provided by the manufacturer. Workgroup Connection and Windows for Workgroups use a type of driver known as an NDIS driver. Most vendors put the letters NDIS in the file name of their driver.

From the network adapters list select Network Card Not Shown on List Below. Insert the manufacturer's driver disk in a floppy drive. At the prompt, enter the path to the proper driver and press Enter. WCSETUP loads the driver and moves you to the adapter settings screen.

Understanding NET and the Connections Menus

Windows for Workgroups and Workgroup Connection share a common utility: the NET.EXE utility. After you install this utility on your computer, you can use it to perform the functions of a workgroup client—that is, connect to and disconnect from shared directories and shared printers.

You can use NET in one of two ways—as an easy-to-use menu system or as a command-line utility. The menu for using shared directories is called the Disk Connections menu, while the menu for using shared printers is called the Printer Connections menu. The Disk Connections menu is the default menu.

You can access the Disk Connections menu in one of two ways. If you chose to load the pop-up during setup, you access the Disk Connections menu by pressing Ctrl+N (unless you changed the default shortcut key from N to another letter). If you didn't install Workgroup Connection as a TSR, change to the directory containing the Workgroup Connection files and run the NET program by typing **NET** and pressing Enter. The Disk Connection menu appears (see fig. 8.7).

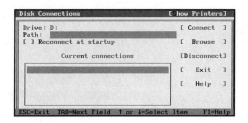

FIG. 8.7 *The Disk Connections menu.*

The following table summarizes the options available on this menu. You can move to any Disk Connections option by pressing Tab or by pressing Alt plus the letter boldfaced in the option name.

Option	Description
Drive	Lists the drive letter you want to connect. You can connect drive letters from A to the last drive letter specified in your CONFIG.SYS file.
Path	Lists the path, which consists of two backslash characters (\\) followed by a computer name and a directory name. To access a directory called SOUNDS on computer WILBUR, for example, you type **WILBUR\SOUNDS**.
Reconnect at Startup	If selected, reconnects this drive each time you run Workgroup Connection and log on
Current Connections	Displays a list of currently connected drives and their paths

continues

Option	Description
Show Printers	Switches you to the Printer Connections menu, through which you can view and control network printing
Connect	Connects the drive letter to the path you select
Browse	Looks at the network to see what computers and shared directories for each computer are available
Disconnect	Disconnects the drive letter from the path
Exit	Exits the Disk Connections menu
Help	Provides help on using the Disk Connections menu

Notice that one of the listed options, **S**how Printers, displays the Printer Connections menu. Most of the options in the Printer Connections menu are the same. The following table shows the differences between the Disk Connections and Printer Connections menus.

Printer Connections Menu Option	Description	Disk Connections Menu Replaced
Port	The printer port name to assign for your computer	Drive
Show Disks	Switches between the Disk Connections and Printer Connections menus	Show Printers
Show **Q**ueue	Displays the activity on a shared printer and enables you to **P**ause, **R**esume, or **D**elete a print job that you sent to the shared printer	None replaced

A quicker way to manage disk connections and printer connections is to issue NET commands at the DOS command line. You can use a number of command-line parameters with the NET command to manage your connections.

The syntax you use to issue command-line parameters is as follows:

NET *parameter*

Table 8.2 lists the different parameters you can type after the command NET.

Table 8.2 NET Command-Line Parameters

Parameter	Description
/?	Displays a list of the command-line parameters
command /?	Reveals additional options available for a *command*. Commands such as NET USE and NET PRINT have a dozen additional options each. To get help from the DOS prompt on the NET LOGON parameter, for example, type **NET LOGON /?**
CONFIG	Displays the computer name, user logon name, software version, redirector version, where Workgroup Connection was loaded ("root"), and workgroup name
HELP	Displays a help screen listing the various NET parameters
LOGOFF	Logs you out of the network
LOGON	Logs you onto the network. If you have any connections marked as **R**econnect at Startup, those connections are established at this time.
PASSWORD	Enables you to change your logon password
PRINT	Enables you to print and manage jobs you already have printed to a shared printer queue (see "Using a Shared Printer" later in this chapter)
START	Starts Workgroup Connection. If you specified the pop-up memory resident program when you installed Workgroup Connection, the Connections menus are

continues

Table 8.2 Continued

Parameter	Description
	loaded into memory. The Basic or Full redirector loads into memory. You also can start without being prompted to enter a user logon name. Start options are listed after this table.
STOP	Stops Workgroup Connection and the pop-up menu if it is resident in memory
TIME	Synchronizes the time on your computer with the time on a Microsoft LAN Manager time server. This command includes option flags that enable you to specify another workgroup.
USE	Connects a drive letter or port to a shared directory or printer on the network. Additional options are mentioned throughout the chapter.
VER	Displays the version of Workgroup Connection you are using
VIEW	Displays a list of computers and shared resources. To view the resources on a particular computer, type **NET VIEW** *computer*, where *computer* is the name of the computer.

The START parameter uses the following options:

- *POPUP*. Loads the pop-up menu interface

- *BASIC*. Loads the basic redirector

- *FULL*. Loads the full redirector

- *WORKSTATION*. Starts the default redirector (specified during installation)

- *NETBIND*. Binds the protocols and network adapter cards

- *NETBEUI*. Loads the Microsoft NetBIOS interface

- */LIST*. Lists Workgroup Connection components loaded so far

■ */YES.* Starts Workgroup Connection without waiting for you to enter a logon name and password. This option assumes the default logon name and password.

Logging On and Off the Workgroup

Before you can use any of the features of Workgroup Connection, you must log into the network. If, when installing Workgroup Connection, you selected the option Run Workgroup Connection and Log On, you will be prompted to log onto the network every time you boot your computer.

Logging onto the network consists of entering your user name and a password, if you selected a password when you first logged onto the network. Because Workgroup Connection remembers the user name chosen when you installed Workgroup Connection, entering your user name amounts to nothing more than pressing the Enter key. If you elected to use a password, you next are prompted to type your password and press Enter.

You can log on and log off the network using the NET command from the DOS command line. The syntax for logging on is as follows:

NET LOGON *username password* /YES

If you type only **NET LOGON** and press Enter, you are prompted to enter your user name and password. You can, however, enter your user name and password on the command line, as you see in the syntax. If you include the optional /YES switch, your default user name and password are used to log you onto the network.

After you log onto the network, you can log off. The syntax for logging off the network is as follows:

NET LOGOFF /YES

The /YES switch is optional. Typing simply **NET LOGOFF** at the command line will log you off the network.

Note that if you log onto the network and then try to log onto the network again, Workgroup Connection assumes you are another user trying to log onto the network. You will see the following prompt:

```
You are currently logged on as username.
You must first log off before logging on again.
Do you want to log off? (Y/N) [N]:
```

8

If you press Enter, you choose the default no and remain logged onto the network. However, if you press Y and then Enter, you are logged off the network and are prompted for a user name to log onto the network. If you are attached to a shared directory or a shared printer, you also are prompted to disconnect from them before you are logged off.

Stopping Network Connections

Each time you start your computer, you also start the network connection because of the NET START command that WCSETUP placed into your AUTOEXEC.BAT file. When the network is started, you can access any of the Workgroup Connection features.

You may stop Workgroup Connection, however, by using the STOP parameter. The syntax to stop network connections is as follows:

NET STOP *option*

In place of *option* you may use one of the following:

Option	Description
POPUP	Unloads the NET pop-up from memory but doesn't stop the network connection
BASIC	Stops the Basic network redirector
FULL	Stops the Full network redirector
WORKSTATION	Stops whatever redirector was the default redirector
NETBEUI	Stops the NetBIOS interface

Simply typing **NET STOP** stops all access to the network. If you are logged onto the network and connected to a shared directory or shared printer, you are prompted to stop the connections and log off before stopping the network connection.

After you stop network connections, you can start them again. The syntax for starting a connection is as follows:

NET START *option* /LIST

The /LIST switch displays which of these options are loaded into memory. The following table lists the options to use in place of *option*.

Option	Description
POPUP	Loads the NET pop-up into memory as a TSR
BASIC	Loads the Basic network redirector
FULL	Loads the Full network redirector
WORKSTATION	Loads the default redirector
NETBEUI	Loads the NetBIOS interface

Why would you want to stop and then restart a connection? Suppose that you are using the Basic redirector, and now need to use features of the Full redirector. You can enter the command **NET STOP BASIC** followed by the command **NET START FULL**. Now the full redirector is loaded into memory for use. Suppose instead that you want to load NET as a TSR. Issue the command **NET START POPUP**. NET loads as a TSR and can be activated by the hot key.

Using a Shared Directory

Probably the feature that is used the most with Workgroup Connection is sharing directories. The following sections show you how to connect and disconnect a network drive.

Connecting a Network Drive

Connecting a network drive assigns a drive letter to a shared directory. To connect a network drive, you can run the NET program or use the pop-up Disk Connections menu.

To connect a network drive using the pop-up menu, follow these steps:

1. Press Ctrl+N to access the Disk Connections menu.

2. Choose the Drive option and then type the desired drive letter.

3. Choose the Path option and then type the desired path. To connect to the SOUNDS shared directory on the server PDS, for example, type **\\PDS\SOUNDS**.

   If you don't know the path, you can use the Browse option, which presents the Browse window (see fig. 8.8). In the Show Shared Directories On list box, select the desired

computer and then press Tab or Alt+D to move to the
Shared Directories list box. Select the desired shared directory. Choose OK to return to the Disk Connections menu.

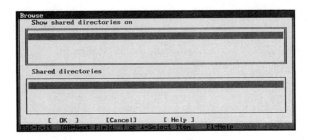

FIG. 8.8 *The Disk Connections Browse window.*

4. Choose the Connect button.

5. Choose Exit to leave the Disk Connections menu.

You also can connect a network drive from the DOS command line
by using the NET command:

NET USE *d*: *server**shared_dir*

or

NET USE * *server**shared_dir*

The * means that the next available drive letter is used, although
you also can use a specific drive letter. For example, NET USE F:
\\PDS\BOOK assigns the shared directory BOOK to your F drive.

Disconnecting a Network Drive

You may find disconnecting a network drive necessary from time
to time, for the following reasons:

■ The computer containing the shared directory went down.

■ The access type of the shared directory was changed while
you were connected.

■ You ran out of drive letters and need to use this drive letter
to connect to another directory.

To disconnect a network drive, follow these steps:

1. Press Ctrl+N to access the Disk Connections menu.

2. From the Current Connections list box, select the drive from which you want to disconnect.

3. Choose the Disconnect option. The drive disappears from the Current Connections list box.

To disconnect a network drive from the DOS command line, use the following syntax:

NET USE *d*: /DELETE

To disconnect network drive F, for example, type **NET USE F: /DELETE** and press Enter.

Using a Shared Printer

Workgroup Connection enables you to assign printing from a local port to a shared printer. When you are running a program, any printing that normally would be directed from one of the parallel ports (LPT1, LPT2, and so on) is redirected to the print queue for the shared printer.

The following sections show you how to connect to, disconnect from, and manage connections to shared printers on your network.

Connecting a Port to a Network Printer

Connecting to a network printer assigns a local parallel port to a shared printer. To connect a network printer, you can run the NET program or use the Printer Connections menu (see fig. 8.9).

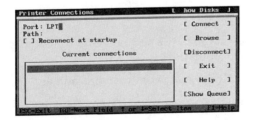

FIG. 8.9 *The Printer Connections menu.*

To access the Printer Connections menu, start the NET menu by pressing Ctrl+N or by typing **NET** and pressing Enter. The default is to the Disk Connections menu. To change to the Printer Connections menu, press Alt+S.

To connect a network printer, follow these steps:

1. Access the Printer Connections menu.

2. Choose Port and then type the desired port number (1, 2, or 3). You can have up to three printer connections defined at the same time.

3. For the Path option, type the desired path. The path consists of two backslash characters (\\), the computer name, another backslash, and a directory path. To access a printer called SPEED_DEVIL on computer TASMANIAN, for example, type **\\TASMANIAN\SPEED_DEVIL**.

   If you don't know the path to the printer, you can use the Browse option, which presents the Browse window (see fig. 8.10). In the Show Shared Printers On list box, select the desired computer. Press Tab or Alt+D to move to the Shared Print Queues list box and then select the desired shared print queue. Choose OK to return to the Printer Connections menu.

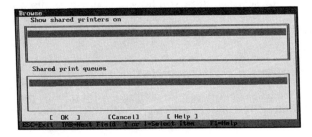

FIG. 8.10 *The Printer Connections Browse window.*

4. Choose Connect. The new printer connection appears in the Current Connections list.

5. Choose Exit to return to the command line.

You can attach to a shared printer from the command line much as you attached to a shared directory from the command line. Use the following syntax:

   NET USE *port#*: *server\queue*

To attach the printer LASER01 from the server PDS01 to your LPT1 port, for example, use the command

   NET USE LPT1: \\PDS01\LASER01

Now, anything that you send to LPT1 is redirected to LASER01 attached to PDS01.

Disconnecting a Network Printer

You may find that you need to disconnect a network printer from time to time, for the following reasons:

- The computer containing the shared printer went down.

- The access type of the shared printer was changed while you were connected.

- You decide to connect different printers to your three allowed ports.

To disconnect a network printer, follow these steps:

1. Access the Printer Connections menu by pressing Ctrl+N and then Alt+S.

2. Select the printer you want to disconnect from the Current Connections list box.

3. Choose Disconnect. The printer disappears from the Current Connections list box.

You also can disconnect a printer by using the NET command from the command line:

> NET USE *port#*: /DELETE

To disconnect the shared printer from your LPT2 port, for example, type

> NET USE LPT2: /DELETE

You no longer are using the shared printer that was assigned to the LPT2 port.

Managing Print Queues

You have a certain degree of control over jobs you place in the print queue for a shared printer. You can view the status of the print queues to determine how busy a printer is. If a queue is busy, you may decide to print to another queue. You cannot affect another user's print job that is in the queue, however; you can affect only jobs you place in the queue. Only the local user using the host computer (where the shared printer is attached) can manage any jobs in the queue.

To view and manage your jobs in the queue(s), you use the Show
Queue option on the Printer Connections menu to display the
print queues available (see fig. 8.11).

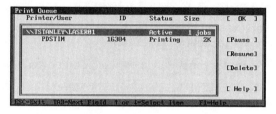

FIG. 8.11 *The Print Queue window.*

The Print Queue window has two major sections: the print queue
contents list and the command buttons. Table 8.3 summarizes the
four columns of information in the Print Queue contents list.
Table 8.4 summarizes some of the print queue management functions you can perform using the command buttons on the right
side of the screen.

Table 8.3 Print Queue Contents List

Column	Description
Printer/User	Displays the *computer name**printer name* of the shared printer. If the printer is now printing a job or has jobs in the queue, the name of the user who generated the job is listed.
ID	Displays an identifying number assigned by Windows for Workgroups so that it can keep track of the job
Status	Lists the status of the printer: Active (ready to print) and Paused (ready but paused by the local user). When jobs are being printed, this column also lists the status of the job: Printing (job is printing successfully) and Paused (for jobs paused by their owners or the local user).
Size	Indicates how many jobs are stacked up for each printer. If jobs are printing, you also see the size of each job in kilobytes.

Table 8.4 Print Queue Command Buttons

Button	Description
OK	Returns you to the Printer Connections menu
Pause	Pauses the currently selected job until you release the pause. You can pause only your own print jobs.
Resume	Enables you to restart a print job that you had paused earlier
Delete	Enables you to delete a job that you have sitting in the queue. You may need to delete a job if you decide to print the same job to another queue. You should delete your first job so that you don't tie up the first printer needlessly.
Help	Pulls up the Help screen

You also can use the command line to manage your print queue by using the following syntax:

NET PRINT *port pjob#*

The *port* option is the port to which you have assigned a shared printer. The *pjob#* option is the print job number that is now in the queue.

You also can add the following options after the NET PRINT command:

/PAUSE	Pauses the print job that you specified
/RESUME	Resumes a paused print job
/DELETE	Deletes a print job that you specified

To examine the queue, type **NET PRINT** *port*. To examine the queue for your port LPT1, for example, type **NET PRINT LPT1:**. If you now have seven jobs in the queue and want to delete job 4, type **NET PRINT LPT1: 4 /DELETE**.

Sending and Receiving Mail

You can set up Mail on a computer running Workgroup Connection the first time you go into Mail. Tell the system which post office to use, enter your password, and fill out the post office account information screen.

After Mail is set up, two things need to happen for you to get into Mail in the future:

- The computer serving as the mail server must be up and running Windows for Workgroups.

- You need to connect a drive to the post office directory.

The concepts for Mail under Workgroup Connection are the same as those for Mail under Windows for Workgroups. For more information on this topic, see Chapter 5, "Using Mail."

Starting Mail

To start Mail from Workgroup Connection, type the following:

MAIL -D*drive mailbox_name* -P*password*

Table 8.5 summarizes the syntax and additional options.

Table 8.5 Mail Start-Up Options

Option	Explanation
-D*drive*	Option to specify the Mail database. *drive* specifies the drive containing the workgroup post office directories (the Mail database).
mailbox_name	The name of your mailbox. This option isn't required. If you don't enter your mailbox name here, you will be prompted for it later.
-*x*	*x* represents the number of lines on your mail screen, from 25 to 50
-C	Flags Mail that you are using a color monitor
-E*drive*:*path*	Tells Mail where your graphics program files (such as Paintbrush) are located. If you are sending messages with graphics images and want Mail to enable you to access them immediately, Mail searches the *path* indicated for graphics programs. If you are

Option	Explanation
	using a program called VPIC.EXE in the GRAPHICS directory, for example, after the MAIL command type **-eC:\GRAPHICS\VPIC.EXE**.
-H or -?	Shows the help screen for the MAIL command
-I*drive:\path*	Tells Mail where to store temporary graphics files it may need to create when processing messages with graphics. If you don't have enough room on your C drive, for example, you may specify a directory called EXTRA on drive D, as follows: -iD:\EXTRA
-M	Tells Mail that the memory-resident programs MONITOR or MICRO are loaded. These programs notify you immediately if you have an incoming mail message.
-N*x*	Mail checks for new mail every *x* seconds. (*x* can range from 1 to 999 seconds.) If you set this value to 1, you receive notice of new mail quickly but may find that your system slows down. A value of 999 checks for new mail approximately every 15 minutes. If you use a value of 0, your computer doesn't check the post office for mail until you get into the Mail program.
-P*password*	Enables you to enter a password from the command prompt rather than have the system stop and wait for you to enter it
-S*type*	Enables you to specify your monitor type: CGA (Color Graphics Adapter) EGA (Enhanced Graphics Adapter) HERC (Hercules Graphics Adapter) VGA (Video Graphics Array) MONO (monochrome)
-V	Reduces the "snow" seen on some graphics screens. If you don't have any screen problems when using Mail, don't use this

8

continues

Table 8.5 Continued

Option	Explanation
	parameter. If you see flickers and what looks like snow on your screen, exit Mail and reenter using this flag.
-X	Sets the notification method
-W*x*	Sets the color scheme, where *x* represents any number from 1 to 15. These numbers correspond to the set of 16 foreground/background colors standard to DOS.

For this example, assume the following:

- The WGPO directory is connected to drive G.

- The mailbox name is Eileen.

- The password is MELLO.

To take Eileen to her mail screen using these specifications, you should type

MAIL -dG: EILEEN -pMELLO

TIP You *must* know the drive letter and/or directory containing your mailbox data. The directory (usually named WGPO) should contain the workgroup post office. If you don't specify the drive and/or directory, Mail will not start.

Sending Messages

Sending a message involves three main actions:

- *Addressing the message.* From your personal address list or the post office address list, you need to pick names of people you want to receive the message.

- *Composing the message.* Type the text of the message. If you want, you also can *attach* a file to the message. The attached file "rides" along with the message; the recipient can detach the file.

■ *Processing it.* You have several choices after the message is composed: save it to a folder for later use, erase it, or transmit it. A transmitted message is placed on the LAN and sent to the post office. The message resides in a file on the post office computer until the recipients of the message "pick up" their mail. If the recipients don't pick up their mail in the designated time period, the mail is considered undeliverable.

To compose a message, first choose Compose from the Mail main menu. Then fill in the Compose window (see fig. 8.12). Table 8.6 lists the fields in the Compose window. Table 8.7 summarizes the function keys you can use while composing the message.

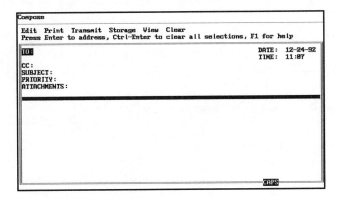

FIG. 8.12 *The Compose window.*

	Table 8.6 Compose Window Fields

Field	Description
TO	Who the message is addressed to. You can select one or more names from the post office list or your personal address list.
CC	Who you want to have a copy of the message.
SUBJECT	The title or subject of the message
PRIORITY	The level of the message:
	1 High priority
	2-4 Moderate priority

continues

Table 8.6 Continued

Field	Description
	5 Low priority
	R Highest priority; causes a return receipt to come back to you when read
	You may not be able to use this option, depending on restrictions set by the workgroup post office administrator.
ATTACHMENTS	Enables you to add files as "riders" on your message
DATE	Today's date. Cannot be changed.
TIME	The current time. Cannot be changed.

Table 8.7 Compose Message Function Keys

Key	Description
F1 (Help)	Calls up the help system, which is available at any time. If you are working on a specific field, pressing F1 can give you help on that field.
F2 (Format)	Formats the text of the message as a paragraph starting with the current line
F3 (Preferences)	Enables you to change preferences while in the middle of composing a message
F4 (Highlight)	Enables you to change the appearance of the highlight. To change a block of text to a specific type of highlight, first select it using F6, and then press F4.
F5 (Include)	Enables you to insert a DOS file in the middle of your message
F6 (Mark)	Starts selecting at the location of your cursor in the body of the message. Use the arrow keys to move to the end of the block of text you want to select.

Key	Description
F7 (Copy)	Enables you to copy the selected text to a paste buffer
F8 (Paste)	Brings whatever is in the paste buffer back to the location of your cursor (useful only when you have text in the paste buffer)
F9 (Cut)	Enables you to cut the selected text to a paste buffer
F10 (Delete)	Enables you to delete the selected text
Insert	Toggles between insert and overtype modes

After you finish composing your message, press Esc. You have several options: you can edit, print, transmit, store, view, or clear the message. Likely, you will want to transmit the message. To do so, from the Compose window choose **Transmit**. If your preferences have the Confirmation option set, choose **Yes**. The message is sent to the post office.

Receiving Messages

You can receive messages in any one of three circumstances:

- When you first enter Mail

- When you choose Update from the main menu

- Every so many seconds depending on the options you specified when you first entered Mail (see table 8.5 earlier in the chapter)

After a mail message is received, you can read it. Follow these steps:

1. From the main menu choose **Read**. A reverse highlighted bar appears on the contents listing screen.

2. On the contents listing screen select the message you want to read. Note that the size of the message appears at the top right side of the screen.

3. Press Enter. You now see the contents of the message.

8

Summary

In this last chapter of *Connecting Windows for Workgroups 3.1*, you learned about changing your workgroup configuration. You can change Windows for Workgroups features such as network adapters or logon passwords, and you can set the performance priority for accessing your resources or using your applications. You also learned how to add a non-Windows computer to your Windows for Workgroups network using Workgroup Connection.

Installing Windows for Workgroups

In this appendix, you install Windows for Workgroups on your PC to create a LAN workgroup. The Windows for Workgroups SETUP program guides you through the installation of the program, whether you are using Express Setup or Custom Setup.

If you aren't familiar with computers, use Express Setup, which determines the type of network adapter your computer uses and the associated hardware settings. Express Setup also asks what printer your computer uses and where that printer is connected.

If you are familiar with computers and want to install only part of Windows for Workgroups or make changes during installation, use Custom Setup. Custom Setup enables you to add printers and select hardware that may be different from what the SETUP program detects. If your hard disk is short on available storage, use Custom Setup to install parts of Windows for Workgroups rather than the full Windows and all accessories. To add Windows features or accessories that you didn't install initially, you can run Custom Setup at any time.

If you have Windows 3.0 or 3.1 installed already, you can install Windows for Workgroups over the existing Windows version. This type of installation preserves your current settings, application groups, and custom drivers. Installation takes about 25 to 30 minutes. If you already have a networking system using Windows, focus on the section "Installing Windows for Workgroups Using SETUP."

Before You Continue ...

You need to be familiar with terms that are used throughout this appendix. A *workgroup* is a group of PCs that share information and other resources like printers and disk storage on a local area network (LAN). A *LAN* consists of nodes, network adapters, and a communication medium, such as cables. A *node* is a computer that can process its own information (a microcomputer). The *network adapter* is the device that converts processed information from the node and transmits this information to the other nodes in the LAN. The *communication medium*, such as wire and cables, provides a communication path.

If you are unfamiliar with these terms, read Chapters 1 and 2 before starting installation. For more general information about networks, read *Introduction to Networking*, published by Que Corporation.

Understanding Your Hardware and Software Needs

Because Windows for Workgroups is a LAN-based system, its operation depends on proper hardware and software installation. The hardware consists of the PC on which you load Windows for Workgroups, the network adapters used to communicate with other PCs in your workgroup, and the cables. Your PC requires a local operating system (such as MS-DOS 5.0).

Before you install Windows for Workgroups, be sure that your PC and the operating system are prepared properly. The hardware and operating system software must meet the following minimum requirements:

■ A computer with an Intel 80286 processor or compatible

■ 1M or more of RAM on a 286-based PC or 2M or more for 386 or 486 PCs. At least 4M of RAM is recommended. The more RAM you have, the better Windows for Workgroups will perform.

■ A Windows-supported graphics adapter card (usually VGA or EGA)

- 5M to 10M of available hard disk storage
- A 1.2M or 1.44M floppy disk drive
- DOS 3.1 or higher (DOS 5.0 provides the best performance)
- One of the following network adapters:

  3Com EtherLink 16
  3Com EtherLink II or IITP (8- or 16-bit)
  3Com EtherLink III
  3Com EtherLink Plus
  3Com EtherLink/MC
  3Com TokenLink
  Advanced Micro Devices AM2100/PCnet
  Amplicard AC 210/AT
  Amplicard AC 210/XT
  ARCnet compatible
  Artisoft AE-1
  Artisoft AE-2 (MCA) or AE-3 (MCA)
  Artisoft AE-2 or AE-3
  Cabletron E2000 Series DNI
  Cabletron E2100 Series DNI
  DCA 10M
  DCA 10M fiber optic
  DCA 10M MCA
  DCA 10M twisted pair
  DEC DEPCA
  DEC EE101 (built-in)
  DEC EtherWorks LC
  DEC EtherWorks LC/TP
  DEC EtherWorks LC/TP_BNC
  DEC EtherWorks MC
  DEC EtherWorks MC/TP
  DEC EtherWorks MC/TP_BNC
  DEC EtherWorks Turbo
  DEC EtherWorks Turbo/TP
  DEC EtherWorks Turbo/TP_BNC
  DECpc 433 (built-in)
  Everex SpeedLink/PC16 (EV2027)
  Hewlett-Packard PC LAN adapter/8 TL (HP27250)
  Hewlett-Packard PC LAN adapter/8 TP (HP27245)
  Hewlett-Packard PC LAN adapter/16 TP (HP27247A)
  IBM Token Ring (all types)
  Intel EtherExpress 16 or 16TP

Intel TokenExpress 16/4
Intel TokenExpress EISA 16/4
Intel TokenExpress MCA 16/4
National Semiconductor AT/LANTIC EtherNODE 16-AT3
National Semiconductor EtherNODE *16AT
NCR Token-Ring 16/4 Mbps ISA
NCR Token-Ring 16/4 Mbps MCA
NCR Token-Ring 4 Mbps ISA
NE1000 compatible
NE2000 compatible
Novell/Anthem NE/2
Novell/Anthem NE1000
Novell/Anthem NE1500T
Novell/Anthem NE2000
Novell/Anthem NE2100
Olicom 16/4 Token Ring
Proteon ISA Token Ring (1340)
Proteon ISA Token Ring (1342)
Proteon ISA Token Ring (1346)
Proteon ISA Token Ring (1347)
Proteon MCA Token Ring (1840)
Proteon Token Ring (P1390)
Proteon Token Ring (P1392)
Pure Data PD1508+ (ARCnet)
Pure Data PD1516+ (ARCnet)
Pure Data PD19025-32 (token ring)
Pure Data PDuC9025 (token ring)
Racal NI6510
RadiSys EXM-10
SMC (WD) EtherCard (all types except 8013/A)
SMC (WD) EtherCard PLUS (WD/8003E)
SMC (WD) EtherCard PLUS 10T (WD/8003W)
SMC (WD) EtherCard PLUS 10T/A (MCA) (WD 8003W/A)
SMC (WD) EtherCard PLUS 16 with boot ROM socket
   (WD/8013EBT)
SMC (WD) EtherCard PLUS Elite (WD/8003EP)
SMC (WD) EtherCard PLUS Elite 16 (WD/8013EP)
SMC (WD) EtherCard PLUS Elite 16 Combo
   (WD/8013EW or 8013EWC)
SMC (WD) EtherCard PLUS Elite 16T (WD/8013W)
SMC (WD) EtherCard PLUS TP (WD/8003WT)
SMC (WD) EtherCard PLUS with boot ROM socket
   (WD/8003EB or WD/8003EBT)

SMC (WD) EtherCard PLUS/A (MCA) (WD 8003E/A or
  8003ET/A)
SMC (WD) StarCard PLUS (WD/8003S)
SMC (WD) StarCard PLUS with on-board hub
  (WD/8003SH)
SMC (WD) StarCard PLUS/A (MCA) (WD 8003ST/A)
SMC 3000 Series
SMC ARCnet PC100, PC200
SMC ARCnet PC110, PC210, PS110, PS210, PC250
SMC ARCnet PC120, PC220, PC260
SMC ARCnet PC130/E
SMC ARCnet PC220/120
SMC ARCnet PC270/E
SMC ARCnet PC600W, PC650W
SMC ARCnetPC
Thomas Conrad (all types)
Xircom Pocket EtherNet I
Xircom Pocket EtherNet II
Zenith Z-Note

You can use other optional equipment in conjunction with your
workgroup environment. Windows for Workgroups supports the
following optional equipment:

- One or more printers or plotters

- A mouse (highly recommended)

- A modem

- Other major networks, such as NetWare, 3Com, LANtastic,
  Vines, LAN Manager, and LAN Server

Windows for Workgroups has two different modes: Standard and
386 Enhanced. Standard mode enables you to switch among multiple applications, but DOS applications that aren't active don't
continue to run. Standard mode suspends these inactive applications until they are selected again. Enhanced mode enables you to
run multiple applications and enables DOS applications to continue to run in the background. Both modes enable Windows
applications to run in the background.

Standand mode is used in 286 and 386 computers with less than
2M of memory. Enhanced mode is used in 386 computers with
more than 2M of memory. The computer and memory requirements for these modes are as follows:

Hardware	Standard Mode	Enhanced Mode
Processor	286 or higher	386 or higher
Memory	1M (640K conventional and 256K extended); more is better	2M (640K conventional and 1024K extended); more is better
Storage	5M to 9M hard disk	5M to 10.5M hard disk

MS-DOS 5.0 is currently the best operating system to use with Windows for Workgroups because it has been tested heavily with Windows for Workgroups. Other local operating system options, such as DR DOS 6.0, are available. If you install Windows for Workgroups on a workstation that uses DR DOS, consult the documentation provided by Digital Research for installation procedures.

When you begin to install Windows for Workgroups, the SETUP program determines what computer equipment you have installed and tries to determine the manufacturer and type. SETUP is generally correct, but if you want to confirm or make changes to the list, use Custom Setup.

Before you start installation, make a list of the following information:

- The drive and directory that you want to contain Windows for Workgroups

- Manufacturer and model number of your computer. If you cannot determine your exact computer model, and your computer has an MCA (Micro Channel Architecture) bus, choose an equivalent IBM PS/2 model. If your computer has an ISA (Industry Standard Architecture) bus, choose an equivalent COMPAQ model. Most computers have an ISA bus.

- Type of display adapter

- Manufacturer and model of your printer

- The parallel port (LPT1 or LPT2) or serial port (COM1 or COM2) to which your printer is connected. If your printer uses a COM port, include that port's settings (baud rate, number of bits, stop bits, and parity).

- Mouse manufacturer and type (if you have a mouse)

- Type of keyboard

- Network adapter manufacturer and type. Also include the adapter's settings (IRQ, base I/O port address, and base memory address). If your adapter uses direct memory access (DMA), you need to know the level.

- Type and version of any other major network your computer is on

The Windows for Workgroups SETUP program asks you for this information during the installation process. If you are uncertain of the manufacturer or type of equipment you use, check your manuals or sales receipts, or call your dealer or corporate PC support line.

TIP	You need 5M to 10M of available storage on your hard disk.

Setting Up a Sample Configuration

This appendix uses a sample network to help you understand better the process of creating a LAN using Windows for Workgroups. The sample network uses Intel 486-based microcomputers and Novell/Anthem NE2000 network adapters. Each computer has 200M of hard disk storage and 8M of random-access memory (RAM). Each computer uses a serial port (COM1), a parallel port (LPT1), a SuperVGA video adapter, a Microsoft serial mouse, and MS-DOS Version 5.0.

The communication medium is thin EtherNet (IEEE/10Base2). Thin EtherNet uses cable type RG-58/U, a 50-ohm coaxial cable, which is one of the simplest cabling systems available.

Preparing the LAN

You can break the preparation process into three major steps:

1. Install and configure the network adapter in your computer.

2. Connect the cabling system.

3. Test communications on your LAN.

The next three sections walk you through each step. In the sample configuration, you install a Novell/Anthem NE2000, connect the cabling between all computers in the workgroup, and then test the cabling system. This process guarantees that information can be sent between all nodes in your workgroup.

Configuring the Network Adapter

The configuration of your network adapter is a very important part of the installation process. The network adapter will not work or will work sporadically if it's incorrectly configured.

Ensuring that system components and devices work together without some parts interfering with the proper function of others is vital to the overall performance of your computer system. For any computer board to be useful, it must be capable of communicating data and other system signals with the microprocessor and other system components. Three fundamental settings for the network adapter to communicate with the CPU are as follows:

- Interrupts (IRQs)

- Memory addresses

- Input/output addresses

> **NOTE** Some adapters use additional settings, including cable type and node address.

Your network adapter's documentation should tell you which settings to be concerned with. The Novell/Anthem NE2000 uses interrupts and input/output address, for example. Its default settings are IRQ3 and base I/O address 300 hex.

Before you try to install a network adapter in your system, determine the actual settings your computer already uses. Refer to your computer's documentation, or run some type of diagnostic software that tests the computer system to see what settings are being used. Diagnostic software you can use includes Checkit, Manifest, and MSD. (MSD, or Microsoft Diagnostics, comes with Windows for Workgroups and Windows 3.1.)

Document the settings your computer system uses. The documentation for the sample workstation looks like this:

	IRQ	*Base I/O*	*Base Memory*
AT type controller	14	1F0-1F8 or 170-177	-
SuperVGA adapter	2	3C0-3CF	A0000-1FFFE
Serial port COM1	4	3F8-3FF	-
Parallel port LPT1	7	378-37A	-

Notice the use of an address range from 0 through F. Most addresses used in a computer are in hexadecimal. Hexadecimal uses 16 digits, 0 through F; 0 through 9 are just like decimal 0 through 9, whereas A stands for 10, B stands for 11, and so on through F, which stands for "15."

You can change settings on your network adapter card in two ways:

■ Change switches or jumpers located on the adapter itself.

■ Use the diagnostic/setup program that accompanies the adapter.

> **NOTE** Consult the documentation that came with your adapter to determine which settings you require and which method you use to make the changes. Remember that you cannot share IRQs, base memory addresses, and input/output addresses. Most network adapters use an IRQ and an I/O address. Certain adapters also need a base memory address, node address, and cable type.

Setting Interrupts

An *interrupt* is a signal sent from a hardware device to the CPU, telling the CPU that the device requires immediate attention. The device that wants the CPU's attention sends the interrupt signal over a special data line called the *interrupt request line* (IRQ).

When the CPU receives the interrupt signal, it stops what it's doing and immediately retrieves from memory special program instructions. The CPU performs the functions dictated by the special instructions. After the CPU completes the interrupt service routine, it returns to what it was doing before it received the interrupt.

The CPU knows which device sent the interrupt signal, because each expansion board and device has its own dedicated IRQ line. You must set the interrupt line on the adapter board when you install it in your computer. If the setting you choose has the same interrupt as another board (or port, such as the parallel or serial port), one of the devices will malfunction.

Duplicate interrupt settings are known as *interrupt conflicts*. You can tell whether an interrupt conflict occurs when your computer refuses to boot, or when it beeps at you when you turn on the power. Take out the adapter card, set it to another interrupt, and reinstall it in the computer. Be sure to write down the setting you finally choose, or run the diagnostic software again.

Setting Memory Addresses

The second way in which an expansion board communicates is through the *memory address*. This address refers to a range of computer memory to which the device has exclusive rights. As in the IRQ, if two boards try to write to and read from the same memory location, information and instructions will become jumbled quickly.

Setting I/O Addresses

The third way in which an adapter board communicates with the CPU is through the *I/O address*. The I/O address, also called the *I/O port*, is for internal communication between the CPU and the hardware device. You must assign each device its own I/O port address.

Using Other Settings

Many network adapters allow different types of cable connections. Each standard EtherNet adapter, for example, has a BNC connector and a 15-pin DIX connector. You must select the proper connection for your network.

Each network adapter has a *node address*, which is a number that identifies each adapter on the LAN. This address must be different from all other adapters on the same physical cabling segment. EtherNet and token ring manufacturers preset the node address on the adapter. Other types of network adapters, such as ARCnet, require you to set the unique node address yourself.

Changing the Adapter Settings

After you determine the settings required for your network card, you must determine how to change the settings on the card. Generally, you can change the settings in three ways:

- DIP switches

- Jumpers and jumper blocks

- Software configuration

Many manufacturers use Dual In-line Package (DIP) switches to configure adapters. Each switch is ON or OFF. (In some cases, the manufacturer marks OPEN or CLOSED, or 0 or 1.) Two main types of DIP switches exist: rocker and slide. On a rocker switch, press the side you want to select. To set a slide switch, move the switch to the proper side.

Some manufacturers of network adapters use jumpers and jumper blocks to configure their products. Jumpers are a series of pins sticking out of the board. Jumper blocks control contact between two pins. To make contact between the two pins, install a jumper block. To open the contact, remove the jumper block. It isn't unusual to find jumpers and DIP switches on the same board.

Some boards enable you to change settings through software utilities rather than by jumpers or switches. MCA adapters and most EISA adapters use this software configuration technique. Consult your documentation to determine the proper setup procedures for this type of adapter.

Installing the Network Adapter

After you change the settings on your network adapter as noted in the preceding section, you are ready to install the network adapter into your computer. Follow these steps:

1. Remove the computer cover to expose the main system board (motherboard). For details on removing the cover, consult the documentation provided with your system.

2. Remove the screws holding one of the empty slot cover plates and remove the plate.

3. Place the network adapter in the slot where you removed the slot cover plate. Make sure that the adapter is seated firmly in the motherboard, and then replace the screw securing the adapter into the system.

CAUTION

Be careful not to bump the switches or jumpers on your network adapter as you install it in the system. If you bump the switches, the network adapter or other type of adapter you are installing will not function.

---

4. Attach the cable to the adapter card so that the computer is part of the network, as discussed in the next section.

5. Before you replace the cover, test the adapter for proper operation. Many computer manufacturers provide system diagnostics that test for any conflicts in base memory, IRQs, or I/O addresses. If diagnostics are provided, test the network adapter operation.

6. After the adapter is functioning properly, replace the cover.

Attaching the Cables

After you place the network adapter in the computer, you are ready to attach the cable to the adapter and test the configuration. Depending on the topology of the network, you may need more than just a cable.

Topology is another word for a wiring scheme. Three main topologies are used in LANs today: bus, ring, and star. In a bus, the cable is daisy-chained from computer to computer. When one computer sends data, all computers on the bus can receive it. In a ring, the computers are wired together one to another, and the beginning of the ring is joined to the end. In a star, all computers are wired to a central device such as a hub or concentrator. The hubs or concentrators are themselves wired together to build the network. Table A.1 lists network adapters and their topologies.

Table A.1 Network Adapters and Topologies

Network Adapter	Topology Used
10Base5 EtherNet	Uses a bus with a 15-pin connector on the network adapter, an external transceiver, and thick coaxial cable
10Base2 EtherNet	Uses a bus topology. Thin EtherNet cable (RG-58) can connect to an EtherNet adapter using the round BNC connector on the adapter card. You need to attach the base of a T connector to the BNC connector on the card. The left and right connectors on the T connector are attached to the BNC connectors of thin cable.
10BaseT EtherNet	Uses a star-bus topology. All network adapters are wired to a concentrator or hub using twisted-pair wire. In this way, 10BaseT resembles a star. When one computer sends out data, all computers can receive the data. In this way, 10BaseT resembles a bus.
Coaxial ARCnet	Uses hubs and RG-62 coaxial cable and is wired in a star fashion. Because all computers can receive data when any of them send data, this type of wiring also resembles a bus.
Twisted-pair ARCnet	Uses a bus topology. Each twisted-pair ARCnet card has input and output jacks, and can be daisy-chained in a bus. You shouldn't have more than 10 twisted-pair ARCnet cards without using an active hub to improve the strength of the signal.
Token ring	Used with a MAU, which is wired in a ring fashion. Because all computers are connected to the MAU, it also resembles a star.

The following list discusses what you need to consider for different topologies:

- *Cabling.* Three types of cable exist: twisted pair, coaxial, and fiber optic.

- *T connector.* This device, which gets its name from its shape, serves as a tap into a long single cable segment. The base of the T connects directly to the network adapter. The left and right top portions of the T connect to the network cable.

- *Terminator.* This device ends a communication signal. A terminator absorbs signals that reach the end of the cable. Such signals can cause noise on the cable. All networks require termination, but only thin EtherNet and ARCnet passive hubs require you to attach physical terminator devices. All other networks build the termination into the network adapters or the other cabling components.

- *External transceiver.* This device amplifies the signal and attaches an EtherNet network adapter to a thick coaxial bus. Thick cable is of type RG-8 or RG-11. The transceiver has a tap on one side that bolts down onto the thick cable. On the other side, a "drop cable" extends to the network adapter.

- *Passive hub.* This simple, inexpensive star-wired coaxial device splits communication signals on one line into many additional lines.

- *Active hub.* This hub provides the same star-wired coaxial capabilities as a passive hub with the addition of signal boosting. This type of hub increases the distance the network can cover.

- *Concentrator.* This device provides the same basic function as a hub but is designed for twisted-pair cabling. A concentrator adds communication management and device management. Concentrators can be programmed to control data flow and prevent congestion, optimizing the efficiency of your LAN.

- *Multistation Access Unit (MAU or MSAU).* Used with token ring, this device provides a data path from computer to computer that maintains the operation of the LAN, even when one workstation on the LAN isn't operating.

- *Wiring closet.* Used with any wiring scheme, the wiring closet is the place where hubs, concentrators, and MAUs are located.

A

> **NOTE** If a thin coaxial EtherNet network is missing a termina-
> tor, the signals sent by the EtherNet adapters reach
> the end of the cable and reflect back, thus causing
> "noise" on the communication line. In this situation,
> a good signal cannot be sent. Using terminators
> prevents this problem.
>
> In bus topology networks, you must place terminators
> on the end of cable segments. In star networks, termi-
> nation is designed in the adapter card. For details,
> consult the documentation provided with your network
> adapter.

Testing LAN Communications

You should test your LAN communications before you install Windows for Workgroups on your computer system. This testing helps
eliminate problems in LAN communications after Windows for
Workgroups is installed.

If you use products following the Institute of Electrical and Electronics Engineers (IEEE) specification, the manufacturer provides
diagnostic software. Some examples of IEEE standards are IEEE
802.3 (which closely resembles EtherNet) and IEEE 802.5 (which
resembles IBM Token Ring). The diagnostic software provided
with these adapters tests the network adapter circuitry and cabling,
ensuring that your network adapters and cabling system are functioning properly before you install Windows for Workgroups.

If your network adapter doesn't follow IEEE specifications, contact
your vendor to acquire network diagnostic software for your
adapter.

Configuring the Sample Workgroup

You now have a good understanding of what you must do to install the hardware components in your workgroup. Now you are
ready to complete each step using the sample workstation:

1. Test each computer, or read the documentation to determine the settings of the components already installed.

2. Document the current settings of each workstation. In the example, each workstation now has components using the following settings:

	IRQ	Base I/O	Base Memory
AT type controller	14	1F0-1F8	-
		170-177	-
SuperVGA adapter	2	3C0-3CF	A0000-1FFFE
COM1 serial port	4	3F8-3FF	-
LPT1 parallel port	7	378-37A	-

> **NOTE** The AT type controller is the standard hard/floppy disk controller used in many systems. SCSI controllers are also a favorite option for installing hard disks in computers. SCSI disk drives provide the best performance available in the industry today.

3. Using the documentation that came with the Novell/Anthem NE2000 network adapter, determine which settings work with the configuration. You should find that the default setting will work. In the example, the default settings for the NE2000 are IRQ3, base I/O address 300h.

4. Follow the procedures in the earlier section "Installing the Network Adapter."

5. The sample network is using thin EtherNet (IEEE 802.3/10Base2) cabling. Connect a T connector to the BNC connector on the back of the network adapter. Then connect RG-58 coaxial cable to each end of the T.

6. Repeat steps 4 and 5 until all network adapters are installed.

7. The cable should be connected from one computer to another in a series. On one end, place a 50-ohm terminator. On the other end, place a 50-ohm grounding terminator. Connect the grounding wire from the grounding terminator to the case of the computer or, preferably, to the center screw of the nearest electrical socket.

8. If available, run the diagnostic software to determine whether each network adapter performs properly and whether information can be sent through all segments of the cabling.

The sample workstation is now ready for you to install Windows for Workgroups.

Installing Windows for Workgroups Using SETUP

After you make a list of your equipment and install and test your LAN, you are ready to install Windows for Workgroups. The following sections provide the steps to install Windows for Workgroups properly.

Preparing for Installation

Before you install Windows, prepare for installation by completing the following optional steps:

1. To protect your original disks from accidental changes, copy them onto a set of backup disks. Then write-protect the original disks and store them in a separate location.

2. Check your disk drive by typing **CHKDSK/f** at the DOS prompt. The /f option tells CHKDSK to search for lost clusters on the disk. If any lost clusters are found, type **y** (for yes) to collect and store them.

3. Run a disk defragmenting or disk optimization application, if you have one. This step makes Windows run faster. Programs such as Stacker (Version 2.0) provide disk defragmentation and optimization that work with Windows for Workgroups.

4. If you plan to use a memory manager such as QEMM386, 386Max, or Blue Max, be aware of specific setting requirements. The files README.WRI and SETUP.TXT in the WINDOWS directory outline these requirements. Read these files before you use a memory manager. To do so, remark out the DEVICE= line referring to your memory manager in your CONFIG.SYS file before you install Windows. After you read the files, you can make the adjustments necessary to use your memory manager.

Running SETUP

To install Windows for Workgroups, follow these steps:

1. Turn on or reset your computer system and return to a DOS prompt. If your computer starts an application automatically on bootup, exit the application and return to a DOS prompt.

2. Insert Disk 1 of the Windows for Workgroups installation disks into your floppy disk drive and then switch to that drive.

3. Type **setup** and press Enter.

4. The first screen that appears is a welcome screen (see fig. A.1). On this screen, you can select F1 (Help) to learn more about the SETUP program, Enter to continue SETUP, or F3 (Exit) to exit SETUP without installing.

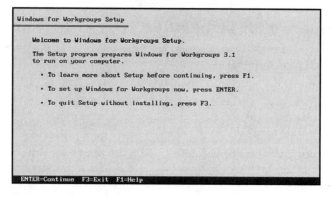

FIG. A.1   *The Welcome screen.*

If you press Enter to continue the installation, you are given two setup options: Express Setup or Custom Setup (see fig. A.2). If you aren't familiar with Windows for Workgroups or with computers, choose Express Setup and continue with the next section. If you want to do customized setup, see the section "Installing Windows for Workgroups Using Custom Setup" later in this appendix.

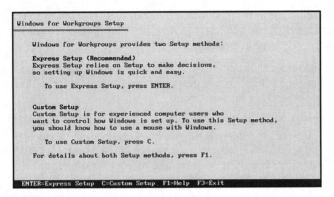

FIG. A.2   *Selecting the installation type.*

Controlling the Setup Options

Express Setup and Custom Setup begin with a series of DOS menus that require the keyboard rather than the mouse. The keystrokes are listed at the bottom of the screen. The DOS part of the installation process appears in two colors, and characters appear as they do at the DOS prompt. After the initial setup software is installed, the SETUP program switches to Windows screens. At that point, you can use normal Windows keystrokes or mouse controls.

At almost any time during the installation, you can get Help by pressing F1. To exit from a Help window during the DOS part of the installation process, press Esc. To exit from a Help window while you are in the Windows portion of SETUP, from the **F**ile menu choose E**x**it.

Installing Windows for Workgroups by Using Express Setup

After you load the SETUP program, you are presented with the option to run Express Setup or Custom Setup. In most cases, you should use Express Setup. If Express Setup doesn't work correctly, you can install or reinstall other items or features of Windows at a later time by running SETUP again (see "Changing the Setup after Installation" later in this appendix).

Express Setup uses settings and hardware configurations that the installation application has determined will work on your system. Follow these steps to run Express Setup:

1. Press Enter to choose Express Setup. You are prompted for a directory in which Windows for Workgroups installs to your system. SETUP assumes the C:\WINDOWS directory. You can accept this directory or change to another directory.

2. If SETUP detects an existing Windows installation, the program asks whether you want to retain the existing setup or create a new windows system (see fig. A.3).

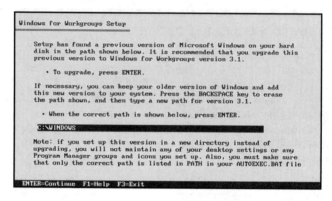

FIG. A.3 *Determining whether to upgrade an existing version.*

If you want to retain your existing Windows installation and install Windows for Workgroups, type a new directory name and then press Enter. To replace your existing Windows installation, simply press Enter. Replacing your Windows installation doesn't affect your program groups or other custom settings that you have made.

3. A screen appears as SETUP copies to the selected directory the files needed to complete the setup.

   SETUP now loads Windows for Workgroups. During this process, SETUP asks you to insert a different disk into the floppy disk drive. From this disk, SETUP loads the proper files onto your computer system.

If Windows for Workgroups doesn't load, consult Appendix B, "Troubleshooting Windows for Workgroups," or the trouble-shooting section in your Microsoft Windows for Workgroups documentation.

The next series of steps pertain to the Windows portion of SETUP. The SETUP program actually loads Windows for Workgroups at this point and runs a Windows version of itself. Follow these steps:

1. At the prompt, provide your name, company, computer name, and workgroup.

   Your company name is optional. "Name" is the name your computer assumes on the network. The workgroup is a name used to refer to a group of computers cabled together on the LAN. Your system sends the computer name to other users within your workgroup. All members of a workgroup must enter the same workgroup name.

2. Choose the Continue option on the bottom of the screen.

3. SETUP asks you to verify the information in the previous dialog. If the information is correct, choose Continue. To make a change, choose Change. Help is also available.

   The SETUP program displays a "percentage complete" dialog as it begins copying files from the Windows for Workgroups disks. SETUP prompts you to change the installation disks many times during this process.

4. After Windows loads into memory, the next dialog enables you to select printers. Use this dialog to install a printer and to specify the port that the printer is attached to.

> **NOTE** If you install Windows for Workgroups on a new computer system, you are asked all the preceding questions. If you install Windows for Workgroups over an existing copy of Windows, you can tell SETUP to keep all your existing settings.

Specifying a New Network Adapter

After you select your printer, Setup determines the network adapter that you have installed in your computer. A dialog displays the adapter that Setup determines is installed. If this adapter is correct, choose **Yes**. SETUP installs the network adapter files and continues. If this adapter is incorrect, choose **No**. Setup displays the Install New Network Adapter dialog, which displays a list of the network adapters for which Windows for Workgroups provides a driver.

From this dialog, select the network adapter installed in your computer to add its driver to your system, and then choose OK. If your network adapter isn't on the list, select Unlisted or Updated Network Adapter. This way, you can install the driver provided by the manufacturer of your network adapter.

After you accept the network adapter that Setup selected or select another network adapter, you see a dialog with the same name as the network adapter you selected. This dialog lists the following adapter settings:

- Interrupt (IRQ)

- Base Input/Output (I/O) Port

- Base Memory Address

Setup tries to determine these settings. If Setup correctly determines the settings, choose OK to continue. If Setup doesn't determine them correctly, you must change the settings, as described in the next section.

Setting Up the Network Adapter

If Setup cannot detect your network adapter's interrupt, base input/output port, or base memory address, you must add the settings yourself. If Windows determines a setting, you see the message (Automatic or Unused). If you must add the settings, use the drop-down list box next to the settings.

Note that in the dialog you can select protocols that you want the network adapter to use by clicking the **P**rotocols button. Protocols are discussed in the next section.

NOTE	You also may see an A**d**vanced button under the P**r**otocols button. For more information, see Chapter 8, "Configuring Workgroups for Windows."

Configuring Other Networks

If you are using other networks with Windows for Workgroups, use the dialog shown in figure A.4 to select the network you are using and to specify that network's settings.

Windows for Workgroups can operate with other network operating systems, such as Novell NetWare. If your workgroup is connected to an existing Novell network, you may want to connect the workstation to the Novell File Server. Select the Novell NetWare option, and then choose the Add button to add the NetWare protocols to this workstation's PROTOCOL.INI file. A *protocol* is a set of rules governing communication. Windows for Workgroups can use more than one set of rules.

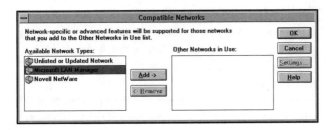

FIG. A.4   *Configuring other networks.*

Setting Up Applications

SETUP searches your hard drive(s) for applications. When it finds applications that it recognizes, it adds them to your Windows for Workgroups.

SETUP lists applications on your system that have the same program file name. You need to choose which application to set up to use with Windows. Choose the proper name, or enter the name you want to use with each application. This dialog appears each time Windows finds a program with the same name.

If you install Windows for Workgroups over an existing Windows version, the current application setup is saved. When you use the Express Setup option, SETUP automatically scans the hard disk for applications. If you upgrade your old version of Windows but don't want to change your existing program groups, use Custom Setup.

The final window that appears during the setup process enables you to run a tutorial about the operations of Windows for Workgroups. Select the Run Tutorial button to use the tutorial. If you don't want to use it, select the Skip Tutorial button.

When you finish, the Exit Windows Setup dialog appears. You can reboot your system or return to DOS. You should reboot your system so that the new Windows for Workgroups environment can load.

Installing Windows for Workgroups by Using Custom Setup

In this section, you complete the options available in Custom Setup. Follow these steps to run Custom Setup:

1. In the screen that prompts you for the setup type to use, press C to choose Custom Setup (refer to fig. A.2).

2. Select the directory in which you want Windows for Workgroups installed on your system. SETUP defaults to C:\WINDOWS. You can accept this default or change it to a directory you select. The screen appears as in figure A.5.

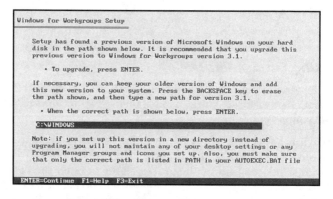

FIG. A.5 *Installing two versions of Windows.*

3. If SETUP detects an existing Windows installation, SETUP asks whether you want to retain the existing setup or create a new Windows system. To keep your older version of Windows, press Esc. A new setup screen appears, enabling you to install a new version of Windows without disturbing the old version (see fig. A.6).

```
Windows for Workgroups Setup

    You have told Setup to upgrade your previous version of Windows to
    Windows for Workgroups 3.1. Please verify this is what you want to do.

        • To have Setup perform an upgrade (recommended), press ENTER. (For
          information about the benefits/effects of upgrading, press F1.)

        • To keep your previous version of Windows and add Windows
          for Workgroups version 3.1 to your system, press ESC.

    Note: If keeping both versions, PATH in your AUTOEXEC.BAT file should
    list only the new version, to avoid running older Windows system
    files. Also, any applications already set up for use with Windows
    must be set up again from this version.




 ENTER=Continue   ESC=Cancel   F1=Help
```

FIG. A.6   *The dialog on upgrading a previous Windows version.*

NOTE   Some applications may not function properly in your new Windows version. If you have available space on your hard drive, you should keep the old version of Windows.

---

4. SETUP scans your system to determine the hardware setup on your computer (see fig. A.7). If the list is correct, press Enter to continue installation. If your list is incorrect or if you want to add items SETUP missed, make the changes here.

```
Windows for Workgroups Setup

    Setup has determined that your system includes the following hardware
    and software components. If your computer appears on the
    Hardware Compatibility List with an asterisk, press F1 for Help.

            Computer:          MS-DOS System
            Display:           VGA
            Mouse:             Microsoft, Z-Nix, or IBM PS/2
            Keyboard:          Enhanced 101 or 102 key US and Non US keyboards
            Keyboard Layout:   US
            Language:          English (American)

            No Changes:        The above list matches my computer.

    If all the items in the list are correct, press ENTER to indicate
    "No Changes." If you want to change any item in the list, press the
    UP or DOWN ARROW key to move the highlight to the item you want to
    change. Then press ENTER to see alternatives for that item.

 ENTER=Continue   F1=Help   F3=Exit
```

FIG. A.7   The System Information Setup screen.

The system information presented on this setup screen must be accurate so that Windows can set up your computer system properly. SETUP tries to select the appropriate setting for you. Most of the time, Windows SETUP is accurate and you don't have to make changes. If any items are incorrect, however, or if your computer model or networking software appears on the Hardware Compatibility List with an asterisk beside it, you must change the information SETUP has displayed for that item.

If you elect to change an item, SETUP displays a list of settings appropriate for that item. Select a new setting and then press Enter. SETUP returns to the System Information screen, which displays your new settings.

5. When all the information on the System Information screen is correct, press Enter to continue with SETUP. The SETUP program now copies the files it needs to complete the setup onto the directory selected previously.

    After the setup files are copied, SETUP loads Windows for Workgroups. If Windows for Workgroups doesn't load, consult Appendix B, "Troubleshooting Windows for Workgroups," or the troubleshooting section in your Microsoft Windows for Workgroups documentation.

    You now move into the graphics-based Windows environment. Use your keyboard and mouse to control information on your screens.

6. SETUP requests information about your networking workgroup. Enter your name, company, computer name, and workgroup. Your company name is optional. "Name" is the name you want your computer to assume on the network. The workgroup is a name used to refer to a group of computers cabled together on the LAN. Your system sends the computer name to other users within your workgroup. All members of a workgroup must enter the same workgroup name.

    After completing this dialog, choose the Continue option on the bottom of the screen.

7. SETUP asks you to verify the information entered on the previous dialog. If the information is correct, choose Continue. If you want to make a change, choose Change. Help is also available.

Using Windows Setup Options

Next, in the Windows Setup Options dialog, you can choose from three optional procedures. These procedures are performed after all basic Windows files are set up on your system. Windows for Workgroups performs all procedures marked with an X in their check box. The available options are as follows:

- Set Up Only Windows Components You Select

- Set Up Printers

- Set Up Application Already on Hard Disk

If you want SETUP to set up all components, remove the X for the selection box next to Set Up Only Windows Components You Select. If you don't want to assign printers, remove the X in the Set Up Printers selection box.

SETUP also can scan your hard disk(s) for applications. This capability can be a good tool if you aren't familiar with Windows operations. To perform this operation, place an X in the selection box.

After you make all selections, choose Continue.

Selecting Windows Components

If you place an X next to Set Up Only Windows Components You Select in the Windows Setup Options dialog, the Windows Components dialog appears. From this dialog, you can select which Windows components to add to your system. This option can be especially useful if you have limited disk space for storing your files. You can select all or certain parts of a component. You may want to set up some Accessories applications, for example, but not others.

If you want the complete component added to your system, place an X in its check box; then choose Continue.

To select specific component files, choose the Files button for the component. Complete the dialog that appears. For help, choose the Help button or press F1 while using the dialog. When you are ready to continue with Setup, choose Continue.

Setting Virtual Memory Options

SETUP creates a swap file on 386 and 486 systems with the information that you provide in the Virtual Memory dialog. Windows for Workgroups uses the swap file to store temporarily data that is taking up space in memory.

Use the Virtual Memory dialog to view or change swap file settings (see fig. A.8). These settings control how your system uses virtual memory. Table A.2 lists the options available in this dialog. To make any changes, choose the Change>> button, which expands the Virtual Memory dialog. To continue, choose the No Change button if you made no changes. If you made changes, choose the Change button.

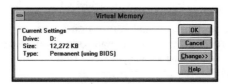

FIG. A.8 *The Virtual Memory dialog.*

Table A.2 Virtual Memory Options

Option	Description
Drive	Lists the local and network disk drives to which you have access. Open the list and select the drive in which you want to save the swap file. The available settings in the Type list and Size box change, depending on whether you choose a local disk or a network drive.
Size	Shows the size you should specify for a permanent swap file to achieve the best performance. Accept the recommended size.
Type	Lists the types of swap files you can create, depending on the drive you have selected. Open the list and select the type of swap file that you want to create. You can choose Temporary, Permanent, or None.

Using a permanent swap file improves the speed of Windows because the swap file is contiguous; accessing it generally takes less time than accessing a noncontiguous, temporary swap file. Because a permanent swap file must be contiguous, you can create a permanent swap file only as large as the largest contiguous free block of space on your hard disk.

Depending on the type of swap file you select, the Maximum Size and Recommended Size values may or may not appear in the dialog. If you choose to create a temporary swap file on a network drive, for example, Maximum Size doesn't appear and Recommended Size changes to Recommended Maximum Size.

NOTE You cannot create a permanent swap file on a network drive.

The SETUP program now begins copying files from the Windows for Workgroups disks. You change disks many times during this process. A dialog showing the percentage of the process completed is displayed.

After Windows loads into memory, you see a dialog in which you select printers. Select the printer(s) of your choice, choosing Install for each printer you select. Choose Continue after you finish installing printers.

Selecting a New Network Adapter

Setup tries to determine the network adapter that you have installed on your computer. Setup displays a dialog, asking whether the program has selected the correct adapter. Choose Yes in the dialog if the selection is correct.

If Setup selects the wrong network adapter, choose No. The dialog in figure A.9 appears, listing the network adapters for which Windows for Workgroups provides a driver. Choose the network adapter installed in your computer to add its driver to your system and then choose Continue. To install an unlisted network adapter, choose Unlisted or Updated Network Adapter. This choice enables you to install a driver provided by the manufacturer of the network adapter.

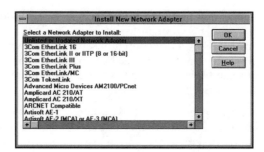

FIG. A.9 *The Install New Network Adapter dialog.*

The next dialog displays the name of the network adapter you selected and the adapter's interrupt (IRQ), base I/O port, and base
memory address. If the driver for the network adapter requires additional settings to work properly, the dialog shows drop-down list
boxes next to the respective settings. In the dialog, specify the settings as described in the manual for your network adapter. For the
example, the network adapter is a Novell/Anthem NE2000 and
should be set to IRQ3 and base I/O address 300h.

Changing the Network Adapter

You can use the Network Adapter dialog to specify the settings of
your network adapter. These settings shouldn't conflict with the
settings used by other devices installed in your computer. If your
network adapter uses built-in settings, or settings set by the driver,
Automatic or Not in Use appears next to the option. You cannot
change these settings. This option is the same for Custom and
Express setups.

Configuring Compatible Networks

As in Express Setup, if you use other networks with Windows for
Workgroups, you can use the Compatible Networks dialog to select the network you are using and to specify its settings. To access
the Compatible Networks dialog, use the Protocols button.

Windows for Workgroups can operate with other network operating systems such as Novell NetWare. If your workgroup is connected to an existing Novell network, you may want to connect the
workstation to the Novell File Server. Select the Novell NetWare
option and then choose the Add button.

After you finish making all the settings for your network adapter, choose Continue to continue the installation.

Modifying Your System Files

The Modify Configuration Files dialog enables you to specify how changes are to be made in your CONFIG.SYS and AUTOEXEC.BAT files. These changes are necessary for Windows for Workgroups to function optimally on your computer.

SETUP can make all changes for you. For SETUP to make all the necessary changes, leave the first options selected and choose the Continue button. SETUP saves old system files as AUTOEXEC.OLD and CONFIG.OLD.

You can review and edit changes in your configuration files before SETUP makes changes. If you select the Review and Edit Changes option, SETUP copies your AUTOEXEC.BAT and CONFIG.SYS files and makes changes to the copies. SETUP displays the proposed new file and your original system files so that you can review the changes and make any further revisions yourself.

SETUP creates backup copies of your original system files and saves the proposed new files as your CONFIG.SYS and AUTOEXEC.BAT files. Backup files are saved as CONFIG.OLD and AUTOEXEC.OLD in the directory where the original files were located.

Running Windows for Workgroups after Installation

After you install Windows for Workgroups and reboot, you can start Windows from the DOS prompt by typing **WIN** and pressing Enter. Windows starts in the most efficient mode for your processor and memory configuration.

> **NOTE** Windows has two modes of operation: Standard and 386 Enhanced. To enable Windows for Workgroups to start in Standard mode, type **WIN /S**. To start in 386 Enhanced mode, type **WIN /3**.

The first dialog that appears prompts you for a logon name. Enter the name that you want to use in the workgroup, and then enter the proper password. The first time you enter Windows for Workgroups, there is no password. You must enter a logon name. The password is optional.

If the screen goes blank when you start Windows, you have installed Windows with an incorrect graphics adapter. To fix this problem, find out what kind of graphics adapter you have (you may need to call the manufacturer) and repeat the installation. Turn off and restart your computer and repeat the installation process, specifying a different graphics adapter.

CAUTION

Don't run CHKDSK/f or programs such as Stacker while Windows is running. These programs may damage Windows. If CHKDSK/f finds bad blocks within the virtual memory file and "repairs" it, Windows has difficulty exiting properly. As a result, damage may occur to the current Windows setup, making it impossible to install Windows for Workgroups over the current version of Windows.

TIP | If you have any difficulty running Windows, try reading through the text file SETUP.TXT or the Windows Write file README.WRI, located in the Windows 3.1 directory. These files contain additional information about Windows for Workgroups that wasn't available at the time the program documentation went to press. You may find many useful tips and tricks in these files.

Changing the Setup after Installation

After Windows for Workgroups is operating correctly, you can make changes without reinstalling the entire application. The SETUP program is located in Program Manager's Main group.

If Windows for Workgroups or a Windows application doesn't operate correctly after the installation is changed, check the Windows Setup dialog to see whether you have the correct settings. Return to the original settings, if necessary, or reinstall Windows for Workgroups, if appropriate.

To change the setup of the display, keyboard, mouse, or network after Windows is installed, follow these steps:

1. From Program Manager's Main group, choose the Windows Setup icon. The Windows Setup dialog appears.

2. From the Options menu, choose Change System Settings. From the Change System Settings dialog, you can change installation settings without reinstalling Windows for Workgroups.

3. After you finish making the changes, choose OK.

4. If a special driver is required, you may be asked to insert one of the original Windows disks or a disk sent by the manufacturer of your display, keyboard, mouse, or network adapter.

5. After the new setup is created, you must restart Windows for the changes to take effect. You can restart Windows or return to DOS.

You also can make changes in your network configuration by using the configuration options discussed in Chapter 8.

Troubleshooting Windows for Workgroups

Troubleshooting is the process of determining a problem and then taking action to correct it. Even the best troubleshooters, however, can fall into common traps that can cost time and money. Taking corrective action before confirming the problem is one of many common traps.

This appendix can help you avoid many problems a beginning network troubleshooter encounters. Although you will not become a superstar troubleshooter overnight, you can become a good troubleshooter with little or no experience. In this appendix you learn the process of troubleshooting as well as detailed information about specific problems and their proper solutions. You can apply the troubleshooting process described to *any* network-related problem.

Understanding the Troubleshooting Technique

Many times, the difficulty in troubleshooting lies in *isolating* the networking problem. You take different actions but none solve the problem. You call in technicians, who quickly indicate that they know what the problem is and take action to correct it. Soon after they leave, the problem reappears. Each troubleshooter had an answer, but the corrected "problem" wasn't the cause of the malfunction.

The first rule in troubleshooting is to verify the problem before taking action to correct it. The best way to verify a problem is to re-create it. If the problem happens each time the same series of events occur, re-creating the problem is easy. However, if the problem you are diagnosing does not occur each time, you need to try to vary the series of events.

Before having the problem corrected, you need to isolate the problem to the component and subcomponent level. In other words, take the problem from the big picture into smaller pictures. Then you can take corrective action to fix the problem. You can break this process into seven steps:

1. Determine the troubleshooting process to use.

2. Obtain physical specifications and network layout.

3. Isolate the problem.

4. Form a theory.

5. Test your theory.

6. Take the proper corrective action.

7. Document the actions taken.

Each step is important. If you complete each step, identifying the problem becomes easier.

Isolating Components in Windows for Workgroups

In a LAN, no single point of failure exists. Because a network-related problem can stem from various sources, not just from a computer or a network adapter, this appendix uses the more general terms *components* and *subcomponents* rather than specific items such as computers and network adapters.

Any major component, its subcomponents, and support components can cause problems on the LAN. Major components of a network include the computers, bridges, routers, software, and other network devices such as file servers, shared modems, and fax servers. Each major component contains subcomponents, such as network adapters, disk controllers, video adapters, and video monitors. Supporting components include the network cabling, hubs, concentrators, T connectors, and terminators.

The major hardware communication components in a LAN are as follows:

■ *PCs.* LANs use multiple PCs to process information. The actual data processing is performed in each PC on the LAN. This concept is known as *distributed processing*.

■ *Network adapters.* To enable the PCs to communicate, you need a network adapter in each workstation. Without a network adapter, a PC cannot share information with other PCs in the workgroup.

■ *Cables.* Network adapter cables can cause the most common problems because LAN users can twist, stretch, bend, and kink cables. You will spend a great deal of time repairing problems with the cables. To make repairs as easy as possible, you should document the location and connection information for the cabling.

Hardware cannot function without a software device driver to activate. The LAN doesn't actually communicate hardware to hardware, but rather the LAN communicates software to software. Without software device drivers, Windows for Workgroups doesn't talk with other computers.

You must use the proper device driver for the hardware being used. In most cases, you need to make certain that the software settings match the hardware settings. You need the following software components:

■ *Network adapter device driver.* This device driver turns the network adapter on and connects to the communication path.

■ *Protocol device driver.* Each network has a set of rules that control the flow of information on the LAN. The protocol device driver controls how data is placed on and removed from the LAN. Without this driver, Windows for Workgroups cannot access the information in the communication path.

■ *Windows for Workgroups.* The final component needed to complete the network is Windows for Workgroups itself. Software used includes device drivers and protocol device drivers software to communicate with other workgroup stations using Windows for Workgroups.

B

Determine the Troubleshooting Process

If the Windows for Workgroups network you are preparing to troubleshoot has been set up properly, the first step—determining the process to use—may involve asking only a few questions. The purpose of the questions is to narrow the problem until you have solved it. Based on the user's answers to your questions and running additional tests yourself, you should be able to form a theory of what is causing the problem. Also ask questions that may result in evidence to support or drop the theory.

First, you should determine whether changes have been made recently, because most problems happen after a change has been made in the network. Start with the person in charge of the overall network. He or she should know whether any major changes—such as the addition of workgroup stations, application upgrades, or hardware modifications—have been made. Next, ask the person using the workstation whether he or she has made any changes. You also can use the Microsoft Diagnostics application (MSG.EXE) to determine the current setup of the workstation.

If you manage the network, get the documentation on the network setup. Compare the workstation setup with the documentation to determine whether any changes have been made.

After you isolate any changes, ask the user to try to re-create the problem. If you are looking for an intermittent problem, see whether the user can re-create it.

The following sections list the type of information needed to troubleshoot the Windows for Workgroups network properly.

PC Information

When you gather information about the PCs, focus on the following information:

- *Manufacturer information.* Determine the manufacturer and the type of computer. The network documentation should include the manufacturer's technical support phone number.

  Before you call the manufacturer, make certain that you have the name of the dealer, the system type, and the serial numbers. Many manufacturers have a bulletin board system (BBS) that you can access (if you have a modem) with the

Windows for Workgroups Terminal program. BBS systems have the latest drivers, which may be what you need to get the system up and running properly. (For more information about the Windows Terminal program, see *Using Windows 3.1*, Special Edition, published by Que Corporation.)

■ *Dealer information.* Document the name, address, and phone number of the dealer. Also document information pertaining to the purchase: the amount, purchase order number, dealer invoice number, and date of purchase.

You also should document the name and phone numbers of the dealer technician who is supporting the network. You should share this information with others in the workgroup. If you are unavailable when a problem occurs, users should know who to call for support.

■ *Architecture.* Determine the computer's architecture, such as Industry Standard Architecture (ISA), Extended Industry Standard Architecture (EISA), and Micro Channel Architecture (MCA). This information and the manufacturer's hardware service manuals can help you determine whether the hardware is configured properly.

■ *Configuration parameters.* The documentation also should include the configuration parameters of each internal component in the system: the base memory address, base I/O address, interrupt request (IRQ) line, and direct memory access (DMA) line. Make certain that no two internal components in a computer system are using the same parameters.

■ *Microprocessor.* The type of microcomputer processor is also important. Windows for Workgroups supports Intel microcomputers and their clones. For best performance, use an Intel 80386 or 80486 microprocessor.

NOTE	An Intel 80286-based system runs Windows for Workgroups only in Standard mode. An Intel 80386- or 80486-based system runs Windows for Workgroups in Standard and Enhanced mode. For more information on the operating modes of Windows for Workgroups, see Appendix A, "Installing Windows for Workgroups."

■ *Serial numbers.* Document the serial number for the CPU and any other system components, including the video monitor.

■ *Video monitor and adapter manufacturer and type.* Document the video monitor and adapter manufacturer and type.

■ *Amount of RAM.* Document the amount of RAM in each workstation on the Windows for Workgroups network. If a PC has less than 2M, Windows for Workgroups runs only in Standard mode. Otherwise, Windows for Workgroups runs in Enhanced mode.

Network Adapter Information

When gathering information about the network adaptor, focus on the following:

■ *Manufacturer and dealer information.* For more details, see the "Manufacturer information" and "Dealer information" discussions in the preceding section.

■ *Network adapter type.* Document the type of network adapter. The most common types of network adapters are EtherNet, ARCnet, and token ring.

> **NOTE** Don't mix network adapter types on a network. For instance, an EtherNet network adapter cannot communicate with an ARCnet network adapter. Both types, however, have a BNC network connector, which means the same type of cable connects to both adapters.

■ *Cable connector types.* Document the type of cable connector used by the network adapter. (EtherNet, for example, can use a BNC connector, a DB15 connector, or an RJ-45 connector.) The cabling system used to communicate with other systems on the network determines the type of connectors you use. The following are cable types for EtherNet cards based on the IEEE 802.3 specification:

IEEE Standard	Connector Type
10Base2	BNC
10Base5	DB15
10BaseT	RJ-45

- *Base memory address.* Some manufacturers design their adapters with a ROM chip on the network adapter. This ROM chip often is placed into the computer's memory addressing scheme through the base memory address. This way, the central processor of your system can communicate directly with the ROM on the network adapter. In other cases, the network adapter uses part of the computer's RAM to store information.

  If the network adapter is using base memory addresses, determine the current memory address setting and document it for later reference. Base memory addresses for network adapters must be in the range of A0000 hex and FFFFF hex in the base memory.

> **NOTE** Base memory uses a block of memory from 0 to 1,024K. This memory is the first 1M of RAM in the system. The architecture assigns 640K of the base memory to DOS. Adapters that require base memory addresses use the remaining 384K of memory address.

- *Base I/O address.* Every network adapter uses a base I/O address, which is the area in the computer's memory scheme where information is drawn from the LAN or placed on the LAN. This address—also referred to as the *I/O port address*—enables the processor to communicate with the adapter. Determine the current setting and document it.

- *Interrupt request (IRQ) line.* Every network adapter uses the IRQ line to interrupt the processor for service. Determine the current setting and document it.

- *Direct memory access (DMA) channel.* If the network adapter has RAM buffers, it assigns a DMA channel, which provides direct access between the RAM on the network adapter and the CPU. If the system is using DMA, determine the channel number and document it.

■ *Node address.* Each network adapter must have a unique network node address. The network uses this address to communicate between cards.

The installer sets the network address on ARCnet network adapters using the adapter's DIP switches. Valid node addresses range from 1 to 254.

The manufacturer sets the network address on EtherNet network adapters. The IEEE assigns each EtherNet adapter manufacturer a unique 6-digit hexadecimal number, and the manufacturer appends a unique 6-digit node number to the IEEE number. As a result, each EtherNet network adapter has a unique 12-digit node address.

The manufacturer sets the network address also on token-ring network adapters. Like EtherNet manufacturers, token-ring manufacturers are assigned a unique number, and the manufacturer assigns a node address.

Network Software Information

The type of software information you need to gather is as follows:

■ *Manufacturer and dealer information.* For more details, see the "Manufacturer information" and "Dealer information" paragraphs earlier in the "PC Information" section.

■ *Windows for Workgroups version.* Document the version and revision of Windows for Workgroups used on each workgroup station. Microsoft's revisions may cause problems on the system.

■ *Communications protocol.* The default communications protocol used by Windows for Workgroups is NetBEUI, which passes data to the network adapter for transmission to others in the workgroup. Knowing that the NetBEUI protocol passes data is useful if you run into network communications problems, especially when several protocols are in use at the same time. The Windows for Workgroups network, for example, can run with a Novell network. Novell uses the IPX protocol. The drivers for the protocol generally are loaded in CONFIG.SYS or AUTOEXEC.BAT.

■ *Protocol version.* Document the version and revision of the communications protocol used by the system.

■ *Network adapter device driver version.* The software that connects the communications protocol with the network adapters is known as a device driver. Problems can result if different versions or revisions of network adapter device drivers are in use. Document the device driver version and revision used on the systems.

■ *Configuration files.* Document the configuration files, including CONFIG.SYS, AUTOEXEC.BAT, and PROTOCOL.INI. You must document each workstation on the network.

B

Other Troubleshooting Tools

Other items are helpful in troubleshooting the Windows for Workgroups system, including the following:

■ *Tool kit.* The basic tool kit should include the tools needed to take apart the computers you will be working on. Compaq computers, for example, require torque screwdrivers.

■ *Computer repair manuals.* If they are available, get copies of the PC manuals—including the hardware service manuals—from the manufacturer.

■ *Windows for Workgroups manuals.* You need to keep with you a copy of the Windows for Workgroups manuals.

■ *Volt/ohmmeter.* A volt/ohmmeter is a valuable tool when troubleshooting a network. Make sure that you know the proper use of a volt/ohmmeter, however, before using it in network diagnosis.

■ *A clean copy of Windows for Workgroups.* Many times, software can become corrupted. To solve this problem, you need to load a new copy of Windows for Workgroups.

■ *A clean copy of MS-DOS.* Version 5.0 or later is recommended. You need a bootable system diskette with no configuration files (that is, a diskette with the MS-DOS hidden system file and COMMAND.COM) to determine whether the hardware can load MS-DOS. Don't include CONFIG.SYS and AUTOEXEC.BAT because these files can create problems during the hardware diagnostic phase of troubleshooting.

■ *Device drivers for all components used by Windows for Workgroups.* Windows for Workgroups requires many different device drivers. Over time, you should acquire numerous versions and revisions of these drivers. Keep copies of all versions and revisions used on the system.

- *Diagnostic software.* You cannot diagnose many hardware problems by sight. In these cases, you need system diagnostic software, such as Checkit or System Sleuth. (You may need to use more than one program to diagnose the system.) Windows for Workgroups comes with a diagnostic program called MSD (Microsoft Diagnostic) that can supply much information about the system.

- *Technical support telephone numbers.* Compile a list of technical support telephone numbers for the manufacturers of all the hardware and software products in the system. The telephone number and contact name of a local dealer technician is also useful.

- *Network adapter diagnostics.* Many network adapters provide diagnostic software with the hardware. If your adapters provide such software, keep a copy nearby.

- *Proper protocol device drivers.* Different versions and revisions of protocol device drivers perform differently. Keep a copy of all device drivers used on the system.

Obtain Specifications and Layout

The physical environment causes many network communications problems. Radio frequency interference (RFI) and electromagnetic interference (EMI) are common in the office workplace and can cause LAN communications problems. Electric motors, fluorescent lights, copy machines, and other electronic office equipment can cause RFI and EMI. Common electronic devices such as radios and TV sets also can cause RFI and EMI. If you suspect some type of electrical interference, don't plug these devices into the same circuit as your computer.

> **NOTE** Most computer manufacters recommend a dedicated circuit with an isolated ground—that is, special plugs just for computers. Orange power outlets indicate such a setup in your office.

Determine the physical layout of the network. Draw a floor plan, including the location of the cables and the devices that can cause interference. Repairing problems with cables is easier if you have documented location of cables and connection information. If communications problems are intermittent, cable layout may help you determine whether electronic interference is involved.

Isolate the Problem

Before you can take action to solve a problem, you need to determine which network component may be causing the problem. To isolate the problem to the component level, you should ask simple questions that isolate the problem to a specific component, such as, "Is the workstation plugged in?" or "Are all the adapters and connections seated and fitting tight?"

The following example shows the process of isolating the problem. In this example, the computer you are troubleshooting is not working at all. You need to isolate the problem and verify that it is the only problem. You should ask these questions:

- *Is there anything on the monitor? Is the keyboard locked up?* These questions can determine whether anything is working.

- *Did the computer function before?* This question can help determine whether the computer has ever worked properly.

- *When did it stop functioning?* This question can help determine whether some event caused the problem, such as a power surge, a change in the network, or some other specific event.

- *Is the fan running?* With this question, you can determine whether the computer is getting power. If the computer isn't getting any power, the next questions to ask would be, "Is the computer plugged in? Is the surge protector (or power strip) turned on?"

  If power isn't the problem, you should continue with questions such as "Will the floppy disk drive read the boot diskette?" This question can help determine whether the computer can boot to the MS-DOS prompt.

- *Did you notice any error messages as CONFIG.SYS and AUTOEXEC.BAT were executing?* By asking this question, you can see whether all the Windows for Workgroups network adapter drivers were loaded properly.

- *If you noticed errors, were they specific to MS-DOS or to Windows for Workgroups?* In the CONFIG.SYS file, the protocol manager (PROTMAN.DOS) must load, a network adapter driver must load, and WORKGRP.SYS must load. (The file name for the adapter driver varies with different types of network adapters. Consult your Windows for Workgroups manual for the proper file name for your network adapter.) If any of these files don't load, Windows for Workgroups

cannot communicate over the network. In the
AUTOEXEC.BAT file, the command NET START must execute. If it doesn't, no network services will be available.

- *If the network adapter software driver didn't load, is the
  software configured to match the physical settings of the
  hardware?* Ask this question to see whether you have the
  hardware and software settings set the same. The settings
  include interrupt request (IRQ), base memory address, base
  I/O address, and DMA channel.

- *Are all hardware and cables in good condition, seated properly in the computer, and securely screwed in place?* By asking this question, you can determine whether the PC you are
  working on can function properly.

- *When you execute WIN.COM, do any errors result?* This question determines whether your Windows for Workgroups application files are loaded properly.

If you were to answer all these questions, you would have a good
idea which component—hardware or software—was causing the
problem. Eliminate as many components from consideration as
possible. Then ask yourself which of the remaining components
can generate the kind of problem being experienced.

Form a Theory

Now that you have isolated the component that you think may be
causing the problem, divide it into subcomponents. Any component or subcomponent, whether hardware or software, may be
causing the problem you are troubleshooting.

Some components have many other parts that make the whole.
The CPU, for example, has a network adapter, a video adapter,
other communication adapters, and other miscellaneous adapters.
Each part is referred to as a subcomponent because they are part
of the whole component.

You also have software components and subcomponents. DOS is a
component; any device driver added to the CONFIG.SYS file adds
additional function to DOS, thus making the device driver a subcomponent of MS-DOS. This process is true in most applications
that are added to your system.

Test Your Theory

Now, you should have a good idea as to where the problem is. You now need to test your conclusion. You have a component or sub-component that you suspect is causing the problem. If it is a hardware problem, try one of the following steps:

■ Remove the component or subcomponent and replace it with one that you know is good.

■ If you have a software diagnostic for the hardware component available, use it to test the hardware component.

If the component or subcomponent you suspect to be causing the problem is software, reinstall the software on your computer. Damage to existing software is not uncommon. Reinstalling the software should solve this problem. If the software problem persists after you reinstall the software, contact the software manufacture to see whether you are dealing with a known bug. Certain problems cannot be solved without the help of the manufacturer.

If the component or subcomponent that you just tested turns out to be OK, you have not found the problem. Return to the process of isolating the problem and continue.

Take Proper Corrective Action

If you have found the problem, you now need to correct it. If the problem is hardware related, you probably need to replace the defective hardware component or subcomponent. In the computer industry today, most components are considered disposable; there simply is no way to fix them.

Software, however, is a completely different item. The applications on your system are never perfect—they will have bugs. If the problem is software related, you can try to solve the problem in three ways:

■ Reload the application software. If reloading the software doesn't solve the problem, you may need to contact your software vendor, or even the software manufacturer, to solve the application software problem.

■ If the problem is software device driver related, make certain that your physical hardware settings match the software settings. If these settings don't match, the device driver will not load.

■ If you cannot fix the problem, you should call in a consultant or technician to help you.

> **NOTE** Don't make more than one change at a time as you are correcting the problem. Otherwise, you may not know which item caused the problem.

Document the Actions Taken

Each computer in your workgroups will have problems from time to time. You need to document the problems and the corrective actions that you have taken. Documentation can become one of your better troubleshooting tools, for three reasons:

■ Remembering all the corrective actions that you have taken over time can be difficult. You can use the documentation to help you remember what actions you took to solve a problem.

■ Some problems seem to be fixed but really aren't. By keeping track of each action you take, you eventually may find the actual problem.

■ Providing technicians with documentation on each corrective action you have tried and the reason you took that action saves them time and saves you money.

Each workstation should have a workstation log that records any changes made to that computer. Each time you add software, update software, or change the software configuration settings, you should record the changes in the workstation log. You also should indicate any changes made in the hardware configuration.

Create a troubleshooting log for each workstation on the network. Each time you have a problem on the network, document the assemblies you tested and the corrective action taken. (The Windows for Workgroups Cardfile is a good place to store this information.) If you follow this procedure, you shouldn't have to repeat the troubleshooting process for the same problems.

The workstation diagnostic log should contain the following information:

■ *Date.* The date you diagnosed and corrected the problem

■ *Problem.* The problem you found during the diagnostic process and a list of the assemblies you tested

■ *Action.* The corrective action taken and a detailed list of each change made

■ *Technician.* The name of the technician performing the diagnostic process and the corrective action.

Understanding Specific Trouble Spots

The rest of this appendix focuses on some specific problems that you may face when working with Windows for Workgroups, particularly in File Manager, Mail, and Schedule+. In this discussion, you also find ways to solve these problems.

Problems with File Manager

Problems with File Manager involve being unable to access the network. When network PCs are set up, shared directories usually are marked so that they can be shared again on start-up. If the computer with the shared directory isn't running or is unavailable due to network failure, users see an error message when trying to connect. To reconnect, they must go into File Manager, select the drive letter, and choose Connect Network Drive from the File menu.

If a drive is connected and the computer with the shared directory goes down or becomes unavailable, Windows for Workgroups doesn't display an error message. Users will not know immediately that a problem exists until they try to access information from the shared directory. Again, a simple correction is to go into File Manager and reconnect the network drive.

Problems with Mail

The Microsoft Mail system revolves around the post office. If the post office computer is down or inaccessible due to network failure, users receive a message in a dialog box telling them that Mail could not connect to the Mail server. The user, however, can click OK in the dialog box and work *off-line*. Mail uses an individual mail file located on the user's computer. The user can continue to work with mail off-line until the post office is again accessible.

Suppose, however, that the individual mail file is corrupted. If the mail file is so corrupt, you see a dialog box telling you so. You can choose the Repair Now button to fix the mail file.

If the mail file is missing, you see the Open Message File dialog box. Select the message file and choose OK. If you cannot find a message file on the system, however, choose the New button from the Open Message File dialog box. A new message file is created.

To avoid major problems, however, be sure to back up your mail messages to a floppy disk. This way, you can restore a file, if necessary. If you send and receive mail quite often, back up your file every day.

Schedule+ Problems

The biggest problem with Schedule+ stems from its use of the Mail system. Because Schedule+ uses the Mail system, the computer with the post office must be accessible at all times. If this computer is unavailable or goes down when a user is scheduling, problems occur.

To prevent such problems from happening, be sure that the local Schedule+ file is on the hard drive of each computer on the network. This way, if the mail server goes down or is unavailable, each computer can continue to perform individual scheduling. If the network goes down in the middle of scheduling an event, Schedule+ asks whether you want to continue off-line. If you choose Yes, you can continue to work with your schedule.

If the user still cannot connect to the mail server when using Schedule+, check the following items:

■ *Is the computer with the post office up and running?* The computer acting as the post office must be running Windows for Workgroups.

■ *Has the computer with the post office completed loading Mail?* If you see the prompt for Mail asking the user to sign in, the mail server hasn't been loaded. The user of the computer with the post office must be signed in before other users can access their mail or schedule on-line.

■ *Is a password assigned to the \\COMPUTER\WGPO directory?* The WGPO (workgroup post office) directory on the computer running the post office should be a shared directory with full access. Don't assign a password to this directory. Otherwise, Schedule+ and the Mail system doesn't stop to prompt the user for the password; instead, the user sees an Unable to connect to Mail Server message. A temporary solution is to have the user connect to the shared WGPO directory and enter the password. The user then can return to Schedule+ and choose Work Online from the File menu.

C

Glossary

A

access type. Security rights or access rights between a user and a shared directory. Access types include read only, full, and password.

active hub. A hub with active electronics that brings the data signal back up to its original strength; associated most often with ARCnet networks using RG-62 coaxial cabling. In a certain sense, an active hub is a signal splitter that doesn't degrade the signal.

association. The link created between an application and a data file. After you use File Manager to create the association, clicking the icon for the data file in File Manager causes the application to be loaded and then the data file.

attributes. See *file attributes*.

B

BNC. A specification for a common connector used on network adapter boards; somewhat similar to the connector used with cable TV cables without the threads.

base memory. A parameter used by many network adapters. Base memory is an area of memory between 640K and 1M used by some network adapters for various purposes. This memory can include mapping the instructions in the network adapter's ROM chip into the computer's main memory. Other network adapters use base memory to point to an area in the computer's main memory used for a buffer.

binary. Numbering system with a base of 2. Binary numbers consist solely of ones (1) and zeros (0). In binary, for example, the number 5 is 101, and 14 is 1110. Computers use binary arithmetic to perform calculations because their memory cells (RAM) are composed of millions of transistors that can be ON or OFF. A 1 often represents ON and a 0 represents OFF. A binary digit is referred to as a *bit*. Eight bits equal a *byte*.

bit. A term that is short for *binary digit*. A bit can be a 1 or a 0 in the binary numbering system. See *binary*.

branch. A term that refers to the way DOS directories and all their subdirectories are organized. The organization method is known as *tree-structured directories*. In this methodology, the top of the structure is known as the *root*. Each directory can be referred to as a main branch, which can have smaller branches.

bridge. A device that connects two LANs together. As far as Windows for Workgroups is concerned, two LANs connected through a bridge are seen as a single LAN. A *remote bridge* connects two LANs over long-distance phone lines.

Bridges generally have a certain amount of intelligence. *Transparent* bridges (also known as *spanning tree* bridges) learn which nodes are on what side of the bridge. Over time these types of bridges can improve network performance because they filter out traffic local to one side or the other. Token-ring bridges are generally *source routing* bridges that require additional intelligence on the part of the nodes.

bus. In the network environment, refers to a type of LAN cabling configuration (topology). A bus is a path that transmits data from one node to all nodes on the LAN. Two of the most popular bus topologies are *linear bus* and *star bus*.

byte. 8 binary digits (or bits). Computers usually address memory one byte at a time. Memory, ever since the original IBM PC, is organized into an array of 9 bits (the ninth bit is used as a parity check to make sure that memory hasn't been damaged).

C

component. Part of the LAN. A major component can include the computers on the LAN, bridges, routers, or other file servers running other operating systems such as UNIX, LAN Manager, NetWare, and so forth. A *subcomponent* is a part of a component and can include any card in a computer such as network adapter cards, disk controller cards, and video cards.

CSMA/CD. Carrier Sense Multiple Access/Collision Detection, a technique of accessing the LAN used by certain types of network adapters, such as EtherNet. If two or more adapters transmit at the same time, a "collision" results. Adapters that use the CSMA/CD technique have circuitry that detects a collision and causes the transmitting adapters to time-out for a random period of time. Using the CSMA/CD technique, the network adapters "listen" to the network bus. If any activity is on the bus, one of the adapters waits. When the bus isn't active and an adapter has data to transmit, the adapter transmits the data.

D

device. Any piece of hardware that can receive and/or transmit data. Devices include boards, ports, network adapters, printers, and mice.

DIP switch. A block of micro switches soldered onto a circuit board. (DIP stands for *Dual In-line Package*.) These switches are used to set parameters on the computer card. Parameters for network adapter cards that can be set by using DIP switches include IRQs, I/O port addresses, and base memory addresses.

DIX. A 15-pin connector found on EtherNet cards. The acronym stands for *Digital Intel Xerox*, the three companies that jointly produced the EtherNet technology.

DMA. Direct memory addressing. A way for the hardware component to send and receive information directly to and from RAM.

E

EISA. Extended Industry Standard Architecture. Compaq Computer Corporation spearheaded this standard in an effort to extend the capabilities of the ISA bus while still maintaining compatibility with ISA cards. (See also *ISA*.)

EMI. Electromagnetic interference, which can cause intermittent or no communication between network adapter cards. Machinery such as generators, electric motors, radar, X-ray machines, and nearby radio transmitters can cause EMI. If you are sharing a file and the LAN experiences strong EMI, the application you are running may crash and the file you have open may become corrupted.

F

file attributes. Properties or features of a file. Attributes include *read only, hidden, system*, and *archive*. The read-only attribute indicates that you can read a file but not delete or change it in any way. The hidden attribute hides the file from the DOS DIR command and from File Manager. The archive attribute indicates that the file has been modified and needs to be backed up.

file lock. A lock placed on a file by an application when a user first opens the file. When the network operating software (or the DOS SHARE program) has granted a file lock, the user has exclusive ownership of the file. Other users cannot make changes to the file until the file lock is lifted.

G

gateway. A device, much like a bridge or router, that joins two networks together. Unlike bridges, however, gateways join two different types of networks. You use a gateway, for example, to join a Novell NetWare LAN with an IBM 3270 mainframe network. Gateways not only enable the two networks to communicate together but also perform file conversions.

groupware. A general label applied to software used by a group of people. This type of software includes "chat" programs, which enable people to converse with each other on-line. Other types of software include meeting scheduling, as found in the Schedule+ feature of Windows for Workgroups.

H

hexadecimal. Numbering system using a base of 16 rather than 10; also referred to as *hex*. In the decimal numbering system, each place of a number cannot exceed 10. In base 16, each place of a number cannot exceed 16. Hex numbers use the digits 0 through 9, and continue with A through F before going to the next place. A in hex stands for 10 in decimal, B stands for 11, and so on.

hub. A signal splitter. Connections on a hub are *bidirectional*. Hubs are used most often with twisted-pair EtherNet (10BaseT) and coaxial ARCnet cabling.

I

IEEE. Institute of Electronics and Electrical Engineers, an international organization of electronic engineers. The IEEE meets in committees to hammer out specifications for the electronics industry. The IEEE is best known in the LAN industry for its set of standards for network adapters. The committees responsible for these standards are numbered starting with the number 802.1. The best known committees include 802.3 (works on specifications similar to EtherNet) and 802.5 (works on specifications similar to token ring).

I/O port. Also known as *base I/O address* or *base I/O port address*. I/O stands for input/output. Computers assign a number—called an *address*—to every device and function of every device. The address fits into the computer's *memory map*, a range of addresses that the computer consults when it wants to access real information. The I/O port is an address where information coming in from the LAN is placed. The LAN sends the computer information, which is placed in an I/O port. When the computer wants to send information out through the LAN, it places the information in the I/O port.

IRQ. A term that stands for "interrupt request." An interrupt is a signal sent from a hardware device to the CPU telling the CPU that the device requires immediate attention. The device that wants the CPU's attention sends the interrupt signal over a special data line called the interrupt request line.

After the CPU receives the interrupt signal, it stops what it's doing and immediately retrieves from memory special program instructions known as an *interrupt service routine*.

The CPU performs the functions dictated by these instructions. After the CPU completes the routine, it returns to what it was doing before it received the interrupt.

ISA. Industry Standard Architecture, a term often used to refer to IBM PC/AT compatible computers. The AT (advanced technology) computer came out in the mid 1980s. A typical AT-style computer has 16- and 8-bit slots on the data bus.

L

LAN. Local area network.

local user. The user who works at the computer in question. In the case of Print Manager, the local user with a shared printer becomes the manager of that printer. In the case of File Manager, the local user becomes the manager of any shared directories that have been created.

log off. The process of disconnecting your computer from all network services. After you log off, other computers on the network no longer recognize you, and you no longer can access network resources such as shared directories or shared printers.

log on. The process of connecting your computer to the network.

M-N

mbps. Million bits per second. This acronym is used to describe throughput.

MCA. Micro Channel Architecture. This technology, introduced by IBM with the PS/2 computer, was an effort to improve performance limitations imposed by the older ISA bus. MCA computers can perform slightly below the level of an EISA computer. The disadvantage is that ISA cards don't fit an MCA slot.

multitasking. The capability of performing several tasks at the same time. Microcomputers don't multitask in the literal sense of the word. Because the microprocessor can operate very quickly, however, the computer seems to multitask.

node. Any network adapter cabled to a LAN. This term sometimes is used to include the computer itself and its network adapter card.

P

packet. A smaller grouping of bytes of data to be transmitted between nodes. Packets are constructed by memory-resident software drivers that manage the network communications protocols. In a Windows for Workgroups network, packets follow Microsoft's NetBEUI standard, the same standard used in a Microsoft LAN Manager network. If you use Windows for Workgroups on another network, such as Novell NetWare, you must add support for Novell's packet type, IPX, by using Control Panel's Network option.

passive hub. A hub without active electronics, used most often in conjunction with ARCnet coaxial networks. This device consists of a small box with BNC connectors on the outside and resistors wired in a star configuration on the inside. Although attractive due to their low price, passive hubs have been known to cause network communication problems because they don't boost the signal to its original specified level and filter out noise. In fact, a passive hub *degrades* the original signal.

paste. An action performed during editing. Pasting inserts in the current application a copy of the data you have on the Clipboard.

peer. A computer that has equal status with other computers in a LAN.

peer-to-peer. A term used to identify a particular type of LAN. In a peer-to-peer LAN, each computer has a status equal to other computers. Peer-to-peer networks are in contrast to client/server-based networks (such as Novell NetWare 2.2 or 3.11), where one computer is designated the "file server," which has greater status than other computers.

port. An interface board or electronic circuitry that provides the computer access to the "real" world. Examples of ports include serial ports used to connect the computer with the phone lines through a modem; parallel ports, which connect the computer to a printer; and I/O ports on a network adapter card.

print job. Another name for a document you have sent to the printer that now is waiting in the queue for its turn to print. This term comes from the mainframe world, where requests to print were submitted to a queue. The requests were often from paying customers, hence the word *job*.

protocol. A term used to describe a set of rules and agreements between two computers. These rules and agreements govern how the two computers exchange information. The TCP/IP protocol used in the UNIX world, for example, defines how information is to be sent, the order of the packets, how the receiving computer is to acknowledge receipt of a packet, and so forth. Other protocols include the NetBEUI protocol used with Windows for Workgroups and the IPX protocol used by Novell NetWare.

Q-R

queue. The process in which a print job must "wait in line" before printing. Some documents may have greater priority than other documents in the queue.

RAM. Random-access memory; also referred to as *main memory* or *primary memory*. RAM is the computer's working space. All programs and files are stored in RAM at one time or another as the computer goes about its business.

Two common types of RAM exist: static and dynamic. Static RAM, often used in devices such as microwaves and cars, requires less support circuitry but is less dense. As a result, this type of memory cannot store as much information as dynamic and tends to be slower than dynamic. CMOS RAM is a type of static RAM used to store the computer's basic system information (such as what disk drives are available and the date and time). Dynamic memory is fast and can be packed densely. Dynamic memory often is shipped in the form of a 4M SIMM chip.

reboot. The process in which you reset the computer. You can reboot a computer by pressing Alt+Ctrl+Del.

remote user. A user working at a client computer who is accessing resources on the computer of the local user. The remote user has limited access to the resources of the local user's computer.

repeater. A device that connects two buses (EtherNet) or rings (token ring) and repeats information exactly as received. Data is bidirectional.

RFI. Radio frequency interference, which comes in the form of radio waves. RFI is a big problem when using unshielded twisted-pair cables, as used in 10BaseT EtherNet and some token-ring cards.

ROM. Read-only memory. ROM chips store basic instructions used to boot devices (such as the BIOS chip found in most computers). ROM chips actually contain programs that literally are burned into the circuitry of the chip. Because the programs are stored on a chip, they always are available. Many network adapters have ROM chips on board to store the programs used to implement how they behave.

S

security rights. Similar to *access type*.

shared directory. A directory that is available to selected users on a LAN. Generally, you can share any files in a shared directory.

spooling. The process of queuing up and redirecting a print job. In the original IBM PC, when a job started printing, it went directly from the program to the printer. Spooling implies sending the print job first to a print buffer of some sort rather than directly to the printer.

stand-alone. A term that refers to computers that aren't networked.

swap file. A file that Windows for Workgroups uses to store background applications and data. Windows for Workgroups uses a "virtual memory" technique that enables swap files to be seen as virtual RAM memory. If you have less than 4M of RAM in your computer, a swap file causes Windows for Workgroups to operate more efficiently.

Windows for Workgroups, like Windows, uses two types of swap files: *temporary* and *permanent*. A permanent swap file is created when Windows for Workgroups is first installed. Once installed, the swap file uses its allocated space permanently, taking disk space away from other applications and data. A temporary swap file is created each time Windows for Workgroups loads and is deleted when the program is exited. A temporary swap file operates like a permanent swap file but isn't as efficient because it takes time to create, making Windows for Workgroups load slowly.

T

task-switching. The process of moving between applications without having to exit each application first. Windows for Workgroups operating in 386 Enhanced mode enables you to task-switch out of an application but still leave the application running in the background. This process is an example of *multitasking*.

terminator. A BNC connector with a resister soldered in place; used with network adapters connected with coaxial cable in a bus fashion. A terminator prevents excess signals from reflecting back and forth across the LAN. The value of the resistor must match that of the cable used. For EtherNet using RG-8, RG-11, or RG-58 cable, use a 50-ohm terminator. For ARCnet using RG-62 cable, use a 93-ohm terminator.

throughput. The rate (in bits per second) that data is transmitted from a sending node to receiving nodes.

token ring. A technology for a device to access a network developed in the early 1980s by IBM. Token-ring devices include mainframe cluster controllers (such as a 3174), minicomputers (such as an AS/400), and PCs. Token ring is the main competitor for EtherNet in the LAN world. Information in a token-ring LAN travels around in a logical ring through a series of hubs known as Multistation Access Units (MSAUs or MAUs). Token ring has certain advantages over EtherNet, including prioritization of network adapters, error checking, and self diagnostics.

traffic. Data traveling on the LAN.

U-W

user. A person working on a computer connected to a LAN. To become a user, the person must be logged on so that the network operating system recognizes that person as a user.

workstation. A computer that runs applications and serves as an access point to shared network resources.

INDEX

Set Access Privileges,
232
Sound, 262
File Manager, 89-90
Print Manager, 123-124
organization of workgroups,
35-37
OSI (Open System Interconnection), network operat-
ing systems, 17
Outbox (Mail), 148, 158-159

P

packets, 17, 39, 112, 375
pages Local ClipBook, 246,
252-254
Clipboard
copying, 254
saving contents,
252-253
sharing, 255-257
viewing, 253-254
passive hubs, 375
passwords, 36, 80-82
changing, 292
logon, 61
printers, 119
start-up, 60
pasting, 375
DOS information to
Clipboard, 249-250
pausing printers, 137,
140-141

PCs
LANs, 355
troubleshooting, 356-358
peer-to-peer networks, 19,
22-24, 375
controlling, 23
documentation, 23
operating systems, 22
troubleshooting, 23
Performance Priority
option, 279
permanent directory sharing,
99-100
personal address book
(Mail), 148
personal groups (Mail), 149
adding/deleting users, 177
creating, 176
deleting, 177
editing, 177
Personal Groups command
(Mail menu), 176
personal scheduling,
207-218
physical layout (networks),
troubleshooting, 362
Planner (Schedule+), 54
Request Meeting button,
55
window, 54
meetings, 227
plenum cable, 31
Port command (Printer
Connections menu), 308